DISCARDED
Fordham University Libraries

Lotze's System of Philosophy

George Santayana

LOTZE'S SYSTEM

O F

PHILOSOPHY

Edited with an Introduction and Lotze Bibliography by

PAUL GRIMLEY KUNTZ

Indiana University Press

BLOOMINGTON / LONDON

Published in Canada by Fitzhenry & Whiteside Limited, Don Mills, Ontario

Library of Congress catalog card number: 72-135008

ISBN: 253-33610-4

Manufactured in the United States of America

Dedicated to my children

SARAH ZABRISKIE,

JOEL DUBOIS,

TIMOTHY ROMEYN,

SUSAN DEBORAH GRIMLEY

Contents

	Page
Editor's Acknowledgment	ix

Introduction: RUDOLF HERMANN LOTZE, PHILOSOPHER AND CRITIC

Santayana and Lotze	*3*
Lotze as Critic of His Predecessors	*12*
Lotze's System: A Theory of Order	*21*
Lotze's Influence on Anglo-American Philosophy	*48*
Lotze's Relevance to Contemporary Philosophy	*68*
APPENDIX: Santayana's Reading of Lotze's *Logik* and *Metaphysik* Revealed in Marginalia	*95*

LOTZE'S SYSTEM OF PHILOSOPHY

I.	Lotze's problem—His relation to natural science	*109*
II.	Lotze and the Kantian philosophy	*130*
III.	Lotze's atomism: his argument for idealism	*155*
IV.	Monism—Causality—Indeterminism	*182*
V.	Personality of God—Aesthetics—Optimism	*211*
	Note on Lotze's Life and Works	*227*
	ERRATA ET CORRIGENDA	*229*
	LOTZE BIBLIOGRAPHY	*233*
	INDEX	*271*

vii

Editor's Acknowledgment

THE EDITOR WISHES FIRST TO THANK Daniel Cory, Santayana's literary executor, for permission to publish *Lotze's System of Philosophy*. Encouragement and approval also came from Clifford K. Shipton, Custodian of the Harvard Archives, and Rogers G. Albritton, Chairman of the Department of Philosophy, Harvard University.

The 322 pages of manuscript were microfilmed and reduced to 109 pages of typescript. In this process the few footnote references (thirteen in all) were inserted into the text, enclosed in parentheses. The editor has introduced corrections of spelling, altered the punctuation, eliminated reduplicated words, occasionally inserted a word or a phrase, occasionally completed a word or even substituted a correct or more contemporary word for an incorrect one or an archaic usage. Since the reader may be without Greek, Latin, and German, the editor has introduced translations to accompany Santayana's quotations. A full list of these additions and corrections follows in *Errata et corrigenda*.

The editor thanks Mary Susan Gould and J. Michael Young, who helped him establish the text.

For sympathetic and intelligent counsel in this project the editor owes thanks to many friends and colleagues: Robert W. Adamson, Richard J. Bernstein, Peter A. Bertocci, Julius S. Bixler, Ivan Boh, John J. Compton, J. Harry Cotton, Joseph Dorfman, Loyd Easton, Kimball C. Elkins, Roderick Firth, Max H. Fisch, Rubin Gotesky, Otto Kraushaar, John Lachs, Donald

M. Love, Victor Lowe, John Passmore, Henry A. Pochmann, Herbert Schneider, John E. Smith, Herbert Spiegelberg, Newton P. Stallknecht, Warren E. Steinkraus, Tyler Thompson, Joseph F. Wall.

I owe a special debt to a score of librarians: of Grinnell College (especially Richard Ryan), of Emory University (especially Joyce Werner), of Haverford College (especially Craig Thompson), of the Free Public Library Service of the State of Vermont (especially Kent Gray, Verna Guatney, and Herbert Beckwith), of Wells College (especially Marie G. Damron), of Yale University (especially Dorothy W. Bridgman), of Oberlin College (especially Lelia F. Holloway), of the University of Chicago (especially Harvey Arnold), of the Universities of Indiana, Iowa, Pennsylvania, and Wisconsin, the Johns Hopkins Library, Notre Dame University Library, and others who supplied materials by interlibrary loan.

This work has been facilitated by grants from the Research Committee of Emory University and the American Philosophical Society, after having been helped at an early stage by Dean (later also Provost) James H. Stauss of Grinnell College. The editor expresses his deep gratitude now to the Woodrow Wilson International Center for Scholars of the Smithsonian Institution for support, and to his wife, Dr. Marion Leathers Daniels, for inspiration.

Emory University
Atlanta, Georgia 30322

"Three Ponds"
South Woodbury, Vermont 05671

The Smithsonian Institution
Washington, D.C. 20560

Lotze's System of Philosophy

INTRODUCTION

BY

PAUL GRIMLEY KUNTZ

RUDOLF HERMANN LOTZE,

PHILOSOPHER AND CRITIC

Santayana and Lotze

THE SUBJECT OF GEORGE SANTAYANA's doctoral dissertation at
Harvard was Rudolf Hermann Lotze (1817–1881), a German metaphysician of the mid-nineteenth century who although
perhaps the most highly regarded German philosopher of his
day has now fallen into obscurity. Later I shall try to show the
extent of Lotze's influence not only on Santayana but on James,
Royce, and other great names in Anglo-American philosophy; I
shall suggest also that, unless one belongs to that school that
finds all metaphysics meaningless, Lotze's work is still relevant
to modern philosophic concerns.

This book is George Santayana's first, and it tells us more
about this American philosopher in early manhood than he tells
us directly of himself. Santayana was a youthful poet and essayist,
and the grace of style for which he became famous was not
lacking in the young man of twenty-six. Santayana wrote well
in spite of the oppressive circumstances of producing a dissertation. Writing under Josiah Royce, his director, Santayana
satisfied the harshest condition in earning the Ph.D. degree:
conforming to another's choice of topic, and perhaps in part
also, another's mode of handling it. Because Santayana would
have preferred Schopenhauer at the time, and Hegel in retro-
spect, it is natural that he regarded *Lotze's System of Philosophy*
as a journeyman's task imposed upon him by his master. The
author, therefore, seems never to have recommended that anyone
read the manuscript deposited in Harvard Library, nor do we

have any evidence that he considered its publication. It may be asked, then, whether this book should be published.

The reasons justifying this publication are complex. One might argue that since 1889 Harvard University has received but one other doctoral thesis by a candidate who later made as great a name in literature. T. S. Eliot's *Knowledge and Experience in the Philosophy of F. H. Bradley* was deposited in Harvard Library in 1916. By urging of his wife it was published in 1964.[1]

Beyond this argument from a parallel case, a better reason for publishing Santayana on Lotze is that it illuminates the development of a major philosopher and critic. A few curious persons have read Santayana's book, 322 pages in neat handwriting. The editor became convinced twenty years ago that much of what was worked out later in *The Life of Reason* and *Realms of Being* was already there in *Lotze's System of Philosophy*. It may seem a bit indecent to examine the embryo, especially when one has the well-born children; however, whatever the personal significance, the public importance of Santayana's work is found in the dependence of much American philosophy of the nineteenth and early twentieth centuries on German models. This has long been obvious in the case of Royce, but it has been ignored in Santayana's development. Specifically what has been ignored is the connection between German philosophy and the rise of realism. Generally we have thought of post-Kantians as idealists; Santayana himself stressed their belief in the omnipotence of mind; indeed, he took it as the dominant theme of German thought. Even perceptive readers of *Egotism in German Philosophy* are not prepared for the tone of writing. It is not scorn or vituperation, but respect. One has even the surprise of having Lotze's philosophy recommended to us as the antithesis of egotism, a wise and moderate paganism.

Might one enjoy reading about Lotze even if one does not care for Santayana? We might well be interested in Lotze's problem because it is ours also. An attraction to Lotze is that his philosophy springs from his life; he scorned the merely aca-

demic. Lotze was much like William James. Both were by training men of science but deeply sympathetic with religion and the
arts. Indeed, the specific professional path was through the M.D.
to physiology and psychology, including the morbid side, and
finally to philosophy as such. In Germany there was a parallel
in Lotze's day in Wilhelm Wundt, and perhaps closer in our
own day in Karl Jaspers. The question is asked still: now that
we have scientific knowledge, should we not outgrow poetry
and put it away as a childish thing? Are not all the arts outmoded by progress? Lotze, who was himself a youthful poet,
was led into philosophy as much because of aesthetics as of the
problem of man's place in nature. He opposed efforts to examine
the arts solely for their intellectual content. Modes of culture
and language are irreducibly many. Santayana, in his essay
"Lotze's Moral Idealism," picked the first sentence of Lotze's
Microcosmus as a statement of this pluralism. "Between the demands of our emotional nature and the results of human science
there is an ancient ever-raging strife." Is this not what we call
the problem of "the two cultures"? It would be, argued Lotze,
as foolish to condemn science because it is bad poetry as to be-
little poetry because it is bad science. It is a prime philosophic
task to bring information to bear on man's aspirations and also
to bring man's ideals to bear on discoveries and inventions. In
short, feeling and knowledge are not exclusive opposites, but
polar opposites. Since one requires the other, whatever the
superficial conflict, there is an underlying harmony.

Another reason for Santayana's sympathy with Lotze is more
characteristic of the twentieth century with its piecemeal treatment of problems. Lotze was unimpressed by the great systems of
philosophy. He knew the official answers of the Kantians, the
Fichteans, the Herbartians, the Hegelians of his day. Indeed
he scarcely treats of any topic without restating the commonly
accepted views. But in contrast to the barbaric customs of the
schools of philosophy in dismissing each other as worthless,
Lotze is almost always unfailingly courteous. His courtesy springs
not from having no position of his own, but from knowing

the limitation of any position, particularly one's own. Much later Santayana spoke of himself as quite capable of seeing both sides of a dispute and choosing neither. Santayana enjoyed, in the study of philosophy, considering strange solutions that he would not have thought of himself. So, apparently, did Lotze.

Hermann Lotze was the darling philosopher of religious liberals of the 1880's and 1890's and of the period through World War I. In Germany, Albrecht Ritschl had reinterpreted religion on a Lotzean basis as a matter of judgments of value. In Oxford a group around T. H. Green, also with active interests in reforming society, sponsored the translation of Lotze's *System of Philosophy: Logic* and *Metaphysic*. Lotze became a German philosopher of repute comparable to that of Kant or Hegel. In America the interest was fanned chiefly by theologians, particularly Congregationalists, and by philosophers with religious concerns. These were obviously seeking to maintain something of traditional theism and to preserve the youth from either identifying God with the laws of nature, then so gloriously evident through scientific discovery, or abolishing soul altogether and settling for sheer mechanism of material atoms. Either pantheism or atheism fails to do justice, Lotze argued, to the reality of persons. And, indeed, personality is ultimately the type of reality. Hence it is easy to see a metaphysical defense of the doctrine of divine personality and significant human freedom. One gathers the use to which Lotze's metaphysics was put at Yale College, Oberlin College, and Grinnell College; and this merely suggests the places where Lotze was taught and studied. In the Preface to Lotze's *Outlines of the Philosophy of Religion*, George T. Ladd, a Congregational minister, Professor of Philosophy at Yale, writes:

> It is my earnest hope that a large number of those whose work it is to teach religion will make a somewhat careful study of this brief philosophical treatise. It seems to me admirably adapted for an exercise in that fundamental thinking on the most important of subjects presented to the human reason, which no one can safely despise, and which few are in a position wisely to neglect. . . .

6

It is an effort to treat of 'Religion within the limits of mere reason.' But it is also avowedly very far from that 'barren rationalism' which overlooks the 'aesthetic' (in the widest sense) elements of human nature; it makes constant reference to, and attempts to afford satisfaction for, our indestructible religious needs. . . . What may be said to be, 'speculatively' considered, either determinable or unknowable, is by no means necessarily the same when considered from the point of view occupied by the investigator of the specific truths of Biblical revelation. In other words, a large amount of speculative agnosticism is not incompatible with a firm conviction as to the truthfulness of the system of doctrines called Scriptural, and scientifically formulated by dogmatics.[2]

Santayana must have been well aware of the pious use of Lotze's philosophy. Santayana's friend at Yale, William Lyon Phelps, took notes on Lotze from Ladd's lectures. Some years later Santayana was the guest at Oberlin College of Henry Churchill King, who taught Lotze's *Microcosmus* to every candidate there for the A.B. degree.

How Santayana responded at the time of writing the dissertation we can only surmise. Probably he had not yet taken a strong dislike to Protestant theology, particularly in its liberal form.

The only discussion of Lotze in all Santayana's subsequent writings, other than the account of writing the dissertation in *Persons and Places,* is in *The Last Puritan: A Memoir in the Form of a Novel.* Mrs. Alden, mother of Oliver, "the last puritan," has a brother, Harry Bumstead, who is a graduate of Williams College. He intends to become a "liberal clergyman or professor."

Mrs. Alden's younger brother Harry was at that time pursuing his theological studies in Göttingen, where tepid philosophical currents, set up by the eloquence of Lotze, continued to temper the truth to the shorn lamb. Among those red-tiled roofs and modest gardens, he lodged in the house of the widowed Frau Pastor Schlote, whose elder daughter gave German lessons to the foreign boarders.[3]

Santayana had himself learned German from Fräulein Schlote, who earlier, when Lotze still flourished, had taught R. B. Haldane (later Lord Haldane of Cloan). Haldane had gone to

Göttingen to study under Lotze. A young Scottish Baptist, he was indeed troubled about his faith and much comforted by Lotze's position and personal counsel. Haldane caught from Fräulein Schlote also an enthusiasm for Goethe that never waned. A whole generation of Americans and Britons was educated there, Royce being one, who learned to think and feel that life was important even when philosophical arguments went lame.

Fräulein Schlote, Irma in *The Last Puritan,* was recommended by Harry Bumstead as nursemaid and tutor of little Oliver Alden. Mrs. Alden had doubts.

> . . . wouldn't a clergyman's daughter tend to be bigoted and narrow? However, her brother reassured her, explaining how far Fräulein Schlote, though deeply religious in her feelings, was from forming any *abstract* notion of religion, or seeing God anywhere but in Nature and Society and the conscience of man. In fact, if anything Harriet [Mrs. Alden] would find her too liberal, too *pagan,* because she was a great admirer of Goethe, and felt how beautiful a healthy sensuality was to round out the character.[4]

Santayana surely at that time questioned the optimistic assumptions of Lotze. One of these is the trust that whatever scientific progress may force faith to give up is not of any religious, moral, or aesthetic value anyhow. Can we adjust our expectations without limit to what we discover to be there? Santayana was also disturbed by what he thought resembled any justification of the ways of God to man. The young rebel turned to the pessimism of Schopenhauer and apparently suggested a thesis on Schopenhauer to Royce. Why did Royce recommend Lotze instead of Schopenhauer? There may have been a touch of prudence. James was quite hostile to Schopenhauer's system. If there were to be a place for Santayana in the department, it were better not to alienate a senior colleague. On the other hand, there may have been a bit of self-interest. Royce was becoming less pluralistic and more absolutistic in his metaphysics at that time. To get Lotze's alternative to Hegel clearly in mind Royce may have wanted a graduate student to reexamine the contrast.

Santayana was already known as an independent critic and was sure to provide a stimulating opponent in conversation. But one can be certain that a thesis director would stress the value to the student. Santayana's ways of thinking needed discipline. Lotze would force him to tighten up his arguments. Moreover, the young poet may have appeared to indulge himself in *Welt-schmerz*. A little healthy workaday optimism was just what was needed for a proper balance of attitude in a teacher. Probably we shall never know the exact relation between Royce and Santayana concerning the writing of this book. How much it owes to the director may be surmised.

Santayana found the task of reading Lotze not unpleasant, for Lotze wrote a good philosophic German. The thesis was produced in a year, and commended by James. The young author got an article out of the thesis, which was published in *Mind*,[5] and was given an opportunity to teach. Perhaps there is some value in holding Santayana's example before present candidates for the Ph.D. But one hesitates to think of what the pedants on a thesis committee would say of a dissertation with but thirteen footnote references to Lotze's texts, very rarely a German term to explain, and but a casual reference to the literature about Lotze! Moreover, the professional philosopher would expect quotations from articles in learned journals, not from the poems of Lucretius and Goethe. Nevertheless, one might hope that Santayana's Lotze could be used as a model in defending graduate students who introduce a light touch now and then into what can be hundreds of pages of unrelieved dreariness.

Perhaps Royce forced Santayana to limit his attention to Lotze's metaphysics; that is, what there is (ontology) and how things belong together in a world-order of space, time, and matter (cosmology). Such references as there are to aesthetics, religion, history, psychology, and generally the works of man, are only incidental to understanding Lotze's view of the world. In terms of Santayana's future development, this first work deals with *Realms of Being* rather than *The Life of Reason*. But Santayana follows Lotze in seeing likenesses between the cosmos and man, and here exercises his poetic gift for drawing parallels. Sometimes there is a casual simile, sometimes an extended metaphor. In the midst of argument Santayana makes the point vividly. For example, when defending the unity of a thought, he says:

> If not united a thought would be simply so many detached and mutually unattainable thoughts, each no greater than the sphere of its own content. To talk of uniting thought, as if it were naturally separate, is like talking of uniting the three dimensions of space which nothing but abstraction could ever sever. The only question is, is there any thought at all? If there is its unity is taken for granted. [below, p. 151]

The most striking use of an extended trope is where Santayana uses a parallelism to chess in presenting Herbart's view of the soul-atom and acts:

> The soul acts in the same sense in which the pieces act in a game of chess. As the *King's* interests may be said to be represented in the player's imagination, and as all his ideas may be called acts of self-preservation of the *King,* reactions on the *King's* part against danger; so the ideas of a man are acts and precautions of his soul. The soul is no more really threatened, no more really acts, than the wooden or ivory *King* on the chess-board. The soul is only that atom whose vicissitudes in the constellation of atoms a series of ideas represents. And, just as the pieces, when the game is over, are thrown into the box, and remain inwardly unchanged although their relations have ceased to call for representation by an interesting series of ideas; so the atom called the soul, before it enters the brain where its game is played, and after it passes out of the brain, remains itself unchanged, but is not the occasion for any ideational process. [below, p. 148]

Santayana's irony and independence of mind were well established in this book. He may have sympathized with Schopenhauer's pessimism, but he pokes fun at the pretensions of the pessimistic system-builder just as he does at Leibniz. "Schopenhauer, in spite of his heretical worldliness and maliciousness, is at bottom a discoverer of the secret of the universe, like Fichte and Hegel" (below, p. 142).

Santayana once boasted in writing "Some Meanings of the Word 'Is'" that the analytic work of distinguishing meanings came easily to him. Santayana shows this skill in his first book. For example, both Herbart and Lotze continued to use the old-fashioned word "soul." Santayana comments: "a certain acceptance which Lotze has found in conservative circles is perhaps due to insufficient considerations of his meaning" (below, p. 153). He scores also against Herbart: "Thus it might turn out that what Herbart religiously calls a soul is an atom of nitrogen" (below, p. 154). Santayana distinguished sharply between the conceptual and the real: "We have not yet heard of the cohesion of a molecule and a point, or of the friction of the earth upon its axis" (below, p. 172).

These linguistic points are not trivial in Santayana. They spring from a deep Socratic irony, peering beneath the level of discourse to the logic of the argument. Has Lotze consistently and without contradiction moved from naturalistic premises to an idealistic conclusion? Santayana is meditating on the relation between what he later calls "The Realm of Matter" and "The Realm of Spirit."

> Thus the idea of body, the idea of extended objects moving as units and remaining internally unchanged in that motion, far from leading in itself and by virtue of attentive analysis to any other conception of reality, inhibits and prevents any other conception. . . . These various conceptions have their own seeds in the mind, and they will spring up there if the soil be congenial. But the grapes of idealism do not grow on materialistic thistles. [below, p. 180]

One wonders, reading Lotze and Santayana, the extent to which our present linguistic philosophies are expansions and concentrations of what was in their philosophic generations a recognized phase of inquiry.

This dissertation does more than show technical skill, sometimes held to be the goal of such an exercise. Santayana is clearly discovering not only his own power as a philosopher, but also his own position. He takes the view that a thing cannot be a process or a series of stages, a history or a melody, but must be a substance, and this means material substance. This he holds against Lotze. With Lotze he prefers the empirical approach to the data of aesthetics, and the term "sense of beauty" occurs here seven years before Santayana published the results of teaching the theory and history of the subject at Harvard College (1892–1895). Santayana has not only found his style and shown professional skill, he also has discovered his own philosophy and his field of special competence. Josiah Royce and William James may not have cared for the conclusions Santayana had reached, but they could not help, each in his own way, respecting him and accepting him as a philosopher. We know better how Santayana qualified his esteem for his teachers than we know of their reservations about him.

LOTZE AS CRITIC OF HIS PREDECESSORS

ONE LEARNS, in reading Lotze, as did Santayana, to orient his views to those of his predecessors. One may have been already reminded of Immanuel Kant, because Lotze, too, wishes to do full justice to both the natural order and the moral order. His way is not, however, to limit reason to make room for faith, or more precisely to establish by moral postulate a realm of freedom independent of a natural realm of necessity. In the next section we will examine his system. The model of Kant was there, and also that of Herbart, Lotze's predecessor at the University of Göttingen. Santayana gives a good account of Lotze's relationship to Kant and Herbart, spiced by Santayana's defense of Herbart's atomism and materialism against Lotze (below, Ch. II). But we need to place Lotze not only as a post-Kantian, but also as an empiricist opposed to the whole rationalistic tradition. Only then can we understand why Lotze's "system" did not seem to his contemporaries and most of his successors like a system of philosophy at all. We shall be concerned with how Lotze viewed himself as a European philosopher.

Lotze was trained as a humanist as well as a scientist. That is, he was a classicist trained, through study of Greek and Latin, to study a few texts thoroughly. He belongs to an earlier period than our own, when a scholar felt himself to be part of an unbroken tradition. His own dissertations had been composed in Latin, and not only could he lecture in Latin, but as relaxation he translated the *Antigone* of Sophocles into Latin verse. Surely this was a strong bond of sympathy with Santayana. We have occasional references to Plato and Aristotle, generally to make the Aristotelian point that a real thing is part of the changing world rather than of the timeless Platonic heaven of pure forms. But Lotze sometimes pays as much attention to Lucretius as to the Greek philosophers, and there is complete silence about mediaeval philosophers. What Lotze knows of modern philosophy is the rationalist tradition, Descartes, Spinoza, and Leibniz. Lotze read his predecessors not to see them in their own historical setting, but, as a scholastic reads texts, to see answers to perennial questions. What, for example, are the least parts? This question controls much of Lotze's writing about Lucretius and Leibniz. Lotze was close to Herbart in viewing the world as composed of many real things. Here lies the explanation of Lotze's concern with Lucretius, on whom we have a Latin essay, and also Lotze's preference for Leibniz among the seventeenth-century rationalists. Lotze was deeply influenced by the theory of monads, and is sometimes therefore called a Leibnizian, although he disagreed sharply with the theory of a pre-established harmony.

The great mass of comment is on Leibniz, Kant, Fichte, and Hegel. We hear also of figures even more obscure to us than Lotze himself: Hermann Fichte (the Younger); Hermann Weisse, originally a Hegelian who became critical and independent, and who introduced Lotze to philosophy; and Lotze's friend (and sometimes medical patient), Gustav Theodor Fechner. Lotze is barely aware of Kierkegaard, though Lotze agrees with the anti-Hegelian position that existence is never exhausted by essence. On other German post-Kantians and post-Hegelians who are well known to us, such as Schopenhauer, there is silence; and of course the philosophic works of Nietzsche belong to the period just after Lotze's death in 1881.

Lotze belongs to the period before international congresses of philosophy. He had no friends among philosophers practicing in other countries, and paid no attention to French, English, Italian, or Spanish philosophy other than an occasional nasty remark about John Stuart Mill. One gets the impression only of a rich local field of activity. Lotze, however, never *says* that a German has nothing to learn from the outside world. He was happy to have his books translated, and almost at the end of his life had a controversy with Charles Renouvier in the pages of *Revue Philosophique*,[6] and contributed in the same year to *The Contemporary Review*.[7] Lotze was far from an arrogant nationalist, probably thanks to his classical training. In spite of his rich German humanistic culture, and attention from the outside world (including students, whom he received with great courtesy), he remained provincial. This is not to be read with a sneer, for Lotze had the virtue of his vice. He was an intellectually modest man, almost as docile as an historian of philosophy who does not claim himself to be a philosopher. In an autobiographical sketch in which he differentiates himself from Herbart, declining to be called a Herbartian, he expressed his position as one produced by a tradition:

> Since philosophy has developed over so long a period of time and all possible positions have been more than once discovered and abandoned, there is now no need for originality, only for exactness. To set aside the past that has made us what we are, and particularly a past in whose development we have come to be, would be as futile as it is foolish.[8]

Lotze, however, is not to be set down as simply "tender minded," to use James' development of Renouvier's *Esquisse d'une classification systématique des doctrines philosophiques* (1885). Lotze's "tough minded" rejection of the whole rationalistic tradition rather reminds an American reader of Charles Sanders Peirce's rejection of Descartes. Lotze examines the arguments of his system-building deductive predecessors, and we are taught to observe their fallacies.

Although Lotze is humble before so great a wealth of insight and skill as that presented by the rationalistic tradition (including German idealism) , and encourages us to learn its wisdom, he is clear that the tradition is based upon a mistake. What, then, of Kant and his followers in epistemology who substituted for statements about the nature of reality questions about whether we can know reality? Is not the critical philosophy a cautious modification of rationalism, studying first man's capacities and limitations? Lotze is also clear that the subject matter of philosophy cannot be limited to ways of knowing.

One epigram of Lotze's is known to many who do not know its source: "The constant whetting of the knife is tedious, if it is not proposed to cut anything with it." [9] What of the idealists— Fichte, Schelling and Hegel—who overcame, so they thought, the dualism of phenomena and the thing-in-itself by identifying mind and reality in an Absolute? These, too, continue the perversion, and, if anything, make the intellectual disease more difficult to cure.

I believe that we can trust Lotze's autobiographical account in "Philosophy in the Last Forty Years." [10] Lotze took his first courses in philosophy at the University of Leipzig from a former student of Hegel, the aesthetician and philosopher of religion, Hermann Weisse. Lotze turned to philosophy out of interest in aesthetics, as he tells in an earlier autobiographical sketch.[11] What Lotze credits to Hegel is "many incitements to . . . doubts." [12] The whole of German aesthetics is based upon a mistake, Lotze tells us in his *History of Aesthetics in Germany*.

One easily observes . . . an error, which for long has spoiled German aesthetics. Science [*Wissenschaft*], which rightly seeks the solution of its own problem in knowledge alone, is always exposed to the temptation to take its own form of activity, cognitive knowledge, as the whole or as the supreme instance of spiritual life. . . . For [science's] tasks consist only in relating, comparing, distinguishing and connecting meanings, which by itself it cannot produce, and unless provided by other activities of consciousness, it would be without object and impossible. The experiences of colors and sounds, which stimulate our senses, the experiences of space in which we find the external world together, the kinds of likes and dislikes which we experience and all the judgments of value, which are more or less clearly known to us, all these are regarded as mistaken endeavors. . . .[13]

Lotze considers, on the contrary, that the intellectual tasks of science are not the original and native modes of thinking. Even in aesthetics, German philosophy, with the exception of Winckelmann, failed to go to the experiences of the arts first, and only then to reflect upon them.[14]

Lotze again reminds us of William James, for he readily admits that he entered philosophy with "prejudices still ignorant of their destination." He questioned the rationalist's search for one single principle from which to deduce the manifoldness of the world. He questioned Descartes's assumption that the most certain thing in the world is the most fruitful thing to know. These doubts seem to be rooted in the objections to "intellectualism," which we saw exemplified in his rejection of rationalistic aesthetics, the assumption that "knowledge [is] the sole portal through which that which constitutes the essence of real existence can enter into connexion with the mind." [15] German idealism, especially Hegel, is rooted in the intellectualist fallacy that the highest principle of all can be exhausted in a single idea or thought.

Lotze's appeal, as against claims to special insight, is to pluralistic inquiry. He is opposing the beliefs of the system-builders, which he summarizes: "that their highest principle cannot possibly be contradicted; that their method, which is usually everywhere the same, is simple; and finally, that the logical structure of the system in which they gather together the results they have attained, rests throughout on intuitive evidence." [16] The truth is, claims Lotze, directly opposite and contradictory to rationalism: there is no one starting point, but innumerable starting points. There is no one universal method applicable to all phenomena; an investigator must use whatever method is applicable to the particular problem at hand. And lastly, the philosopher may not safely presume a systematic unity of principles prior to investigation.

In one word, what is wrong with philosophy, according to

Lotze, is *pretension*. Lotze rarely found it possible to say in a single word, much less a sentence, what he found wrong in even one of his predecessors. One recalls Santayana's condemnation, also in one word, *egotism*. We may demur that the post-Kantian idealists are great because of their influence on subsequent history. Out of this circle, after all, came the impressive influences called Marxism and Existentialism, and also, by reacting against Hegelianism and reviving an aspect of Kant, Positivism and Pragmatism. Nineteenth-century German philosophy is apt to impress us as the seedbed of most of what is philosophically alive in the twentieth century. But Lotze is not an historian of thought, but rather a systematic philosopher seeking to judge among alternative views which comes closest to the truth.

As an example of pretension Lotze cites the dominant system of his youth, that of Fichte. Fichte required "that no theory of the world should pass for truth and science which was unable to explain all the particular parts of the world's history as independent consequences of a single general principle." [17] The element of truth, says Lotze, is that philosophy's subject matter is the world itself. But to demand of an all-embracing system that it "make all particular parts of it pass before [us] in the majestic succession of an unbroken development"! Who could satisfy this demand but God? "It seemed to me that only a Spirit who stood in the centre of the universe which he himself had made, could, with knowledge of the final aim which he had given to his creation" see the whole.

> But we finite beings do not sit at this living root of all existence, but somewhere among the branches which have spread out from it; and only with many roundabouts, and with careful use of all the means of assistance which our position affords us, can we hope to acquire an approximate knowledge of the ground on which we stand, of the system to which we belong, and of the direction in which the motion of the great whole carries us along with it. [18]

Throughout his writings, as in these autobiographical sketches, Lotze has a sharp eye for fallacies. Indeed one should say that Lotze, like every other philosopher, reveals his own position by detecting fallacies in rejected positions. For example, Idealism commits the "fallacy of *incomplete disjunction*."

> . . . Idealism urges with perfect justice that the representation of the external world is only a representation of ours and nothing more. But when it proceeds to deny the existence of the world because of this subjectivity of our representation of it, it completely forgets that this must be so in any case. Our representation must be subjective, not merely if there were no external world, but it must be subjective also if there is. Even of a real world we could have no other kind of representation than we have, a representation reproduced through our own subjective activity, and the subjectivity of all our knowledge, which is so often emphasized, decides absolutely nothing as to the reality of its object and the accuracy of our representation of it.[19]

No set of formal rules can preserve a philosopher from error.[20] To keep us aware of our limitations, Lotze recommends that we study philosophers with whom we do not agree. "The best preservative against this kind of fallacy is the existence of hostile opinion. It is indispensable, besides developing our own doctrine, to familiarise ourselves with ideas which proceed from points of view opposed to our own." [21]

Materialism and mechanism often fall into the fallacy we call reductionism. Rather than take an example from some philosopher, Lotze observes how students reason once they have learned a bit about the physics of light.

> Now when the student has learnt that these changing sensations proceed from mathematical differences in the light waves, he generally becomes inclined to assert that colours *are* nothing whatever but different vibrations of ether; though he may perchance bethink himself at this stage of his scientific knowledge and admit that they do indeed *proceed* from those vibrations, but yet are in themselves something new and different, namely special states of psychical excitation in us. But now perhaps he learns in psychology that we have reason to regard even these qualitatively different impressions . . . as mere phaenomenal forms . . . which qualitatively are quite homogeneous, and are only quantitatively or formally different. . . . he easily grows accustomed to look down upon the many-coloured qualitative variety of mental phaenomena with a certain feeling of superiority as a sort of juggle of which one has penetrated the secret.[22]

Lotze was not in method an anti-mechanist. He pushed mechanism in physiology, and regarded the method as universally true of all processes. But it is only an aspect of nature, not the whole truth. He opposed, however, the idea that soul had to be either material or spiritual. It need not be a substance at all. F. A. Lange, in *The History of Materialism,* does not meet Lotze's argument but responds with an *ad hominem:* Lotze, "joint-manufacturer of the genuine Göttinger soul-substance with the title of a speculating Struwelpeter." [23]

Lotze's *Logic,* now little read, has much more of value in analyzing philosophical arguments. Unlike contemporary logic texts, the examples of invalid conclusions are drawn from philosophy. The cases are not merely what he has copied from Aristotle or some other textbook writer. He finds habits of mind called "doctrinairism" and "narrow-mindedness" that illustrate traditional invalid processes called "de dicto simpliciter ad dictum secundum quid," and "de dicto secundum quid ad dictum simpliciter."

> The doctrinaire is an idealist, who refuses to see that though ideas may be right in the abstract, yet the nature of the circumstances under which and of the objects to which they are to be applied must limit not only their practicability but even their binding force. The narrow-minded, on the other hand, can recognise and esteem no truth and no ideal, even the most universally valid, except in that special form to which they have become accustomed within a limited circle of thought and personal observation.[24]

Lotze proceeds to the perennial case of how some condemn all lies on principle, but then allow exceptions.

Philosophers have sometimes attempted to find in their logic the universal law and plan of the cosmos. One such clue that was trusted by many idealistic Germans was the dialectic. Lotze does not deal with the familiar thesis, antithesis, synthesis of Hegel but deals with the idea of a dialectic method. It is to guarantee

> the completeness and certainty of the formulae in which [the idealistic systems] unfolded the true content of the universe. They di-

rected their attention but slightly to the riddles of experience. To a much greater degree they had allowed themselves to be affected by the concentrated impression of all the imperfections by which the world outrages at once our knowledge, our moral judgment, and the wishes of our hearts. In opposition to that impression there arose in their minds with great vivacity but, as was not denied, in complete obscurity the forecast of a true being, which was to be free from these shortcomings and at the same time to solve the difficult problems of rendering the presence of the shortcomings intelligible. This forecast, into which they had gathered all the needs and aspirations of the human spirit, they sought by the application of their method to unfold into its complete content.[25]

Lotze feels the attraction of dialectic:

. . . it sought in a series of intuitions, which it unfolded one out of the other, to convey an immediate insight into the very inner movement which forms the life of the universe, excluding that labour of discursive thought which seeks to arrive at certainty in roundabout ways and by use of the most various subsidiary methods of proof.[26]

The illusion of dialectic is that although it is at best a way of arranging already discovered truths, it yet is presented as a form of *discovering* truth. There lurks in dialectic the metaphysical error, according to Lotze, of characterizing reality after our development of thought.

Yet Lotze himself employed stages, beginning with the many, to lead us to conclude with him that the many cannot be comprehended unless they are one. Santayana, although he never mentioned Lotze's *Logic* beyond the "Preface," shows that he has learned well how to turn an argument against a man. Writes Santayana:

Lotze wishes to coerce the mind with arguments, he wishes to make idealists of us by an artificial process. He tries to compel us to admit conclusions suggested by metaphysical and poetic insight as the results of an *argumentum ad hominem* addressed to the positivist. And the artifice employed to this end is the familiar one of constructing a series of stages, so that by imperceptible variations the unsuspecting student may be led from his native conviction to a diametrically opposite assertion. The Platonic Socrates has with admirable irony shown us how a man thus led to contradict himself may

by the same arts be recalled from his perplexities and happily be restored to his familiar thoughts. Lotze might undoubtedly have cancelled and retraced his entire argumentation, had he desired to
bring us back to positivism; . . . [below, p. 181]

In spite, then, of all Lotze's criticism of rationalism, of the
idealistic arguments, and his spotting of fallacies, was Lotze
really liberated from the basic belief of an idealist? Santayana
suggests not completely, yet he had no desire to bring us back to
positivism or to "doctrinaire" idealism. Let us inspect Lotze's
system itself.

LOTZE'S SYSTEM: A THEORY OF ORDER

LOTZE CONTINUED to show great sympathy for the monistic vision
of the world, although he abandoned the deductive method in
reaching the idealistic conclusion that reality was a single infinite and absolute mind. Can reasoning from many principles
rather than from one be justified? Time does not permit examin-
ing more than one basic line of argument, but this one seems the
most important in Lotze's system; it has proved an endeavor
fulfilled in various ways subsequently by those who had studied
under Lotze or who had read his books, and is still, I believe, a
position of value for contemporary philosophers to know.

More precisely, Lotze's question is how to get from the many
things presented to our senses, with which the sciences, arts, and
common sense deal, to the unity of the world, this ordered cosmos without which the many cannot be. If this plurality is not
to be dismissed as mere appearance, in what sense does it remain
real after we have achieved our vision of cosmic unity? If there
are distinct orders, a world of existence and a world of values,
and we cannot by beginning in one get logically to the other,
how is this discontinuity, gap, chasm, or break in reality compatible with there being a world that is an interrelated whole? Can
Lotze's results be called a "system"? Many contemporaries refused
him the name of what Fichte, Schelling, and Hegel had, whether
validly or invalidly, achieved. Lotze's critics have sometimes

classified him as an eclectic, for he chose parts of realism and parts of idealism. How can this patchwork be, as Santayana says it is, strikingly free from contradiction? Perhaps the question should be put linguistically: shall we extend the word "system" to include a theory of several logically independent realms of being? Can there be, in this sense, a pluralistic as well as a monistic system?

The basic line of argument I shall follow is Lotze's concern with relation and order. Lotze is famous for his dictum "to be is to be related," which recurs in almost every chapter of his metaphysics; and since metaphysics is the basic stem of philosophy, we hear of this basic concept of a thing in the other disciplines which branch off from metaphysics. Lotze's brief presentation of his own system in his "Encyclopaedia of Philosophy" stresses the centrality of the problem of the one and the many. Since things related are a whole made up of parts, and a whole that cannot be without parts, perhaps in studying relation and order we shall find that Lotze had a solution to a problem that has perplexed philosophers throughout Western development.

Earlier I mentioned that Santayana had picked up Lotze's metaphor that to be is like being a melody. Santayana, had he developed this as a root metaphor, might have made the discovery about metaphysical types made fifty years later by Stephen C. Pepper.[27] I believe that Lotze had a basic insight into what a thing is and extended this to the universe.

> We may compare the essence of a thing to a melody. . . . The successive sounds of a melody are governed by a law of aesthetic consecutiveness, but this law is at the same time recognised as one perfectly individual. There is no sense in regarding a particular melody as a kind, or instance of the application, of a general melody.[28]

Sometimes Lotze stresses the note related to the others as predecessor, successor, or accompanying notes in the chord. Other times Lotze stresses melody as a whole. He thinks it obvious that music could not be without both. Hence the aptness of the metaphor in expressing musical order as a solution to the problem of the one and the many. This is in contrast to using logical order as a model of the cosmos.

Other aspects of Lotze's root metaphor, that the world is like a melody, have escaped the attention they deserve. We may approach the world, as music, statically or dynamically. In *Microcosmus* we have the analysis of the world of sound comparable to the analysis of mathematical relations.

> Without spatial images of height and depth and intervals, the relations between tones would not be clear to us in thought, although in sensation we are conscious of their simply qualitative nature. . . . A note . . . has its own immutable place in the scale, . . . like a truth which has its own definite place in the system, coming between those upon which it depends, and those which depend upon it— everything has its own definite place, in the fabric of reality, between other things which are related to it with different degrees of nearness or contrast. And, moreover, in correspondence with this intellectual order, everything will appear to a soul in which its influence encounters a capacity for spatial intuition. . . .[29]

Lotze knows the limit of his metaphor: music, in the world of time and change, cannot altogether represent "the order of immutable and eternally valid systems." [30] Characteristically Aristotelian and anti-Platonic, he has given the primacy of actuality to things which change (the concrete) in contrast to the things that are eternal (the "essences" as Santayana called them), which are abstract. This is made explicit when Lotze analyzes sound dynamically.

> . . . the only reality given us, the true reality, includes as an inseparable part of itself this varying flow of phenomena in space and time, this course of Things that happen. This ceaselessly advancing melody of event—it and nothing else—is the metaphysical place in which the connectedness of the world of Ideas, the multiplicity of harmonious relations, not only is found by us but alone has its reality. Within this reality single products and single occurrences might be legitimately regarded as transitory instances, upon which the world of ideas impressed itself and from which it again withdrew. . . . But the whole of reality . . . could not properly be separated from the world of Ideas as though it were possible for the latter to

exist . . . before realising itself in the given world, and as though there might have been innumerable other equivalent instances . . . besides this. . . . Just as the truth about the individual Thing is not that there is first the conception of the Thing which ordains how it is to be, and that afterwards there comes the mere unintelligible fact, which obeys this conception, but that the conception is nothing more than the life of the real itself; so none of the Ideas is an antecedent pattern, to be imitated by what is.[31]

A thing is like a melody and the world of things a *"ceaselessly advancing melody of event."* Whitehead in *Science and The Modern World* uses the same metaphor for the pattern of an enduring object: "Thus in the organic theory, a pattern need not endure in undifferentiated sameness through time. The pattern may be essentially one of aesthetic contrasts requiring a lapse of time for its unfolding. A tune is an example of such a pattern. Thus the endurance of the pattern now means the reiteration of its succession of contrasts." [32]

Since the prime subject of philosophy is things in the process of the world, what does this make the philosopher? Clearly if he does not perceive harmony, how things belong together, he cannot be a philosopher. But perceiving harmonies does not distinguish him from other scientists and other artists, nor from one who has a religious vision of divine harmony. The finest statement Lotze achieved of the philosophic search for coherence, removing contradictions from the "riddles by which our mind is oppressed," is from *The Encyclopaedia of Philosophy*. It is paragraphs long, but worth contemplating as a whole, for it defines the search that rests upon studying evidence from all the sciences, not to synthesize their results, as some critics accuse Lotze of attempting, but to see the limitations of their principles.

'Philosophy' should not be considered as an employment of the thinking faculty, which attempts to solve problems of its own, that are . . . otherwise unheard of; and which, therefore, makes its appearance as a kind of luxury superfluous to our real life. The rather is it nothing else than the strenuous effort of the human spirit, by a coherent investigation, to find a solution, that is universally valid and free from contradictions, for those riddles by which our mind is oppressed in life, and about which we are perforce compelled to hold some view or other, in order to be able really to live at all.

Life itself involves, in that which we are wont to call 'education,' numerous attempts at such a solution. As well concerning the nature of things and their connection under law, as concerning the grounds of beauty in phenomena, and, finally, concerning the rules obligatory for human conduct, education is accustomed to establish a number of trains of thought that excite a great interest on account of the liveliness and warmth which they possess as witnesses, not for unprejudiced reflection but for life's immediate experience. Their disadvantage, however, consists in this, that they are not connected systematically together, are often contradictory of each other, and are as a rule interrupted before they have attained the ultimate ground of certainty. Aroused by certain events, which happen to one man in one way to another in a different way, all these reflections retreat in a lively manner some steps backward, in order to discover the reasons that will explain such experiences. They then ordinarily come to a halt, and regard as sufficiently ultimate principles certain points of view, which themselves include what is yet more of a riddle. It is natural that many such trains of thought, setting out as they do from different points of view, should not coincide in one whole but leave gaps and contradictions between them.

The same relation maintains itself with the individual sciences. They attach themselves to single domains of actuality, and are satisfied when they discover principles which are constantly valid within such a domain, but which at once become doubtful in their application on being carried over to any other domain. Thus the conception of a cause that acts according to law is undoubtedly valid in physics. But the consideration of organic life, as well as ethical speculations, frequently oppose to it the conception of a cause that is determined only by its ends and not by laws, or of one that acts with a complete freedom. It is the problem of philosophy to determine the claims of these different principles and the circuit within which they are valid.

Accordingly [philosophy] admits, for the present of being defined as the endeavor, by means of an investigation which has for its *object* that which is the *principle* of investigation in education and in the particular sciences, to establish a view of the world that is certain, coherent, and of universal validity.[33]

Clearly, Lotze's program in its content can be described as Whitehead describes his type of thought: "a transformation of some main doctrines of Absolute Idealism onto a realistic basis." [34] Lotze is far closer to Whitehead than to his own contemporary Herbert Spencer. Like Whitehead, Lotze was a critic of abstractions. The object of the search, "a view of the world that is certain, coherent, and of universal validity," may have been the basis of Whitehead's definition: "Speculative Philosophy is the endeavour to frame a coherent system of general ideas in terms of which every element of our experience can be interpreted." [35] (I shall, in my study of Santayana's marginalia in *Lotze's System of Philosophy,* show that even Lotze, the pluralist, sees the cosmos not without a degree of logicality and necessity when he uses the model of interdependence of discourse.)

Why should realism, belief in many independent things, be combined, if indeed it can, with idealism, belief that the world is an interdependent whole? On the face of it, it is contradictory to hold that relations are external to things and also that relations are internal to things. The program might seem to be not the way to coherence but be a sure way to incoherence. Yet coherence is saved by asserting that things-in-relation is the actuality.

Lotze's answer is that all philosophers, and all who search for truth of any sort, believe in an order of things. Lotze expresses this fundamental presupposition of the sciences in many different ways. One expression is "Nature cannot bring to pass what is self-contradictory." [36] Another is epistemological rather than logical-ontological: "the supposition of a universal relation of mutual dependence of all things real . . . [is] the common foundation of all scientific investigation." [37] When Lotze states the postulate carefully, he does not claim that we know prior to acting on this faith that there is "conformity to universal law." [38] Moreover, there are many sterile forms of this faith, among them absolute idealism because it claimed to know the nature of the order in advance, and because it took the form of a teleological plan.[39] Platonism, similarly, is a misleading form of the faith in order. "Now it is not once for all nor in a systematic order that this real world unfolds ectypes of the ideas." [40]

The basic postulate may also be stated that there is some

truth about things that we can discover. Both contrasted views, realism and idealism, "are at one so far as this, that the world must be a unity; and consequently the perfected cognition of it must be, as it were, a closed system, which can contain no parts that are not united, or that stand toward each other without any ordering whatever." [41] Of course, human cognition is never perfected; consequently the claim of metaphysics is ever to be fulfilled.

Why, then, begin one's search for the order of things realistically? Idealism would begin with the one and attempt to derive from it the many. Not only is this impossible, but also Lotze prefers to begin with the many and to attempt to discover the unity in them. This has several advantages. For one thing, it respects the logical independence of different realms.

> We require, on the one hand, certain investigations concerning that which *exists;* and, on the other hand, concerning the *value* we attach to what is actual or to what ought to be. We now see that nothing in relation to its value follows immediately from insight into the origin and continued existence of anything actual whatever; and nothing in relation to the possibility of its being actual follows from insight into its value.[42]

In another way the realistic principle helps us face the "riddles, . . . contradictions, gaps, and lack of coherence" that idealism often ignores or underestimates. Realism does not confound the thought of a thing with the real thing, nor does it take the logical to be the real. This error is illustrated in supposing that because our judgment takes the form of subject-copula-predicate therefore we can discover

> a somewhat that is without all predicates. . . . and that there can be predicates which were somewhat previous to their being actualized in some subject; and, finally, that there is in *rerum natura* some 'cement,' as it were, similar to the logical copula by means of which the predicates are thought to 'inhere'—as the customary expression goes—in the subject.[43]

Why try to finish one's search idealistically? We cannot be satisfied with the "pursuit of special investigations which are attached to single groups of problems." How, for example, do the realms of fact and value belong together in our world? Realism is partial and fails to discover the basis of cosmic unity or a "supreme Ground of actuality." [44]

Without attempting to derive the many out of the one, or confusing a "series of subjective operations of thought" with the object, Lotze affirms the key doctrine of Hegel realistically.

> . . . that the self-developing being *is* not yet that which it is to *become*, but that at the same time the possibility of its becoming . . . lies in it alone. . . . 'Being' is never simple, unchangeable 'Position,' but is constant movement through the three 'Moments.' . . . this one Absolute does not remain a wholly empty name for an obscure point, but has essentially the nature of the Spirit, and its development is the advance from the 'being-in-itself' of unconscious existence [through being other-than-self] to the 'being-for-self' of self-consciousness.[45]

We must stress two advantages Lotze sees in his combination of realism and idealism. One concerns causality and the other knowledge. Realism stresses parts independent of one another and therefore in external relations. It results in the " 'mechanical view' of forces working blindly according to general laws." But to say that the world is *"mere* 'mechanism' without any power of Ideas or final purposes" is absurd. Therefore it is truer to combine idealism with realism. The result is that we "are not bound to constantly uniform laws of . . . action, but modify . . . mode[s] of behavior at every moment with a teleological reference to the result for which [ideas] strive." [46] This spells out one aspect of the philosophy encapsulated in the root metaphor of a melody.

Not only does Lotze intend to have a truer view of causality, but also, by combining idealism and realism, to have a truer view of knowledge.

> The Realism of common opinion is wont to regard the world, apart from cognition, as a ready-made matter-of-fact that subsists complete in itself; and cognition is only a kind of appendage by means of which this subsisting matter-of-fact is simply recapitulated for the

best good of the cognizing being, but without in this way experiencing any increment of reality. Now Idealism establishes the truth that the process of ideation itself is one of the most essential constituents of the world's ongoing course; . . . that . . . the whole spiritual life is a goal, to the attainment of which is summoned the entire world of objects that do not share in the process, and the entire ordering of relations between them.[47]

Part of Lotze's epistemology is a theory of truth which was later developed conspicuously by Bertrand Russell. Lotze states that "cognition cannot be 'true' in the sense that it copies the essence of objects in form similar to the objects themselves; but at most in the sense that it repeats the relations between things in the form of relations of their mental images." [48]

Lotze does not define "relation," because it is too fundamental a concept, or "order," perhaps because he had not seen the possibilities that opened to Bertrand Russell when Russell developed his theory of relations. ("Order" is a "relation that is asymmetrical, transitive, and connected," etc.) But Lotze does indicate in discussing "chaos" what it would be like for the world, contrary to fact, not to be a cosmos. Lotze was, after all, not as concerned with the formal types of order (such as those developed also by Lotze's student Josiah Royce in his *Principles of Logic*) as he was with the actual series, networks of series, causal regularities, analogies, and processes that are encountered, not merely thought.

In passages dealing with "chaos" Lotze indicates by negation the extraordinary richness of meaning packed into the belief that there is an "abiding order of Nature." The first meaning of "order" is *"regularity* of mechanism," and its lack, then, is that "any combination of two or more elements will be just as likely to occur as any other combination of the same number." The second meaning of "order" is an *"inherent equilibrium to secure . . . preservation,"* and its lack is "falling to pieces." The third meaning of "order" is *"design"* or *"intelligent contrivance,"* which is not to be confused with "simple, undeveloped, rigid forms of being," for design may secure "things complex, manifold, yet in their manifoldness orderly," in contrast to things "mingled together as we could suppose them to have sprung together from the impartial haphazard of chaos." [49]

Can there be sheer lack of any order, in senses one, two, or three? The answer, and on this Lotze is simple and clear, must be no. The ancient atomists made a "wholly unwarranted assumption" in postulating

> infinite motion and mixture in infinitely various ways and directions. No one who means to think clearly can form any idea of the existence of such an infinite agglomeration of countless possibilities. However manifold we may suppose the original relations of the elements to have been, they must yet have constituted a total condition of the universe that was exclusively actual, and it is impossible that the other infinitely numerous conditions of the universe that might have been in the absence of this one, can have co-existed along with it. Hence the abyss of indefiniteness, to which we formerly gave the name of chaos, is unthinkable. . . .[50]

The argument of Lotze is an enthymeme: we need to supply the assumption—part of his faith in the order of things, no doubt—that what is not thinkable is impossible, and what is impossible cannot be actual.

The minimum orderliness, then, is for there to be some distinction between beings and between their states. But this gives no license whatsoever for asserting that the order of nature is simply mechanism (definition one), or equilibrium (definition two), or design (definition three). The alternative quickly disposed of is definition two. Although there is nothing "essentially unadaptable," there are accidental monsters or "contradictory . . . formations, which . . . could not themselves endure. . . ." Although such forms may aid in producing better products, they cannot mechanically continue. Out of the combinations produced blindly, we should expect some monsters. Apparently this is preferable to calling them "a selection made by designing purpose." [51]

Universal design is the most objectionable theory:

> . . . it cannot be demonstrated that all parts of Nature indicate ideal significance and definite ends; along with myriad phaenomena

that undoubtedly do create that impression, occur myriad others that comport themselves as if they were unintentional and incidental results of a chance-formed combination of atoms—results which in accordance with a deliberated plan by no means *ought* to have come about, but which *have* come about, and once in existence have maintained themselves, because they were not out of conformity with the mechanical conditions of existence.[52]

Lotze is equally severe with two forms of design, the Hegelian idea and divine predestination. The Hegelian plan of order requires not only "that all that exists is rational but further that all that is rational exists." [53] Lotze asks scornfully:

Do then all fair dreams perish, and is the actual all that can be desired? Does not even imagination in its independent creations add fresh ones to the list of forms of Nature? The actual world does not show those winged angel forms in which religious art delights, and yet we cannot show cause why these forms, to whose ideal significance our reverence is a testimony, have not deserved to exist. . . .[54]

On the other hand, we have no reason why Nature should have produced animals with such curious modes of locomotion as the giraffe and the kangaroo.[55] Divine predestination, with its doctrine that "the actual be always right," also cheats "human feeling [which] is consciously under the obligation to realize a not yet existent ideal." [56]

The only actual universal order that can be affirmed within a universal logical order is therefore a mechanical order. That order, we have already seen, can account for examples of order$_2$. But is order$_1$ compatible with examples of order$_3$? Far from universal mechanism disproving particular teleology, in principle, as we have seen, mechanism is unthinkable without some teleology.

Lotze defends this universal mechanical-particular teleological view from

. . . Nature directly, not modified by any theory of the schools, . . . there is in it much that is purposive and harmonious, yet that on the whole its existence seems to have no special significance, and that on the other hand we do not find realized all that might appear to offer a possible end to intentional design.[57]

It is clear also that an ordering of elements may occur by mechanical means and chance, without design:

. . . any motion which can be given to the elements by the propulsion of an ordering hand, could also possibly be given to them by the purposeless propulsion of an accident. In fact, it needed only a certain succession of gales in alternate directions gradually to raise the pile of the pyramids from the several grains of sand in each.[58]

A great theme of nineteenth-century thought was "order and progress," to use the watchword of Auguste Comte. Earlier we cited Lotze's metaphor that the world is a "ceaselessly advancing melody of event." Obviously, then, the order of nature is not a static order that excludes change and chance. It is one in which species emerge and evolve, though not necessarily in the merely mechanical way Darwin supposed. Lotze had reservations about the adequacy of Darwin's evidence, and looked primarily at the metaphysical problem of evolution, on which contemporary theory was, according to Lotze, deficient. Moreover, the popular use of evolution to mock human ideals as merely developments of ape-like responses struck Lotze as fallacious argument and destructive of human dignity.[59]

Although Lotze had rejected the notion of law as imposed upon nature, and reasoned metaphysically to a notion of law as immanent in the process, he did not accept what might have seemed the application of this to biological species. The explanation of his student John Theodor Merz is probably correct. Lotze had determined the main lines of his metaphysics, as a young man of twenty-four, in his first *Metaphysik* (1841). Darwin's theory came along eighteen years later, and rather than generalizing biological evolution into a process philosophy, which philosophers did later on in the century, Lotze was not particularly interested metaphysically by the *Origin of Species* and *The Descent of Man*. He saw in it more mechanism, a deficient metaphysic by itself, and the basis for reductive fallacies, of which the Germans had enough, according to Lotze, in the 1840s and 1850s.

Lotze has, we must conclude, distinguished between different meanings of "order" found in then prevalent philosophies. He has managed a "dialogue between the contending parties," and, in this case, has come to a coherent result. If this can be said for his philosophy of natural order, which Harald Høffding considers Lotze's best work, can this also be said for his general theory of relation and order?

Order is important for Lotze's philosophy of nature because the central idea there is that nature is a cosmos. Order is important for Lotze's psychology and philosophical anthropology, including epistemology, because the central idea there is that man's thoughts are in series. Hence we can easily see how the idea of parallelism or analogy is central to his whole position, expressed in the title *Microcosmus:* man is a little cosmos. The central questions are then "How are things related?" and "How are ideas and acts related?" The truth of knowledge, including philosophy, depends upon the relatedness of the inner to the outer order.

Lotze's writings are a battleground for the idealistic conception that all relations are internal and all order is mental conception, and the realistic conception that all true relations are there between things and order is there external to us to be discovered. Has Lotze succeeded in his program of beginning with the many and ending with the one, or of putting idealism on a realistic basis? Has he removed the contradictions between a theory of relations external to things and a theory of relations internal to things? Has he achieved a coherent system, or does it remain an incoherent patchwork?

The answer to all these questions must be no if we collect from his writings the passages on relation and order. On the one hand we find flat idealism. Relations and orders

> exist only in the unity of observing consciousness, which, passing from one element to another, knits all together by its comprehensive activity, and in like manner all efficacious order, all laws, that we are fain to conceive as existing between things independently of our knowledge, can exist only in the unity of the One that binds all together.[60]

On the other hand, in the same work we read:

> We have already had repeated occasion to distinguish between the relations which seemed to belong to things themselves and others into which they are merely brought arbitrarily by our thought. It is only in the first class that we shall now seek to find these relations, to be in which constitutes the existence of things; and yet those of the other class are not less important, and it is only apparently that they are foreign to the nature of things. For to establish by arbitrary conjunction relations which have no foundation in the content of things conjoined would be not thought but mental aberration; even a relation of comparison must, in as far as it is correct, have its root in the actual condition of that which is compared. If we compare things as contrary, or, greater or smaller, it is not our comparison that makes them contrary, greater or smaller, but the things compared actually had these relations to one another before we came to consider them, and the relations are found, not invented, by our thought. . . . Sometimes the contrasts are brought together and exhibit their opposition only in our thought; sometimes they encounter in reality and cancel one another; sometimes in our thoughts the greater is opposed to the less without affecting it, sometimes in conflict it makes its superior power felt. It will easily appear from a generalization of these examples that the former relations afford definite grounds for the form and content of *future* action, and that the latter are the effective conditions of *actual* action, in which the related elements do and suffer as those conditions indicate.[61]

There seems to be no sense to why Lotze is sometimes idealistic and sometimes realistic, except that the idealistic passage is from a section on the Soul, and the realistic passage is from a section on the world. But this explanation goes counter to Lotze's doctrine of panpsychism: that things are ultimately soul-like. We must shun initially the theory that there were two Hermann Lotzes, for there are some passages in which he does seem conscious of the contradictions and attempts to mediate between the two.

Metaphysic, second section of *The System of Philosophy,* seems more successful than *Microcosmus* in avoiding contradiction. The best integrated document on Lotze's realistic-idealistic theory of order is in the *Outlines of Metaphysic,* posthumously published from student lecture notes. Lotze's strategy of beginning with realism and ending with idealism emerges here when one follows the argument of the whole work.

The basic ontological question with which *Metaphysic* begins is, "What is a Thing?" The traditional answer continued to be, from the ancient Greeks, a substance with attributes. Therefore, to know the thing, one had to get at the substance and define the attributes. Then one had the existence coupled with essences. Lotze is most radical as a philosophic critic in rejecting this tradition. It is wrong because it attempts to separate substance from attributes, for we never know anything without qualities and relations. It is wrong also in trying to account for change, for the substance is considered independently real, and change involves dependence on other things. Change cannot be merely a change of qualities, for these are simple and do not change into anything else.[62]

On the other hand, if a thing is "a multiplicity combined into unity," we might say that the thing is "only the bond which connects it together, as constituting this essence." Can we identify the thing with a law? This theory "makes it appear as though it were only a thought, which itself, in turn, is a net-work of relations between various points of relation. If quality, therefore, was too simple, then a law is not simple enough to form the essence of a 'Thing.' "[63] A thing is "an actual power over its properties," but a

'law' is merely a valid rule, or a truth that prevails in the connection of our ideas, or in the connection of events as well. Of a 'Thing,' on the contrary, we demand a great deal more; it is required to be a subject, that can fall into states, and be affected and produce effects.

Nothing of this kind, however, appears possible as occurring in the case of a *truth*, which is always valid, which always is what it is, and which, since it never changes, can never pass through any experience. Every such 'law' is rather comprehensible by us merely as that mode of relation which flows from the inner nature of somewhat else; and it is in this somewhat else that we are now looking for the essence of a 'Thing.'[64]

Thus Lotze guards himself initially against confusing "to be is to be in relation" with "to be is to be a law." He wishes also not to have his question about relations and cosmic order confused with the question, why is there something rather than nothing: it is like

> raising the inquiry, how 'actuality in general' is made. But no one can tell precisely how it is brought about that, in general, something *is*, instead of there not being anything at all; or how it is made possible that something *enters existence* through coming to pass, instead of everything remaining as it was of old.
>
> This problem is not merely hopeless, but also contradictory. For every attempt to show how actuality originates assumes antecedent actuality of some conditions or other, out of which, or according to which, it originates. We can therefore never deduce all actuality, but always merely one form of actuality from another. And the problem of metaphysic is actually this: To discover the laws of the connection which unites the particular (simultaneous or successive) elements of actuality.[65]

Lotze defends what he believes is the "ordinary order" of things standing in relation to each other.

> While the things, that is to say, disappear from our perception, they still continue to stand in all kinds of relations with one another, and it is these 'relations,' in which, while they are not being observed, the 'Being' of things consists, and by which it is distinguished from 'not being.' [66]

In opposition to this philosophy he has tried to substitute pure Being; that is, that which is prior to all relations.

> Accordingly, the 'Being' of things can consist neither in their relations to us, nor in their relation to one another; it must rather be thought of as a perfectly pure and simple 'position,' 'affirmation,' or 'putting,' which excludes all relations, but forms the ground of the possibility of becoming related at all.[67]

This mistake is made by Hegel, who draws, according to Lotze, the correct conclusion: 'Being = Nothing.' Lotze's doctrine of relations is an effort to avoid this final denouement of traditional metaphysics (prolonged today by Heidegger).

When Lotze therefore writes of things as "subjects enter[ing] into . . . relations," he means not the abstract category of relation, but particular relations. We recall the point made about a melody. Each melody has a particular pattern, and it is rather useless, says Lotze, in understanding music to classify melodies. This is particularly evident in Lotze's solution to the troublesome ontological problem: what is the "soul"?

> Since we only have to do with elucidation, it is left altogether undecided whether this idea is of itself perfectly correct, or whether it, like perhaps our own result as thus far reached, stands in need of a further elaboration.

> (1) No one looks for the 'being' of the soul in an altogether relationless, self-sufficing 'position'; but the soul *is* only so far as it *lives*—that is to say, stands in manifold relations, of affection and action, to an external world.

> (2) No one looks for its essence in a 'simple quality,' so that the true nature of the soul would consist in this quality, while the entire manifoldness of its further development would only contain . . . incidental succession of consequences, which would be wrung from this quality by circumstances. Rather do we look for what is most essential to the soul in its *character;* that is to say, in that quite peculiar and individual law which appertains to the coherency of all its manifestations,—a law which always remains identical, while the occasions for these manifestations are variously changed.

> (3) We have no thought whatever, at least in common life, of taking this personal character of the soul to be an 'Idea,' of itself devoid of all effect, which as pure form is attached to a 'soul-stuff' that is in itself formless, but for this reason, all the more real. On the contrary, . . . to be thinking of the entire essence of the soul; . . . the subject of all spiritual affection and action, and, accordingly, the reality of the soul.[68]

One would want to know whether law could be identical, if further development of a person is subject to choice. How free is one if one is controlled by an essential law? At least it seems clear that for Lotze being means things and not thinghood, and soul means particular persons in relations to a particular world.

If Lotze had had more dramatic sense he would not have ended his chapters on being so modestly. He could have written that all previous metaphysic was founded upon a mistaken doctrine of substance and pure or independent being, whereas this new doctrine is founded on a doctrine of relations, hitherto neglected as largely subjective, and of dependent or related becoming. Lotze could have said that traditional metaphysic died with Hegel, but here is the new metaphysic. Such showmanship was left to Henri Bergson and others, founders of what is now called "Process Philosophy."

Lotze might have ended his ontology with a realism that distinguished objective relations by "a resistance which things really offer to one another." [69] Other relations are subjective or merely logical. But Lotze, sometimes called the first of problem-solving philosophers, was also, according to some histories of German philosophy, the last of the idealistic system-builders.[70]

How can we get from the pluralism of real things, unique but comparable with one another, individual in their peculiar relations and hence with unique laws, to the unity of things in a cosmic order?

Lotze seems to have seven arguments, that, if valid, carry us from pluralistic realism to monistic idealism. Each argument resembles some great founder of idealism: Plato, Spinoza, Leibniz, Berkeley, Kant, Hegel and Goethe. They are not presented in temporal order, and I shall deviate from the historical sequence, since the attention is on the logic of the strategy, running right through the three divisions of Lotze's metaphysic: ontology, cosmology, and phenomenology. (The term "idealism" as Lotze and Santayana use it is very general, and as used here covers positions on being, knowing, and valuing.)

Berkeleyan argument

One of the relations most carefully analyzed by Lotze is cause. Of this he says every "change of something actual" requires a cause. Earlier we took as an expression of relation-and-order-idealism the doctrine that relations and orders "exist only in the unity of observing consciousness." One argument of realism is that the individual things, in external relations to one another, are perfectly unchanged. Lotze uses this argument as a premise and produces a proof of the necessity of real change. The proof takes the form of considering not what it is, but to whom does it appear. It is Berkeleyan because if change appears, then it is. This realistic theory

> even when most strictly carried out, can only suffice to eliminate from all *external* nature any change in reality itself, and to reduce it to mere variation in relations; but that, on the contrary, an actual *interior* changeableness must, all the more inevitably, find a place for itself in that real being for which, as for the perceiving subject, the . . . appearance of an objective change is assumed to originate. For in order that something may appear, a being is necessary to whom it appears. This 'appearing,' however, has no significance except that of 'being experienced.' Now, in order that the cognitive being may experience, sometimes α and sometimes β, it must manifestly pass over from one state, in which it previously was, into another, which previously was not. And we certainly cannot assume that this passing-over is only a variation in the external relations of this being to other beings. . . .[71]

> Phenomena are . . . always phenomena *of* something or other, *for* some subject or other. The theories which make use of this expression have on this account, as a rule, come to the conclusion, not to deny all reality, but only the independent reality of individual things; and to regard the latter as 'phenomena' of a single infinite Reality,—whether in the sense that this Reality causes the things to appear to us as objective, or that it, so far as it shapes also the nature of our soul, merely produces *in us,* in a general way, the idea of a world of things without its having any actual existence.[72]

On substance Lotze is clearly a Berkeleyan realist: to be a substance means nothing more than to appear as a substance.

Hegelian argument

Lotze, as we noted earlier, wants to have a ground of unity established so that we may understand the world order. He rejects the common causal model that God created the world and established its order, and also the seventeenth-century metaphysical versions called Occasionalism and Leibniz's doctrine of the Pre-established Harmony.[73] Nevertheless, we cannot understand causal efficacy if things are independently real.

39

Now as long as *a* and *b* have the value of beings independent of each other and self-subsisting,—no matter how similar, comparable, or related their natures may otherwise be,—so long is the above assumption without a reason for its possibility; the states of *a* have nothing to do with *b*, and conversely. All the pains-taking, however, to bring these 'Things,' which are themselves quite isolated, into some relation . . . by means of ideas of the 'passing-over' of some influence, have been shown to be perfectly fruitless.

If, therefore, causal action is to appear possible at all, this assumption of the independence of 'Things' toward one another must be denied absolutely. . . .

The foregoing requirement can be met only by the assumption that all individual things are substantially One: that is to say, they do not merely become combined subsequently by all manner of relations, each individual having previously been present as an independent existence; but from the very beginning onwards they are only different modifications of one individual Being, which we propose to designate provisionally by the title of the Infinite, or the Absolute $= M$.[74]

Elsewhere, in his *Metaphysic*, Lotze explains what he means by *M*, or the unity of the whole:

. . . this eternally present condition of an interchange of action, unremitting but varying to the highest degree of complexity. For neither does this unity ever really exist in the general form indicated by this conception and name of unity and by this sign *M*. It really exists at each moment only as a case, having a definite value, of the equation for which I gave the formula, and in such form it is at the same time the efficient cause of the actuality of the state next-ensuing as well as the conditioning ground of what this state contains. Thus the stream of this self-contained operation propagates itself out of itself from phase to phase.[75]

Kantian argument

Lotze's argument proceeds from causal relations to spatial and temporal relations. Can space and time be the substance or medium in and through which things are related? Space cannot be "a ready-made, empty, and yet self-subsisting 'form'" which precedes and furnishes a place to whatever is real.[76] This conception, derived by analogy with space-containing vessels, is misleading. A vessel is not only a container of material, it is itself material, and therefore not empty.[77]

Space is not 'the arrangement of things' but "only the *possibility* of all this." [78] "If space were actually a cohering totality of relations *between* 'Things,' then, for that very reason, it could not possibly have any existence of its own, independent of things and comprising or preceding them." [79]

> Accordingly, if relations of space cannot pass for inner states of 'Things,' but are obliged and designed merely to pass for external relations between them, then it follows that they can only exist as inner states of the spirit which is percipient of the things,—that is to say, as forms of our intuition; but they have no such existence of themselves as to make our intuition a mere means for perceiving them.[80]

Lotze thus established the ideal character of space, modifying, as he acknowledges, the Kantian view. Kant set his intuition of space and time "over against 'Things' " but for Lotze there are no things to be related spatially and temporally and we, reciprocally, can have no intuition of empty time and space.[81]

Lotze, like other post-Kantians, was dissatisfied with the notion of the thing-in-itself, absolutely unknowable. He argues for a world of intellectual relations beyond the phenomena:

> . . . we perceive in space different phenomena at places which we cannot perceive in another order at our pleasure, but must see as they are. There must, consequently, be a reason in the things which assigns to them these determinate places. That is to say, even if Things are not themselves spatial, and even if no relations of space subsist between themselves, still there must be other non-spatial or intellectual relations, which can be portrayed in general by means of space-relations, and which . . . furnish the reason why, whenever they are apprehended in space-form by any intuition, each thing must appear to be at a determinate point of space.[82]

Leibnizian argument

Lotze's Leibnizian argument is a development of the theory of space coupled with a conviction that ultimately the real things are mental in nature.

All real elements can act immediately at and from any degree of remoteness; and it is just by means of these actions that they prescribe to one another the places in space at which they are to appear.

Matter consists, therefore, of a multiplicity of real beings, each of which is of a super-sensible nature and unextended, and all of which, by means of influence acting at a distance, prescribe to one another the reciprocal position that belongs to each as a spatial expression for all its intellectual relations to all the rest.[83]

If this is Leibnizian monads without Pre-established Harmony, there is *M*, which is constantly re-establishing harmony. In the world of internal relatedness, Lotze notes that physics illustrates the symmetrical relation of one thing to another: force is never "the force of a single element, but always [as of attraction] the force which two elements exercise upon each other." [84]

Spinozistic argument

So extreme becomes Lotze's statement of the oneness of all things that the plurality is almost completely swallowed up in the unity.

On considering the conception of causality, it was found that the various real beings which underlie the course of nature, when taken together, must be, either directly or indirectly, comparable; that none of them need be a *Unicum* whose nature were disparate from that of all the rest; but rather that all the contents which constitute the nature of 'Being' must form a coherent system in which each of them has a fixed place. It was further shown that all real beings ultimately can only be modifications of one single infinite Reality.[85]

Santayana in Part V raises the issue of whether Lotze has not given up the claim of freedom of the parts and capitulated to the claim of necessity of the whole.

Goethean argument

Lotze has a characteristic argument of the Romantic reaction against the Newtonian mechanism which so delighted the rationalist's sense of order. Mechanism is an order of things external to each other. Organism is an order of things internal to each other. Mechanism also separated inquiry into the general laws and "the Plan which rules in the combination of things and occurrences." [86]

Mechanism is not false in calculating the relationships of elements to each other (position and distance, etc.).[87] Nor does Lotze quarrel with "general laws, according to which this particular result ensued from this particular beginning, while from another beginning a quite different result would have ensued." [88]

> In opposition to the above view another is advanced, which discovers not impossibility, to be sure, but absurdity, in the thoroughgoing maintenance of this mechanical doctrine. . . . the thought is held to be insupportable that . . . organism . . . is assumed not to develop from within itself, but to be merely the inevitable resultant of many conditions in themselves indifferent to one another, and only co-operating as a matter of fact.
>
> For this reason it is denied that everything in nature is the necessary result of circumstances; and the conception of an organic or dynamic 'impulse' is opposed to that of physical or mechanical 'force.' . . .
>
> 'Force' was never known to pass over from one form of causal action to another without a definite inducement; 'Impulse,' on the contrary, begins its effects, starting from a state of rest, by means that lie within itself.
>
> Now it is through its own action that the living totality to which impulse appertains, is held to define for itself its own form and the connection of its development; but the external real elements it employs as means in its service.[89]

Lotze now proceeds to extend the concept organism to the "single real Being," and to attribute to it adaptation to "the changeable circumstances with a changeable activity, in such manner that the latter is at the same time always adapted to a definite final purpose . . ." [90] Then in this Being there must be represented that which is to be, but as yet is not, such that it can exercise its co-determining influence upon these reactions. This can only be if the Being "has a consciousness of the final purpose," unless the Being itself operates in a merely mechanical way. Either way, there must always be purpose finally as well as mechanism, and circumstances alone cannot account for development.[91] Lotze admits that this line of argument may be deterministic; and although this cannot be disproved, "Our mind wants that not all in the world be 'mechanism,' but that some One be 'freedom' as well; that not all be shaped by external conditions, but that some One at least shape its own being and its own future for itself." [92]

Platonic argument

The last argument from the plurality of things to the unity of the cosmic ground is Platonic. Although Lotze was sharply critical of Plato's doctrine of ideas as a theory of order, just as he differed from Berkeley, Hegel, Kant, Leibniz, Spinoza, and Goethe, still in the end he agrees with certain of his essential positions.

The first Platonic point is the connection between the spirit and the supersensible world. What is common to spirit is self-apprehension, or what Hegel had barbarously called "Being for self." This is common, says Lotze, "to all forms of *spiritual* life, to feeling, to representation, to effort, and to volition." [93] We must admit, he adds,

> that to be spirit *is* the only conceivable reality: that is to say, only in the idea of spiritual life do we understand with a perfect clearness what 'real Being' means; and . . . every as yet non-spiritual but 'Thing-like' reality is conceived of by us only through the instrumentality of a collection of abstract conceptions that make upon us the demand for somewhat more, of which we do not know precisely in what way it is to be fulfilled.[94]

The second Platonic point is the nature of the really real.

> . . . the morally Good . . . we besides conceive of [as] the 'beautiful,' too, and the 'happy,' or 'blessedness,' as united with this Good into one complex of all that has *Value*. And now we affirm: Genuine Reality in the world (to wit, in the sense that all else, in relation to It, subordinate, deduced, mere semblance or means to an end) consists in this Highest-Good personal, which is at the same time the the highest-good Thing. But since all the *Value* of what is valuable has existence only in the spirit that enjoys it, therefore all apparent actuality is only a system of contrivances, by means of which this determinate world of phenomena, as well as these determinate meta-

physical habitudes for considering the world of phenomena, are called forth, in order that the aforesaid Highest Good may become for the spirit an object of enjoyment in all the multiplicity of forms possible to it.[95]

The final achievement of order is then hierarchical and not progressive. In terms of the great watershed described by A. O. Lovejoy in *The Great Chain of Being*, Lotze belongs in his conclusion to the earlier phase of the ladder leading to perfection. Yet in Lotze's initial realism he belongs to the later phase of evolutionary thought, a temporal ordering from less to more adapted. It is most instructive historically to find a thinker trying to hold together both modes of cosmic order.

Has Lotze succeeded in bridging the gap between pluralistic realism and idealistic monism? Has he created a coherent and consistent system? On the basis of the evidence I believe the answer must be no. As Santayana wittily concludes, Lotze's monism is the price he had to pay for his pluralism.

Two pragmatists, James and Schiller, went over Lotze's argument for monism and rejected it.

The idealistic argument of Lotze is, according to James, a *reductio ad absurdum*. The realist contends

> that things, though in some respects connected, are in other respects independent, so that they are not members of one all-inclusive individual fact. Well, your position is absurd on either point. For admit in fact the slightest modicum of independence, and you find (if you will only think accurately) that you have to admit more and more of it, until at last nothing but an absolute chaos, or the proved inability of any connexion whatever between the parts of the universe, remains upon your hands. Admit, on the other hand, the most incipient minimum of relation between any two things, and again you can't stop until you see that the absolute unity of all things is implied.[96]

James then restates Lotze's argument that causal efficacy or "transeunt" interaction is impossible unless multiple things are parts of a single real being, *M*.

A pretty argument, but a purely verbal one, as I apprehend it. *Call* your *a* and *b* distinct, they can't interact; *call* them one, they can. For taken abstractly and without qualification the words 'distinct' and 'independent' suggest only disconnection. If this be the only property of your *a* and *b* (and it is the only property your words imply), then of course, since you can't deduce their mutual influence from *it,* you can find no ground of its occurring between them. Your bare word 'separate,' contradicting your bare word 'joined,' seems to exclude connexion.[97]

Lotze has fallen into the very kind of fallacy he rebuked in Hegel: mistaking the abstract for the concrete. Hegel, according to Lotze, had a merely verbal formula as a solution to the problem of reality. And Lotze, according to James, has a merely verbal solution. The names "one" and "many" don't enable us to understand interaction any better.

We have now given verbal permission to the many to change all together, if they can; we have removed a verbal impossibility and substituted a verbal possibility, but the new name, with the possibility it suggests, tells us nothing of the actual process by which real things that are one can change at all.[98]

Earlier we saw Lotze's attention to fallacies. There was the idealist's fallacy, that of doctrinairism: refusing

to see that though ideas may be right in the abstract, yet the nature of the circumstances under which and of the objects to which they are to be applied must limit not only their practicability but even their binding force.[99]

Lotze, as we saw above, was harshly critical of the intellectualism of German philosophy. James brings this very charge against Lotze:

The treating of a name as excluding from the fact named what the name's definition fails positively to include, is what I call 'vicious intellectualism.' . . . As well you might contend . . . that a person whom you have once called 'equestrian' is thereby forever made unable to walk on his own feet.[100]

Schiller, also, concluded that Lotze's proof of monism had failed. In his own summary the reasons are:

(1) A Unity of the Universe or Absolute, on Lotze's own showing, is not needed to explain the interaction of things, and in its sole tenable form is insufficient to refute Pluralism. (2) Lotze is not entitled to hypostasise his unity, nor is its immanent causality more intelligible than the transeunt causality of things. The argument from commensurability is invalid. Can commensurability be conceived as a fortuitous growth? (3) The Absolute guarantees neither causality, nor orderly succession, nor change, nor rationality, nor the existence of spiritual beings. (4) Its identification with *God* assumed and not proved, and really impossible. (5) It aggravates the problem of Freedom, Change, and Evil. A real 'God' must be a moral being and provable *a posteriori* from the facts of our actual world. All the *a priori* proofs are worthless because too wide.[101]

My own objection would be that Lotze's order monism is untrue to the distinctions between the realms of fact, laws, and values. Lotze's monism abandoned the distinctions between fact and value, between the abstract general and the concrete, and was untrue to his order pluralism. Pluralism corrected the error of the tradition that subjected all creatures to the absolute law of the cosmos or God.

My explanation of Lotze's failure is not that he lacked insight or knowledge, but that in his modesty, he lacked the courage of a great philosopher. Lotze concluded his *Metaphysic* with both faith and doubt. His faith is in order:

It is a true saying that God has ordered all things by measure and number, but what he ordered was not measures and numbers themselves, but that which deserved or required to possess them. It was not a meaningless or inessential reality, whose only purpose would have been to support mathematical relations, . . . but the meaning of the world is what comes first; it is not simply something which subjected itself to the order established; rather from it alone comes the need of that order and the form in which it is realised. All those laws which can be designated by the common name of mathematical mechanics, whatever that name includes of eternal and self-evident truths, and of laws which as a matter of fact are everywhere valid, —all these exist, not on their own authority, nor as a baseless destiny to which reality is compelled to bow. They are . . . only the first consequences which, in the pursuit of this end, the living and active meaning of the world has laid at the foundation of all particular realities as a command embracing them all. We do not know this meaning in all its fulness, and therefore we cannot deduce from it what we can only attempt, in one universal conviction, to retrace to it. But even the effort to do this forces upon us a chain of ideas, so far-reaching that I gladly confess the imperfections which, without doubt, can be laid to the charge of this attempt of mine.[102]

Lotze concludes with an Oriental proverb: "God knows better."

LOTZE'S INFLUENCE ON ANGLO-AMERICAN PHILOSOPHY

SANTAYANA BELONGED to a generation of students in the British and American universities who were, when possible, sent to Germany to do part of their professional training in philosophy. Santayana was too late to have studied under Lotze, for Lotze had died in 1881, five or six years before Santayana's sojourn at the University of Berlin. Clearly during the 1870s Lotze was the German academic philosopher who was best known to the outside world and who proved peculiarly attractive to young Anglo-Americans. I call them such because in both English-speaking countries there was the common background of a rising neo-Hegelianism and all of them except Santayana were Protestants troubled about their religious faith. Both their native empirical beliefs and their biblical faith were in trouble. Lotze was known as the man who could see them through the difficulties of adjusting the old biblical authority to the new authority of science.

We must examine first Lotze's personal influence on such young pilgrims (one of them was Josiah Royce), which is interesting because it includes many of the leaders of philosophy in Britain and the United States in the period 1880–1920. At least if we include not only Lotze's students, but also his admirers like Bernard Bosanquet and William James, we can see why an encyclopedia of the period was only slightly exaggerating in calling Lotze the most influential philosopher: "in the U.S. his influence is stronger in academic philosophy, perhaps, than that of any other author." [103] The philosophic significance of Lotze for James and others is that he formulated the problems for them and managed in his eclectic or dialectical way to state the alternatives that seemed viable: idealism, realism, and pragmatism. Consequently, all the flourishing schools appealed to his authority, although they had to make apologies for his lapses and to press his argument to conclusions he himself was unwilling to reach. The best study of the period, John Passmore's *A Hundred Years of Philosophy*, calls Lotze the most pillaged source.[104] Because of the centrality of Lotze we can see the young Santayana placed in a very favorable vantage point for seeing the alternatives. It is, I believe, significant that this period of transition chose as its most characteristic recent continental philosopher a man who is himself a transitional figure. I call the period 1880–1920 therefore "the Lotzean period."

Thirty years ago Otto Kraushaar, writing of Lotze's influence, referred to him as a "barely recognizable name to most younger members of the present generation of American philosophers." This is even more the case now than in 1938, for we would have to add older members today. Kraushaar spoke of the dust "steadily accumulating" on Lotze's works. It is now thicker, and even covers the books of most of those he influenced.[105] By now many of those who quoted Lotze are themselves obscure, and we must strive, if we are to read Santayana's book sympathetically, to imagine ourselves living in that period. Clearly lists of names, such as appear in histories of philosophy, will not now suffice.

The most vivid personal account of studying under Lotze comes from Richard Haldane, later Lord Chancellor and Viscount Haldane of Cloan, 1856–1928. Young Richard became dissatisfied with his father's fundamentalism, and in perplexity joined the Edinburgh University Philosophical Society. His great friend there was Andrew Seth (later Professor Andrew Seth Pringle-Pattison). Haldane went to Göttingen with a letter of introduction, written by a professor in Greek, to Lotze. We have his letters home mentioning his Bible-reading and his longing for hymn-singing on the Sabbath in Scotland. One of the letters home tells of the relationship:

I spent a very pleasant afternoon with Professor Lötze on Monday. I had a long conversation with him on the relation of Philosophy to religion, on materialism, the immortality of the soul, and so on. He said that a lifetime's reflection on these subjects (he is 65 and about my father's build, and like him very active) had convinced him that no ascertained truth in philosophy clashed with religion. Speculation might, but time had shown that speculations were untrustworthy till proved in accordance with facts, and he said that he was convinced that none of the Schools even of Mill or Bain had ever succeeded in bringing a single *fact* forward against Christianity. He did not believe that philosophy and Christianity had much in common—they were not necessary to each other's existence, but the reason of this was that their spheres were different. Philosophy could never perform the functions of Religion. . . . Materialism, he was sure, was a mere speculation and his research had convinced him that it was unscientific. He lent me a very rare book to read, and told me to come to see him very soon again. He was so very sociable and pleasant that one could scarcely realize that one was speaking to the greatest living metaphysician. He seldom sees people, as he lives a sort of solitary life in the country where his home is, about half a mile from Göttingen, and is looked upon as unsociable.[106]

We may smile at his simplistic version of Lotze, particularly at the failure to observe that the grounds of nonfalsification are offered for the truth of a religion; since all religion, according to Lotze, is a matter of value-judgment, and if there is a logical gap between judgments of fact and judgments of value, would not any religion be then justified? None could be falsified.

On another occasion Lotze affirmed that knowledge rests upon faith. Haldane wrote:

He said that people talked of philosophy as something different from and opposing faith and particularly Christianity, but that such people were in reality muddling up human experience with philosophy, whereas his idealistic system at any rate quite led one to expect a revelation such as Christianity. Altogether his philosophical speculations had led him to the belief that sciences in trying to explain beyond a certain point became unscientific and that a materialistic philosophy was the most unscientific of beliefs as it did not comprehend the problem before it. I proposed to him some difficulties that had come up in an analysis that I have been making lately of Causation in Willing, whereupon he got quite excited in pointing out how by faith philosophy raised itself above such difficulties in the freedom of the will and yet took the most scientific course. . . . I told him that philosophy was . . . very insufficient unless it culminated in faith. That he said rejoiced him to hear, for he felt himself convinced that without faith all fell to the ground. Then he told me of a book to read on Psychology. He was quite recovered of his rheumatism but his face tells of much suffering. I am afraid he will not live much longer and his body looks washed away and quite inadequate to the support of his gigantic head. When he goes, all scientific Germany will be materialistic with the exception of one or two second-rate men.[107]

This letter, toward the end of Haldane's sojourn in Göttingen, shows some gain over the earlier. Lotze's pedagogical skill must have been partly in taking anyone's philosophic problem seriously and in holding out a solution to encourage him.

Thirty-six years later Lord Haldane, in the midst of a lecture at Aberystwyth on "The Soul of a People," recollected Lotze:

He has produced a deep effect on German thought, and his influence has crossed the seas to Britain and America. The theological teaching of his fellow-professor Ritschl, and of Harnack later on, seems to me in large part the outcome of the principles of Lotze. They turned away from controversies about the Gospels . . . to seek in the origins of Christianity for a foundation which should require no metaphysical assistance, but should be its own witness. Whether they have succeeded time will show. It may be that they, and Lotze too, will turn out only to have opened anew the door to scientific doubt. But their work has been a great work, alike in the extent of its influence and the spirit in which it was conceived. I have spoken to you of Lotze—not merely because he was a notable figure, representative of some of the finest qualities of the soul of the great German people. He was great as a teacher, whether or not his thinking was more than that of a profound critic of other systems. He was equally great as a moral figure. . . . Thirty-six years ago I was bidden to choose for myself whether I would go to Oxford or to a German university, and I chose Göttingen because Lotze was there. I was only seventeen, little more than a boy. I remember now vividly how spiritually as well as intellectually anchorless I felt in the early days of my residence in the old University town where lay the

Hanoverian centre of learning. Göttingen was in those days full of great men. Gauss and Riemann and Weber were dead, but Wohler was there, and Benfey and Sauppe and von Jhering and Ritschl—names that stood in the "seventies" for what was highest in Germany in science and classical learning and jurisprudence and theology. Yet the figure that stood out above all the others was that of my old master, Hermann Lotze. I had the privilege, boy as I was, of seeing him often in his study as well as of listening in his lecture-room, and to the end of my life I shall hold the deep impression he made on me—of a combination of intellectual power and the highest moral stature. It seems to me but yesterday that he used quietly to enter the lecture-room where we students sat expectant, and, taking his seat, fix his eyes on space as though he were looking into another world remote from this one. The face was worn with thought, and the slight and fragile figure with the great head looked as though the mind that tenented it had been dedicated to thought and to nothing else. The brow and nose were wonderfully chiselled, the expression was a combination of tolerance with power. The delivery was slow and exact, but the command of language was impressive. Our feeling towards him as we sat and listened was one of reverence mingled with affection. Such was Hermann Lotze as I knew him.[108]

Haldane then quotes Browning's "Christmas Eve" and wonders whether the professor is not Lotze (a suggestion no Browning authority has noticed).

Some of those who went to study under Lotze adhered far more closely to his teachings. Among these was George T. Ladd, Congregational minister, Professor of Philosophy at Bowdoin and at Yale College, who later translated six volumes of the lecture notes into English, and whose own philosophy bears constant traces of Lotze's influence. Lotze was taught at Yale, and thus disseminated wherever Yale's influence pervaded, eminently in the Congregational denominational colleges. Even closer to Lotze was Borden Parker Bowne of Boston University. Boston's influence was widely felt, and although particularly strong in the Methodist colleges, pervaded far more widely. Bowne's third book, *Metaphysics,* was "Dedicated in grateful recollection to the memory of my friend and former teacher,

Hermann Lotze." [109] Bowne is credited with introducing the term "pluralism" into American usage, where it now has a richness of applications.[110]

Some of those former students of Lotze became prominent in educational administration. Among them were college and university presidents. George A. Gates, who was president of Grinnell College and later of Pomona College, heard lectures in Göttingen in 1878–79. His problems were similar to those of Haldane, and he was invited to take walks with Lotze.[111] The future American university president who had gone to Göttingen to learn to philosophize with Lotze was Jacob Gould Schurman. Although Schurman was an admirer, and was in company with Haldane's friend Andrew Seth from Edinburgh, and with another Scot of great promise, John Muirhead, he was not as fortunate in making personal contact. Dr. Schurman, later president of Cornell University and subsequently Ambassador to China and Ambassador to Germany, recollected:

> Unfortunately the great man gave in the summer *semester* of 1880 only elementary courses for beginners, and he had no *seminar.* After a short time we dropped out of the lectures, and concentrated on writing our theses for the Hibbert Trustees. . . . We owed much to Göttingen—but nothing to the professors.[112]

We learn from Seth's letters at the time: "We have heard two lectures of Lotze's on *Praktischen Philosophie.* His face has the quaint old-fashioned intelligence of a little shoemaker, but is sweet in its expression. . . . The *Metaphysik* we leave because it would break up the forenoon, and read his book instead." Two months later he visited Lotze, then revising his *Logik,* who berated Mill's *Logic* as tedious. Seth was indebted to Lotze for

his "undaunted reassertion of the fundamental truth of the view of the world implied in moral and spiritual experience." The permanence of Lotze's influence in particular is shown by the frequent references in Seth's later writings; and his deliberate judgment was that Lotze had "exercised a more pervasive influence than usually falls to the lot of any one who is not a thinker of first-rate originality and genius." [113]

There are of course many others who merely mention Lotze as one among other philosophic influences: one such is Robert M. Wenley.[114] George H. Howison, who was in Berlin at the time of Lotze's death, had no great opportunity to know him well. On the death of Lotze in 1881, William James wrote to his friend: "As you are in Berlin I suppose you are lamenting Lotze's loss. He seems to me the most exquisite of contemporary minds." [115] Howison was later Professor of Philosophy at the University of California, which once had a flourishing department with a tradition rivaling Harvard's.[116]

Histories of philosophy commonly contain lists of those influenced by Lotze whether personally or through his writings. For example:

> After 1880 we observe a fresh force in academic thought, the force of Lotze's writings. Several of the younger school of English idealists attended the lectures of Lotze at Göttingen and the effect of his views on all facets of philosophical exploration, on psychology, logic, epistemology, metaphysics, ethics, and aesthetics appears in the later expressions of idealism. It is seen in the thought of Martineau, George Croom Robertson, Charles Upton, Sir Henry Jones, Pringle-Pattison, and James Ward; it infiltrates into the Hegelianism of Bradley and Bosanquet.[117]

Rudolf Metz in his *A Hundred Years of British Philosophy* adds to this list: W. R. Sorley and Hastings Rashdall, readers of Lotze who were personal idealists rather than Hegelians, and John Theodor Merz and John Cook Wilson, both of whom studied under Lotze.[118] Merz took Lotze as the central figure in his four volume *History of European Thought in the Nineteenth Century*.[119]

But mere lists and names tell us little of how Lotze came to be a great influence. It is of more significance to know that George Croom Robertson (1842–92) was first Editor of *Mind*. Surely this journal has done more than any other agency to set the style of scholarly work in Anglo-American philosophy. In its pages we find frequent articles on Lotze, beginning with R. M. Lindsay's article in 1876, critical notices by Robert Adamson of the

Oxford translations of 1884, and an article on Lotze's realism in 1892.[120] Under the editorship of G. F. Stout, who had himself been under Lotze's influence, there appear occasional articles such as that of F. C. S. Schiller, "Lotze's Monism" in 1896, quoted in the last chapter, and "Lotze, Bradley and Bosanquet" by Agnes Cuming in 1917. Probably James or Royce advised Santayana to send his Lotze article to Robertson at University College, University of London. World War I triggered a revulsion against German philosophy in Britain and the United States, and one ceased to see the name Lotze in *Mind*. Such is fashion in politics and philosophy. The significance of these articles is that in them we see the forces of idealism, realism, and pragmatism battling one another.

Lotze's influence depended not only on acquaintance with students and the concern of editors, but also on translators. Philosophers at Cambridge and Oxford helped dissemination throughout the English-speaking world.

At Cambridge there was Sorley, Knightsbridge Professor of Moral Philosophy, who was deeply influenced, and Sidgwick, Professor of Moral Philosophy, whose meticulous studies in *Methods of Ethics*, 1874, parallel Lotze's work. A former student of Lotze, James Ward, was a powerful influence on the rising generation of philosophers.

That James Ward fell under Lotze's influence was no accident. "Lotze combined the interests—scientific, philosophical, and religious—which were struggling in Ward's mind and which dominated his career. . . . [Lotze's] thought appealed to Ward who was equally alive to the demands of exact science and to the claims of moral and religious values." [121] Ward's theological liberalism, like Gates' non-creedal Christianity, was unacceptable to Congregational authorities. Ward's specific personal doubt was of the personality of God, a belief equally threatened by universal mechanism, pantheism, and Hegelian absolutism. It was precisely Lotze's metaphysical and moral personalism that gave Ward what, in his own words, he needed: " 'the line of apology for Christianity . . . that shall rest on first principles.' " [122] Much like Haldane, Ward was writing letters home about theological problems that seemed to clear up under Lotze's influence; that is, the young man could then philosophize without excluding " 'personal communication with God from the world altogether' "; [123] that this motivation ran deep in Ward's subsequent development which Lotze helped to shape, can be seen in *Essays in Philosophy*.[124]

One of Ward's students tells of the life-long emphasis upon science and religion:

> Ward had grown up during the period of the discussion of the biological theory of evolution. He insisted that his students should study some biology and himself gave definite attention to the philosophical problems arising from the fact of living organisms with their genesis and strivings. The conceptions of physics are not enough for the understanding of the world. In his second series of Gifford Lectures, *The Realm of Ends,* he emphasized the purposive aspects of life.
>
> In contrast to MacTaggart, Ward maintained that the hypothesis of Theism was the most satisfactory one in philosophy. There are too many uniformities and unities in the (so-called) physical world and the psychical nature of men for them to have arisen out of the interaction of a multiplicity of beings. The hypothesis of a dominant mind was necessary. . . . in the development of his theistic philosophy he had given no attention to the religious experiences of mankind, but . . . they required specific consideration. (I made that one of my own tasks.) He accepted the belief in human immortality but did not give it much discussion. In his writings and his lectures he rarely referred to traditional Christian dogmas. I am inclined to think that the sadness of his period acting as a Christian minister was due to the painful discarding of doctrines in which he had been reared. In his generation many went through profoundly disturbing experiences of theological doubt.[125]

Ward's students came to hold Lotze in high regard. They were taught that Bergson did not deserve all the attention he got. The reality of *durée* was taught by Lotze.[126]

Men of Whitehead's day in Trinity College, Cambridge, were brought up on Lotze: G. E. Moore, Bertrand Russell, C. D. Broad. Ward set Moore "to read pieces of Lotze's *Metaphysic* and to write essays on these pieces, which essays [Ward] then," wrote Moore, "discussed privately with me. His lectures, which were attended by three or four of us, were also very stimulating. They were on what in Cambridge is officially 'metaphysics' . . . a subject which includes the whole of philosophy except Moral Philosophy." [127] What Russell read of Lotze was on the theory of space, on the one and the many, and on Leibniz's monadology. Russell, like Moore, came to think of Lotze's thinking as he thought of Ward's: "often very confused." Russell had read Lotze closely and calls attention to his poor historical scholarship in commenting on Leibniz.[128] Russell characteristically preferred his philosophic types unmixed: if it were monism, then Hegel; if pluralism, then Leibniz; but not "monadism-monism"! [129] Lotze was one of the philosophers set for examinations at Cambridge. C. D. Broad, who won the Burney Prize with an essay on *Lotze's Philosophy of Religion,* tells of working in the years 1908–10

for Part II of the Moral Sciences Tripos in the Section of Metaphysical and Moral Philosophy with the History of Modern Philosophy. The two philosophers set for special study on that occasion were Leibniz and Lotze. Lotze was rather a bore, though there is plenty of good stuff in his voluminous writings, and one cannot help liking a philosopher who refers familiarly to the Absolute as 'M.' Leibniz was exciting in himself, and was made more so by Russell's then recent *Philosophy of Leibniz* and by the fragments . . . published by Coutourat.[130]

The leader in translating Lotze into English was the very distinguished Thomas Hill Green (1836–82), Professor of Moral Philosophy at Oxford, who set out to do for British public life what Florence Nightingale had accomplished in nursing. Green's student, Cook Wilson, went to Göttingen to hear Lotze, and returned to his lifelong career as a fellow of Oriel College and Professor of Logic. The Editor's Preface to *Logic* says:

Since the present Translation of Professor Lotze's 'System der Philosophie' was begun, both the author himself, who cordially welcomed the undertaking, and Professor Green, who first definitely proposed it, have been removed by death. These two distinguished men, however different in method and style of thought, had some fundamental tendencies in common; and it may be of interest to Professor Lotze's admirers in this country to know that Professor Green not only executed an important part of the Translation, but intended to take upon himself the task of revising and editing the whole, which was not entrusted to the present Editor till after Professor Green's death.[131]

Bosanquet thanks various dons for their cooperation. John Cook Wilson is singled out in both this preface and that of the *Metaphysic* for assistance in translating technical passages dealing with mathematics and physics. The staff included the literary scholar A. C. Bradley and the Plato scholar R. L. Nettleship, both fellows of Balliol, and others, including a priest, not now regarded as illustrious.

A year later, a translation of the *Microcosmus* was first published (1885) under the distinguished name of Hamilton. The translation was begun by Miss Elizabeth Hamilton, daughter of Sir William Hamilton. Death ended Miss Hamilton's work on page 659 of Volume I, and it fell to Miss E. E. Constance Jones of Girton College, Cambridge, to complete the work (783 additional pages). Miss Jones thanks two Cambridge dons for advising her: Sidgwick and Ward.

As though this were not prestige sufficient to make Lotze one of the immortals in the philosophic pantheon, one of the Oxford dons who helped translate the *Logic*, F. C. Conybeare of University College, published the posthumous translation by his (Conybeare's) wife of Lotze's *Outlines of a Philosophy of Religion*. She was Emily Mary Müller, daughter of the eminent philologist Max Müller (one of the celebrities of Oxford who supervised translating *The Sacred Books of the East*). The touching 'Preface' gives us a picture of practical Lotzean religion, hinted at by Haldane in the Ritschlian emphasis on good works rather than on correct doctrine. Emily Mary Müller was under the influence of Arnold Toynbee at Oxford and therefore deeply concerned with the poor. In her charitable work she is said to have

> continued . . . indefatigable . . . to the last. The work of visiting the poor was thoroughly congenial to her, and she knew how to sympathise with them in their wants and difficulties; how to advise and help them without patronising them. . . . the belief in the brotherhood and equality of men is very easy to entertain and air as a drawing-room conviction. . . . she had no ulterior motive for her charitable visits, no anxiety to get her people to go to church.[132]

The most thorough studies we have of Lotze's influence reconfirm the impression that the admirers of Lotze were on the "liberal" rather than the "conservative" side of the political fence, quite unlike the admirers of Hegel and Nietzsche, and some other German philosophers.[133]

English and American readers of these translations seem to have followed Lotze's advice in the "Preface" of the *Logic* "to regard it as an open market, where the reader may simply pass by the goods he does not want." Ward passed by the idealistic monism and what Moore, Russell, and Broad (perhaps Whitehead also) were given at Cambridge was realistic pluralism. What Oxford students got, except from Schiller, was Lotze the last great Hegelian, a modernized version to make allowances for empirical science. Schiller, of course, isolated the pragmatic strain in Lotze, separated from what Schiller regarded as Hegelian nonsense.

Some Lotze articles were written by critical realists, like those of the very able Robert Adamson, who held with him that thought must be sharply distinguished from thing, and that therefore truth was correspondence of thought to thing, and knowledge was the mind's relation to something other than itself.

> To Lotze himself, as one may gather from many detached criticisms and from the general tenour of his whole treatment, there appeared to be one vast difference between his own conception and that of Hegelianism, a difference extending beyond and lying at the root of the manifest divergence of method. In laying out the matter of

metaphysic, Lotze adopts on the whole the method of Herbart, and generally is of opinion "that it is only inquiries conducted in the spirit of realism that will satisfy the wishes of idealism." But the superficial difference of arrangement only indicates the deeper opposition in which Lotze stands to the Hegelian method. To him that method seemed to imply the view that the ultimate nature of reality was to be found in and was exhausted by a symmetrical interconnected system of thought-determinations, from which in some way the real proceeded, of which the real was in some way the imperfect manifestation or shadow. Even though at times he is forward to acknowledge that in Hegel are found correctives of such a view, he is yet consistently of opinion that the Hegelian method leads to nothing but a rehabilitation of the Platonic impassable and unworkable division between the realm of absolute thought and the changing, variable, transitory and relatively non-beënt world of finite fact. To such a conception he stands in irreconcilable opposition and would press as against it the view that found in Aristotle its early exponent. With a statement of the opposition the *Logic* closed, with a restatement of it the *Metaphysic* opens.[134]

The idealists were indeed aware of realistic tendencies in Lotze, but all these were to be deplored because they led to nothing but incoherence. Since, argues the idealistic critic, Lotze had fixed a gulf between thought and thing, relying upon common sense and the empirical method of scientists, he must think a true judgment corresponds to a fact and a false judgment fails to correspond. But what do we have of the thing but another judgment, hence an impossibility that Lotze can only resolve to his own satisfaction by an act of faith? Lotze "gets on the one hand a hypostatised world of ideas and on the other an unknown world of 'things.' . . . That is the worst of philosophies in two pieces; they have to be inspected twice over. Lotze indeed seems anxious to save us the trouble by trying to weld the two pieces into one, in his philosophy of religion." [135]

Another idealistic critic of Lotze, Agnes Cuming, calls attention also to the dualism of sensation and conception. There cannot, on this basis, be knowledge that is necessarily true:

Lotze's dualism is radical and complete. He makes a cleft between feeling which supplies the material and thought which exercises its purely formal activity upon it. That truth results from this partnership of functions which are utterly diverse is explained by Lotze in words which make it almost seem due to a happy chance. In his *Logic* he says: "The nature of . . . things, of the given thinkable contents, is so constituted, that thought by surrendering itself to the logical laws of these movements of its own, finds itself at the end of its journey if pursued in obedience to those laws, coinciding with the actual course of the things themselves." To bring an element of necessity into the account of thought's dealings with reality was impossible on a theory which had put an abyss between these two factors of the judgment.[136]

The latter idealistic critic seems well aware of the pragmatic elements in Lotze, but neither critic sees anything but the dichotomy between the false realistic theory, correspondence, and the true idealistic theory, coherence. The latter critic summarizes the pragmatism beautifully:

The *aim* of thought is not to be or to copy reality, but to be valid of it; thought is the means or the tool of knowledge. The nature of this tool Lotze deduces from its two limiting conditions: it must fit the thing and it must fit the hand. According to the first condition the forms and laws of thought must "show a constant and regular adaptation to reality," according to the second, which is more important for the understanding of Lotze's peculiar position, these forms and laws are the result of the place which Lotze assigns to the human mind. The mind of man "has a modest position somewhere in the extreme ramifications of reality," and the operations of thought which are made necessary by this position need not therefore correspond to the reality which we are trying to understand, but may be, in Lotze's image, frequently a mere scaffolding, which helps us to construct the building without forming part of it. In other words, thought is a round-about laborious substitute for the "adequate perceptive intuition with which, for some unknowable reason, man is not endowed." [137]

Idealists of the Lotzean period were well aware of the roots of the *Logic* of Bradley and the *Logic* of Bosanquet in Lotze's *Logic*. Dewey's instrumentalist logic was similarly formulated by constant reference to Lotze.[138] Both the idealistic and instrumentalist versions were theories of "the human act of inferring" and not theories of implication. We have been cut off from this other tradition by the prominence of formal logics developed by Whitehead, Russell, Royce, and others.[139] Doubtless the time is overdue for us to reconsider this other tradition. For one thing, as I have shown earlier, it provides a fruitful consideration of fallacies in philosophic argument.

In America, as in Britain, young men found out whether they were to be idealists or realists, or perchance, pragmatists, by writing about Lotze. In this context, when we reread Santayana's account, published fifty-six years after the thesis was completed, we may wonder whether he had not forgotten the philosophic issues:

> On my return to America in 1888 I at once consulted Royce as to my thesis for the doctorate, and suggested for a subject the philosophy of Schopenhauer, because Schopenhauer was the German author that I liked most and knew best. The wise Royce shook his head. That might do, he said, for a master of arts, not for a doctor of philosophy. Instead, he proposed Lotze. I had read Lotze's *Microcosmos* [sic] and liked a certain moderation and orthodoxy that pervaded it, without deeply respecting its principles or its conclusions. Lotze was a higher form of Palmer. But Royce said that his other books were more technical and his metaphysics rather Leibnitzian. That sounded better. I agreed, procured the complete works of Lotze, and set to work to read, digest and annotate them, composing a running summary and commentary, out of which my thesis might be afterward drawn. It was a pleasant task, not at all brain-racking. I was soon absorbed in it, living in complete retirement at my mother's in Roxbury. For exercise I would walk to Boston or Cambridge. I went to weekly seminars, admirable stimulants, given by James and Royce. James read to us from the manuscript, chapter by chapter, his new *Principles of Psychology;* while with Royce we read Hegel's *Phaenomenologie des Geistes.*
>
> I wish now that my thesis might have been on Hegel; it would have meant harder work, and it would have been more inadequate; yet it would have prepared me better for professional controversies and for understanding the mind of my time. Lotze was stillborn, and I have forgotten everything that I then had to read in him and to ponder. I liked Hegel's *Phaenomenologie;* it set me planning my *Life of Reason;* and now I like even his *Logik,* not the dialectical sophistry in it, but the historical and critical lights that appear by the way. I could have written, even then, a critical thesis, say on

Lotze's Influence on Anglo-American Philosophy

Logic, Sophistry, and Truth in Hegel's Philosophy. This would have knit my own doctrine together at the beginning of my career, as I have scarcely had the chance of doing at the end. My warhorse would not have been so much blinded and hidden under his trappings.

My dull thesis on Lotze was duly accepted, and I was told that I was the most normal doctor of philosophy that they had ever created. Retrospectively I may have been, because most of the candidates had been lame ducks; but prospectively, as a doctor who teaches, I was to prove unsatisfactory and irregular. They may have suspected as much; but they were kind masters and not in a position to make great demands. They accepted me thankfully in spite of my lack of a vocation for teaching; and at once a place was made for me among them.[140]

To understand Santayana's handling of Lotze we should put it in the context of the relations of James and Royce to Lotze.

Royce as a young man seems just like all the others who went to study under Lotze. As he tells us in his first book: "The religious problems have been chosen for the present study because they first drove the author to philosophy, and because they of all human interests deserve our best efforts and our utmost loyalty." Such problems are solved, he tells us, not by turning away from doubt, but by pushing doubt to its farthest point. Out of the paradox "what if all be error?" comes a new faith.[141] If Royce passes on no anecdotes of walking with Lotze or visiting him in his country study, it may be because he was too shy to break into the meditations of a retiring man. But impersonally Royce commented in "Present Ideals of American University Life" that it was a privilege to have done graduate study in Germany. "Lotze or Helmholtz, or Mommsen was his master. He could hear and read his fill, in a world of academic industry, and amidst elsewhere unheard of treasuries of books. The air was full of suggestion."[142]

In Germany I heard Lotze in Göttingen, and was for a while strongly under his influence. The reading of Schopenhauer was another strong influence during my life as a student in Germany. I long paid a great deal of attention to the philosophy of Kant. But during the years before 1890, I never supposed myself to be very strongly under the influence of Hegel.[143]

One wonders why Royce does not, like James, quote frequently from Lotze. James both praises Lotze as a genius and disagrees sharply with what he thinks are fallacious arguments.

Santayana was working on a philosopher who touched off sparks between his director, Royce, and the other reader of the thesis, James. Perhaps the thesis was "dull" by comparison with the debates between the two:

> Royce disagreed with the negative criticism of his German mentor by his Harvard colleague. He took Lotze to be no monist but, as he said to Santayana, "rather Leibnitzian." On this point, Royce is certainly nearer the mark than James. Lotze, an adversary of the absolutism developed in post-Kantian idealism from Fichte to Hegel, was one of the thinkers who helped to undermine Hegelianism in Germany—a consummation that James devoutly wished and enthusiastically applauded while he was lamenting the revival of the Hegelian philosophy in Britain and America.
>
> Royce, on the other hand, demurs at the Lotzean metaphysics where James does not. Lotze's appeal to validity falls under Royce's general indictment of critical rationalism, the confounding of actuality and possibility. And Royce would not admit that Lotze accounts for the place of sentiment in the search for truth. Where Lotze wants the truth for the good of humanity, Royce wants it for its own sake and regardless of its impact on our ideals and aspirations: "Doubt should be earnest." Again, Royce was not so convinced as James about Lotze's empiricism, which he judged inferior to Le Conte's on the score of scientific knowledge.
>
> The Lotzean system was, therefore, not acceptable to Royce, who scarcely refers to it while building his own. His legacy from his Göttingen professor was primarily a matter of spirit, approach, method. Lotze hoped to erect a grand synthesis of human knowledge; so did Royce. Lotze intended to remain hardheadedly empirical without rejecting idealism; so did Royce. Lotze wanted to purify old metaphysics with new logic; so did Royce. Lotze argued for a union of facts and values that would save the uniqueness of each; so did Royce.
>
> Lotze achieved with Royce what is doubtless the highest achievement of any teacher with any pupil: He inspired him to creative reaction rather than to pious imitation. After learning Lotze's system

Royce would never again be moved by Spencer's. After mastering Lotze's technique, Royce would become progressively more dissatisfied with Lotze's system. His mind alerted to the dimensions of philosophical problems, he was impelled to look for more satisfactory ways of dealing with them.[144]

The dependence of James on Lotze has been told with great care. Ralph Barton Perry mentions James's admiration; Lotze seemed to him the

'deepest philosopher' of the day, and 'the most exquisite of contemporary mind.' Like James, he had undertaken to reconcile the new science with the old moral and religious earnestness; unlike James, he was a system builder on the grand scale. In his final reckoning with monism, James selected Lotze's proof of monism for special refutation. But while he rejected the argument, he esteemed the man. He was moved by Lotze's moral eloquence. He was attracted to one who could write well in spite of being a German philosopher. And, waiving the fundamental issue between pluralism and monism, there were many doctrinal bonds. James's early and persistent rejection of associationism, in what he called its 'nihilistic' implications, certainly owed something to Lotze, who had distinguished merely external conjunctions from the 'inward kinship' of things that 'belong' together. Again, there was the appeal of panpsychism, to which James never wholly yielded, but to whose attractions he was never insensible. Of even greater importance was Lotze's notion that worth or validity is a radical principle, irreducible to existence; that, in fact, things *are* what they are *worth*. Here are intimations of pragmatism and of many ideas dear to James's mind. Finally, Lotze, like James, was willing that faith, prompted by conscience and feeling, should pronounce the last word.[145]

How had Santayana come to read Lotze's *Microcosmus?* Had he been a few years younger he might have read it with James, for James adopted the English translation immediately in a course, and used Lotze three times in the 1890's.[146]

James's acquaintance with Lotze went back to 1867, when he bought *Medicinische Psychologie* (1852), and James's writings show a close study of Lotze's physiological and psychological writings. James's approach to Lotze the metaphysician was thus through Lotze the empirical, realistic, and indeed mechanistic physician. There is, I believe, evidence sufficient to warrant the generalization that this made a vast difference between James's Lotze and Royce's Lotze. Royce was an expert on the development of German metaphysics, and Lotze must have seemed a rather weak version of Kant, Fichte, Schelling, and Hegel. But there is an advantage to a fresh empirical beginning as well as a long rational tradition. James regarded Lotze as a fresh start, "not as a kind of attenuated Hegelian idealism, but as a promising new philosophy." [147]

Lotze, as we saw earlier, was a sharp critic of the whole rationalistic tradition, especially German idealism. James was a rebel at heart and hated stuffy assurance and security. British and American idealists seemed to James and Santayana to be like their German predecessors, a bit self-satisfied and overbearing, and sometimes too proper and self-righteous. In James's pages Lotze comes alive as a man of flesh and blood, not a disembodied spirit. A whole range of teachings about man appealed to James as the truth: we learn through the senses, and what we notice and remember is to the service of bodily needs. We are moved by love, fear, hatred, and ambition. We are creatures of emotion and will. James agreed with Lotze that the vital meaning of "freedom of the will" is "unrestricted choice between the objects . . . put within its reach." James, in short, agreed with Lotze about what a human being is like, and thus freed the "Dionysian" and original, empirical elements from the "Apollonian" doctrines of his tradition.[148]

Lotze was not only rebellious against intellectualism, and in the old sense of the word, an "anti-intellectual," but also he did not conceal from the reader his doubts and his faith. There are frank statements about the peculiar personal motivation of a problem, not pretending that the philosopher is a pure seeker of truth for its own sake. Philosophy is not and cannot be, for either Lotze or James, a pure or strict science. As we saw above, not to claim necessity and certainty was unforgivable to the idealists. Both Lotze and James detested Hegel's method of dialectic, which was supposed to guarantee completeness and adequacy of the truth. Both Lotze and James wanted to move the reader to action, and made no bones about using the imperative mood. For example, would this sentence fit a James essay? "Moses may stand on the Mountain of speculation and pray that the laws of thought may be faithfully observed; but the facts can only be brought into subjection by what Joshua is doing in the valley." James would have liked to have written it. It has the ring of a call to action.[149]

Three particular doctrines of Lotze are reaffirmed in James: that there is an underlying manyness and variety of things; that reality consists of free agents; and that even if thoughts and things are not congruent, at least our thinking is efficacious in action. All of these are contrary to the monism, the determinism, and the *a priori* rational and deductive methods of idealism. When Santayana was attending James's seminar in 1888–89, hearing *Principles of Psychology* chapter by chapter, had James developed this interpretation of what is original and vital in Lotze? We are told that James had one period of thorough review of Lotze, in preparation for the publication in 1890. Perhaps it was not until the later period that James so expressed his profound philosophic sympathy with Lotze. At any rate, the Jamesian Lotze is not one who would have appealed greatly to Santayana. Although earlier it seemed that Santayana's interpretation was aimed at correcting what he viewed as Royce's incorrigible optimism, perhaps it was also aimed at correcting what he viewed as James's irresponsible romantic irrationalism.[150]

"As to Lotze—see you do *justice* to his valiant effort to be at once a scientific man and a philosopher in times when the latter was no credit, and also to the great solidity and critical watchfulness of the man." So Edward Caird advised his friend Henry Jones.[151]

We have not done Lotze full justice in this sketch of his influence. To do this would require an account of his influence in Germany. He trained or helped train many of the leaders of the next generation: Stumpf, Twardowski, Windelband, Rickert,

Lask, Driesch, Paulsen, Dilthey, Eucken, Wundt, Büsse often are recorded as indebted to him. Of greatest interest are his influences, as yet unexplored, now affecting us strongly through Husserl and Frege.[152] Nor have we begun to show his influence in Scandinavia and other European countries.[153] To be really thorough would involve following lines of influence to Hungary and Russia.[154] Among the interesting claims for Lotze's novelty is that he is the "true founder of modern value theory." [155] Related to this work in value theory, joining together aesthetics and ethics, is his influence through Ritschl on theology.[156] There is also the considerable influence in psychology.

In the light of all this evidence I cannot but conclude, with Philippe Devaux, that Lotze's influence has been considerably underestimated. This essay, although it tends to explain Lotze's pre-eminence sociologically, calls attention to the continuing influence of his type of philosophy, but not his own name. In many ways, as I have already pointed out, Lotze's system is much like Whitehead's. The Belgian critic regards them as philosophical cousins. Since this is one of the metaphysical types most prominent now in the United States, the last question must be answered: "Is Lotze's System Relevant to Our Philosophical Situation?" [157]

LOTZE'S RELEVANCE TO CONTEMPORARY PHILOSOPHY

LOTZE'S SYSTEM of philosophy, the philosophy stripped by James and Schiller of its traditional monistic encumbrances, is a live option today. In this conclusion, obviously denied by those who regard Lotze merely as a post-Hegelian or transitional curiosity, I am making three assumptions.

I am assuming first that both nineteenth-century and twentieth-century positivism have failed to show that all metaphysics is either outmoded or nonsense. I am assuming that those like Lotze who refused the doctrine that only scientific questions are meaningful helped to keep more general questions about reality alive and deserve credit for so doing. When Richard

Falckenberg, an eminent product of Lotze's seminars, told the prorector of Erlangen University, a chemist, that he would devote himself to philosophy, the latter was astonished: " 'To philosophy? Do I understand? Speculative philosophy? That is impossible; philosophy is long since dead!' It was, almost. It was the low-water mark of our pursuit." [158] I do not mean that positivism has been entirely wrong: Lotze is himself deeply sceptical about our ability to answer such riddles as "Why is there something rather than nothing?" He is not trying to tell God how to construct a universe.

I am assuming also that the supposed successors to speculative philosophy—existentialism, phenomenology, and analysis—are but aspects of philosophy and that the need of system is perennial. This system need not be deductive, and indeed, according to Lotze, cannot be deductive: it is against this that there has been a legitimate revolution in philosophy, and Lotze should be allowed a share of credit in such benefits as the revolution has had. I have, in discussing Lotze, already made points about human freedom and choice, the given in experience, and the importance of not confusing the linguistic order with the real order. None of these aspects seems to me of such overwhelming importance that all else of the tradition should be sacrificed; philosophy cannot be only a doctrine of groundless freedom, or only the study of the given, or only the study of language.

The first and second assumptions must have been made also by Santayana. I am doubtful if he would care, however, for my third assumption. It is that the metaphysics inherited from the ancient Greeks, based on the notion of a real substance independent and autonomous, was a mistake. The metaphysics beginning with Parmenides and ending with Hegel was then properly rejected by Lotze. But this left room for a relational concept of being, particularly a concept of being in change and therefore temporal. Lotze was one of the discoverers of this new type of metaphysics. I believe it has become clear that he rejected, as did Whitehead, the "subject-predicate form of expression" as metaphysically inadequate, and rejected the Platonic notion of forms as more real and real antecedent to embodiment in things; he also rejected what Whitehead calls "vacuous actuality" or space and time as real containers of things and events.[159] Santayana recognized some of these heresies in Lotze, because he was searching for orthodoxy. For the same reason he underestimated the new type of metaphysical system as an alternative to the old type.

To bring these considerations to bear on reading Santayana I will first try to trace the lines of the new metaphysics, called "Process Philosophy," in his account of Lotze. I will then try to show that the parallelism of Lotze and Whitehead is not superficial but extends to some of the principles of Whiteheadian metaphysics and encompasses numerous details that seem to mark this off as a distinctive type of metaphysics, not a mere juncture of realism, idealism, and pragmatism.

In writing *Lotze's System of Philosophy* Santayana came to recognize in Lotze a new set of metaphysical positions:

No one, I think, will fail to admire the beauty of this conception of the life of nature, and the ingenuity with which it combines various convictions which we all retain, although philosophy has often found them to be contradictory. The reality of events, the truth of our natural belief that something happens in the world, that thought, the demiurgus, has not yet finished his work, but continues to hammer at matter and transform it into new and unexpected shapes,—this conviction is reconciled with the belief in universal mechanical laws. And the responsible and original decision by which things are what they are is distributed throughout nature and not confined to the adoption in the beginning of a tyrannical constitution, which allows no activity in the world besides that which it itself directs. If the formulation of doctrines that appeal to mankind, if the explaining to men what they really believe and are trying to say of the world, be the task of philosophy, Lotze in this instance would seem to have admirably fulfilled it. If his doctrine were not so subtle, if it did not require such care and moderation in the combination of its elements, one would be tempted to predict that it would some day become the received and orthodox doctrine of the world. But whatever may be its fate, its merit is unquestionable. [below, pp. 204–205]

Let us examine the "elements," as Santayana calls them, that fit coherently into this new pattern now called process philosophy, but which then had no name. To be clear about them we shall name and number them. Since all of them have already been discussed, we may gain by brevity a succinct conspectus.

1. The real things of the world are processes. The unit is in relationship with other things and changing, so that what we can know of it is the series of its states. The mark of reality is effecting changes in other things and resisting changes from outside.

2. The characteristics of things are just what they are, and since they do not change, and neither effect nor resist change, they are not real. They are aspects of real things that we may abstract and consider as possible, and manipulate in thought.

3. There is a plurality of real things in causal interaction with each other. Real changes are effected by one thing in another, so independence and self-sufficiency are not marks of reality but of inactual and merely possible characteristics.

4. There is real spontaneity, or self-induced change. Things are in process of realizing their own immanent aims. There is no absolute beginning or end of the total process, only fixed logical limits such as laws of identity, contradiction, and excluded middle that are discovered holding of things.

5. The minimal regularities of things are mechanical laws. Since these laws state the natural order—how things affect each other in causal change—and since things are not governed by necessity external to them, these laws cannot be fixed for all time.

6. Consciousness or soul is not a substance but a series of events. Being conscious of something else is a higher degree of relationship that is present throughout real things, not limited to human beings. How things are aware of one another is far richer than conceptualizations of characteristics and laws.

7. The interacting totality of real things is a cosmic order. Although there is spontaneous change of the parts, and real

chance is not excluded, yet the resultant totality of effect is har-
monized in keeping with some overall plan.

8. The ground of the overall plan is the ground of all values,
aesthetic, moral, etc. This ground is called "God," and may be
said to be a person, persuasive through the possibilities he provides, but neither an absolute creator nor omnipotent.

I have here schematized and condensed about fifty passages
that spell out the new metaphysics in Lotze. Since this is not
what one had supposed to be presented sympathetically in
Santayana, especially from his very negative reaction against
Bergson in *Winds of Doctrine,* I shall quote Santayana's best
statement or statements of each element of process philosophy:

1. A thing, a being, a substance, is for him the "actualized law of its
behavior" (Verhalten), its unity is its history, the melody or movement of its variations. Now all the objects that enter our world enter it by virtue of their relations in that world; they must occupy
some place in it, figure in its history, and be parts of its process.
This is nothing more than saying that the thing exists . . . [below,
p. 182]

2. . . . the world of reality is for Lotze necessarily a world of
change; were it a world of eternal things it would belong to the
province of logic. Two familiar types of metaphysics are thus excluded *in limine:* materialism, or any philosophy of an unknowable
substance, and Platonic idealism, or any philosophy of eternal entities. [below, p. 156] . . . Reality, as he elaborately shows us, is
not simple, but essentially complex; the reality cannot be in a simple quality, it must lie in the relations of states, in the behavior of
things. [below, p. 186]

3. . . . in order to be one, a being must be composed of elements;
its unity is the unity of a series, which to be realized, calls for a
series of examples or applications. . . . The world, in order to be
real, has to be a series of separate events, a galaxy of distinct realities; . . . its unity is that order, that scheme, which makes each of
these events and realities a member in that series; for evidently a
star that was not in space or an event that was not in history would
be a non-existent star and an imaginary event. This procession,
therefore this order, apart from which nothing can be actual, is
the unity of the world. . . . There is in his conception of the argu-

ment a dynamical element; the emphasis is laid everywhere on the necessity of unity to explain action and reaction; the ability of things to affect one another involves their unity, and we are told that interaction is conceivable between the various states of the same being but not between different beings. [below, p. 186]

4. Lotze . . . introduces a second element of change, which involves a really new beginning, something not a development, not a mere unfolding of a given law, but an absolutely unexpected and unaccountable irruption into the order of nature. For that change in a given element the response to which in all other elements the law of the world determines, need not itself be such a response to that law. It may be a spontaneous change. [below, p. 196]

Now what Lotze wishes to gain by indeterminism is vitality. He does not wish to think that the process of things (and existence for him is essentially a process) is the mere consequence of a single act, of an original state of things. It is the danger, the doubt of what sort of a reality will appear, that gives it a moral value when it does appear; this moral value Lotze does not wish to confine to the original choice of things to appear as they did appear; he wishes to distribute this moral action throughout the cosmic process, to make it possible at every point that a new choice, a new and unaccountable fact, should repeat the original and miraculous choice of things as to be they are. . . . the whole number of atoms did not exist from all eternity, so that the entire virtue and yield of things was the inevitable result of their primeval condition. [below, pp. 203–204]

. . . a merely causal explanation does not require anything but a series of causes, and even requires this series to be infinite. . . . It is not the principle of phenomenal causation that requires a first cause; on the contrary it excludes that idea, for it demands a cause for everything and therefore an infinite regress. [below, pp. 201–202]

That imagined primitive choice or fatality whence all things flow by an efficient law is now seen to be wholly unreal; there is no first fact; every part of nature is equally primitive and shares equally in that metaphysical choice by which things are as they are. No fact is prior to any other fact, and all facts are prior to the laws that express the order of their appearance. [below, p. 208]

5. Relations are to be regarded as projected from real things; a change of relation means a change in the internal condition of the related objects. . . . Relations are not between things because nothing exists at all but things; it is impossible that anything at all

should lie between realities, for either it is nothing or it is itself a reality; and if a reality, then it is not between things but *ipso facto* one of these. [below, p. 152]

Lotze blamed the older metaphysicians for regarding types as fixed, and abstract ideas as realities; he is willing to admit gradual variation. . . . It was the law of things itself that Lotze hoped might be variable, so as to admit of more perfect life. But he shrank from admitting variations according to a given and apparently eternal law, that shows all life to be in a state of unstable equilibrium. . . . He would have welcomed an evolution that pointed out an essential expansiveness and progression in things, that allowed us to conceive the cosmic process as a melody with ever new meaning and augmented beauty. But the evolution that modern science has led many to believe in is only an incidental evolution, followed by dissolution. [below, p. 122]

6. The life of nature . . . is a real life, because it has something on which to feed, something corresponding to an environment. . . . Nature . . . has a life; an internal principle and aspiration, which is its purpose, playing with phenomena which enter its life but are not products of its principle nor necessarily favorable to its aspiration. It is exactly in this way that our own life moves; the person has a certain will, a certain store of accumulated experience and digested knowledge, with certain habits and maxims which constitute the personal character; but these do not run out of themselves into a self-determined development; they are subject to varying conditions, and the life of the man consists in his reactions, the reactions of his character, on what is external to him and not a product of his activity.

. . . if the indeterminism seems to do so much for us in this system it is only because the dynamical monism has threatened us with all sorts of dangers. It has in fact introduced an efficient law, a metaphysical force that dissolves the universe at every instant, annihilating everything, and creating it anew. Thus Lotze conceives the soul, that "substance," as we have been persuaded to call it, as annihilated during unconsciousness, deep sleep, or even between ordinary pulses of feeling, while the "sense of the world" produces anew detached states of consciousness when they are required by its own interests; and any set of these detached states is known to belong to one "soul" only because of certain internal harmonies and similarities between them. [below, pp. 206–207]

7. The only serious fault he finds with preestablished harmony is the determinism it involves. He wishes the plan according to which the correspondences in things appear to be no fixed plan adopted in the beginning and controlling the entire development; he wishes the plan to grow with the work. But the efficiency for which Lotze has been contending is at this point finally explained as the efficiency of a final cause; the power that at each moment arranges the correspondences in things and is the instrument of interaction, is the sense, the meaning, of the world. But essential changes can take place in the world by virtue of . . . a law of development . . . spontaneous change. [below, pp. 195–196]

. . . Instead of preestablished harmony Lotze therefore suggests an ever-reestablished harmony. [below, p. 196]

8. . . . in the case of the divine life, belief in it rests on the sense of the value it would have did it exist, and on the deep-rooted belief that we have in the reality of our ideals. [below, p. 197]

The plan of the world is simply declared not to involve or call for all the changes that appear in the world; the plan or purpose only directs what changes shall ensue in order to maintain order in the world after the unaccountable changes have occurred. There is no contradiction in this idea. [below, p. 198]

Lotze's instinct and aesthetic susceptibility have led him . . . to avoid the rash enthusiasm of those theologians who so magnify their conceptions as to make them formless. A God that accomplishes literally everything no longer has a definite function in nature, he is no longer a power that makes for righteousness, and although we may continue to use his name, we shall use it in vain, and the world will with perfect justice call us atheists. This is notoriously the case with Spinoza; and all pantheism has the same tendency. Lotze may almost be said to have reintroduced the idea of God into philosophy, where the notion of a divine being had been replaced by an aspect of nature. [below, p. 199]

The ideal, the purpose of the world, is for Lotze a real end, which does not determine its means necessarily, but only determines them in view of given conditions. Here again we see how moderation saves the ideal that an enthusiastic exaggeration destroys. If the purpose of the world required, not only that certain values should arise, but that they should arise in given ways; in other words, if what is valuable is the whole world indiscriminately, no distinction is possible any more between ends and means, between good and useful, between purpose and fact. Teleology becomes a merely subjective and arbitrary method; everything is at once end and means for everything else. The attempt to make the world perfect has led to the denial of the validity of the idea of good . . . [below, pp. 200–201]

Certainly Whitehead grew up in a Cambridge in which Lotze's pluralism was regarded as a philosophy with a future. After quoting Lotze, "It is a true saying that God has ordered all things by measure and number," Ward raised the question:

what is the relation of God . . . to these particular realities, which interact according to a system of law and order which he sustains? In other words we are brought face to face with the old and formidable problem of the One and the Many. Can we predicate veritable reality of both, can we say that both are really in some sense free and for themselves? Or if we maintain this reality for the Many does not the One become a fictitious, merely all-inclusive unity or totality; are we not pantheists? If we maintain it of the One does not the reality of the Many become illusory, merely phenomenal? This, it has been said, will be the philosophical problem of the twentieth century. Let us see how the century is approaching it. With such a problem much depends on the side from which we begin. The nineteenth century on the whole, I think, began with the Absolute. Its latest attempt by that subtle Doctor, F. H. Bradley in his *Appearance and Reality,* probably the ablest philosophical work that has appeared in English during the last fifty years, might be characterized as Hegelianism turned sceptical: hence it has been facetiously described as the Disappearance of Reality. For Mr. Bradley the real is one; the self we take to be real is but a phenomenal adjective, and when regarded as real becomes 'riddled with contradictions.' The 'alleged independence' of the Many, in which we empirically believe, he declares, 'is no fact. . . . the plurality sinks to become merely an integral aspect in a single substantial unity, and the reals have vanished.' Nevertheless Mr. Bradley prophesies: 'Monadism, on the whole, will increase and will add to the difficulties which already exist.' The first half of this forecast at least is true. A decided reaction has set in against this Absolutism . . . which Mr. Bradley defends; and Pluralism is now to the fore. And there it is likely to remain so long as philosophy elects to start from, and to stand by, experience as conscious life, and to regard that life as directed to self-realization. For unless human freedom is a reality and not mere appearance, unless we have power on our own act and on the world, what basis of fact have we from which to ascend to a Supreme Reality of a spiritual kind at all? Surely in such a case the universe lapses back into a mechanism, and Naturalism is right.[160]

The Lotzean idea of reaching some idealistic conclusions about the unity of things and a ground of order and value from a realistic and pluralistic basis may have come to Whitehead not directly but through Ward. At any rate, there it is in Whitehead, developed, as Santayana had been tempted to predict, into a contender for place as "the received and orthodox doctrine of the world."

I have already invited the reader to inspect the parallel definitions of philosophy given by Lotze and by Whitehead, and called attention to the close similarity of their programs to elaborate some aspects of idealism on a realistic basis. How is my thesis to be tested that they belong to the same metaphysical type? By a deeper and more careful study of Lotze and Whitehead together, I believe the reader of *Science and the Modern World, Adventures of Ideas,* and *Process and Reality* needs little more than the above eight points to recognize something surprisingly similar. We should not be surprised, according to Philippe Devaux, to find philosophical cousins. For were they not both nineteenth-century Protestants with a keen interest in the ideas of science, as little eager for dogmatic certainty in one as the other? Were they not both deeply committed to faith in an order of things and particularly in an order of nature? Were they not both deeply concerned with man's ability to create a better future, and in spite of qualifications, holding out the infinite possibilities of free pursuit of beauty, truth, adventure, and peace? Were they not deeply concerned with reconciling the discovery of mechanism with the pursuit of value, based on the metaphysical ground of a God similarly described as a power for righteousness, but not an omnipotent tyrant? [161]

There are various well-recognized ways of establishing a common manner of philosophizing. One of these is Stephen Pepper's consideration of the root metaphor. This method is instructive because Lotze's root metaphor was that a thing is like a melody, and the world an on-going polyphonic melody. The root metaphor of Whitehead, according to Pepper, is that the world is like a purposive act. I see no difference here. Another way of establishing identity of type is less convincing: both Lotze and Whitehead are tender-minded about man's rational capacities in general and also sceptical about any particular scientific theory or religious creed. What we now have in any area of study is inadequate and shot through with fallacy, but for this very reason we are urged to press on with zeal. Obviously neither man can be dogmatic and feel it a great advantage to be as positively clear as, for example, Russell wanted his own and others' conclusions to be. Russell's type is always at some extreme or other; the Lotze-Whitehead is always in the middle, trying in a *via media* to adjust extreme claims to each other. The method of muddled suspense of judgment is a good one, according to Whitehead, for it leads to discovery, breaking out of the present deadlocked clash of dogmas. I believe the method of Lotze-Whitehead particularly appropriate to philosophy in an age of specialized science. It has the capacity to point out what is in common as a working faith of all, and what is yet inadequate in the particular results of each. All partial studies are likely to have the "dogmatic fallacy" or the "fallacy of the doctrinaire," or the fallacies of misplaced concreteness and vacuous actuality. I believe a close study of the common philosophic fallacies will show that Lotze and Whitehead were very close in rejecting the same types of arguments. Neither could tolerate Hegelianism with its single principle, all-encompassing single system, and claim to final adequacy. Both Lotze and Whitehead, in contrast, always point out in the end that their own efforts are inadequate. Just as Lotze ended his *Metaphysic* with "God knows better," so Whitehead comments "how shallow, puny, and imperfect are efforts to sound the depths in the nature of things.

In philosophical discussion, the merest hint of dogmatic certainty . . . is an exhibition of folly." [162]

What of the problems that Lotze and Whitehead confront? Some of these are not exclusively philosophic, and are therefore the more immediately relevant. Both are concerned with the whole education of man, and in this they are sharply aware of excessive intellectualism in scholars generally. Those who run educational machinery think only of the passive acceptance and reproduction of matter of fact. But of greater, far greater concern is the emotional development of students, and their ability to go back and forth between theory and practice. Since there is no axiomatic certainty with which to start any study, even geometry, we can only start with *our* axioms, not *the* axioms, said Whitehead. The meaning lies in the application as well as the deduction. "Whatever is found in 'practice' must lie within the scope of the metaphysical description. When the description fails to include the 'practice,' the metaphysics is inadequate and requires revision. There can be no appeal to practice to supplement the metaphysics, so long as we remain contented with our metaphysical doctrines. Metaphysics is nothing but the description of the generalities which apply to all the details of practice." [163]

The specific dominating philosophic problem in both Lotze and Whitehead is that of the many and the one, the relations between the parts that make them wholes, and therefore the problem of order. We can find questions of great similarity such as "What is the basic fact?" "What is a mechanical relation?" "What is a teleological relation?" "What is the relation of knowing?" "How do we get from the concrete given to the abstract points and instants?" "What kinds of causal connections are there?" "What holds societies together?" "What final unity is there in the cosmos?" "What is the basis of this unity?"

The conclusions of Lotze and Whitehead, if they do constitute the conclusions of a single type, would take many pages to place in parallel columns for inspection, particularly if the differences of context are to be respected. Allowing for differences of nation, language, period, backgrounds in different sciences, religions, and arts, the unity of type seems to me the more overwhelmingly clear.

As to the basic problems of the many and the one, we have found Lotze saying that although existence is basically atomic, yet things require each other. Lotze produced a monadism-monism, and so did Whitehead, in solving their problem:

> Though Whitehead's metaphysics . . . is pluralistic, no monist ever insisted more strongly than he that nothing in the world exists in independence of other things. In fact, he repeatedly criticizes traditional monisms for not carrying this principle far enough; they exempted eternal being from dependence on temporal beings. Independent existence is a myth, whether you ascribe it to God or to a particle of matter in Newtonian physics, to persons, to nations, to things, or to meanings. To understand is to see things together, and to see them as, in Whitehead's favorite phrase, "requiring each other." [164]

What is the basic fact? We have quoted over and over again Lotze's answer: an event or a process. Lotze was capable of putting this in the linguistic mode: the model of a real thing is not found in a noun, but in a verb; for a noun is thought to have independent meaning, whereas a verb is a relating of parts.[165] Whitehead, I believe, accepted Lotze's answer. It appears more fully in Whitehead: "everywhere [there is] some process of self-realization, which grows out of previous processes and itself adds a new pulse of individuality and a new value to the world." [166]

How are things related? A logical relation is only one kind, found in thinking, and although we can trust that the logically contradictory cannot also be actual, there is no more than correspondence between logical and real relations, not identity. The real relation is causal efficacy in both Lotze and Whitehead. On transeunt causality, one thing's affecting another, one thing effecting a change in another, this is the basic tie in a process philosophy. The causal relation must be studied by the active agent from within, not merely by some passive observer from without.

Both Lotze and Whitehead were opponents of reducing the causal tie to temporal sequence in which sense data are presented. In a metaphor, both found the world thick rather than thin and tried to introduce the thickness of experienced change into the thinness of philosophic theory. The causal processes we know by willing and feeling as well as by abstracting modes of perception are directed to ends or goals. Neither Lotze nor Whitehead therefore can limit teleology to man, nor can knowing be limited to human modes of cognition. All things participate, in however slight degree, in aims and awareness of aims. Hence, in both there is deep suspicion of the propositional mode of formulating knowledge. We saw in Lotze a suspicion of the subject-copula-predicate Aristotelian model, in spite of the fact that Lotze missed, from our perspective, the significance of Boolean algebra developed by Whitehead and Russell into *Principia Mathematica.*

In many respects both Lotze and Whitehead think old ways of thought were fallaciously dualistic. Body and mind were defined as two substances, objective and subjective were thought spatially separated, and so the whole world of experience-reality was sundered. A person, the model of a real thing, in Lotze is an interreacting and originating whole. So also in Whitehead. Says Lowe of Whitehead's theory and our difficulty with it: "Many philosophers consider Whitehead's doctrine of a self-creating experiencer unintelligible. It certainly contradicts the mode of thought to which we are accustomed—*first* a permanent subject, *then* an experience of it. But how did the subject originally come into being?" [167] Similar difficulties are produced by the traditional dualistic reading of Lotze on the person.

Both Lotze and Whitehead picture the cosmos as a wonderful and entrancing environment, full of variety, novelty, and creativity. It is shot through with value, particularly aesthetic value. Both call attention to the underestimation of *feeling* what things are worth, and their writings on the aesthetic mode are more full than on the moral mode, that of judgment, though there is more of this latter in Lotze than in Whitehead. Nothing, therefore, is absolutely without value, though for any agent engaged in pursuing a specific aim, some things are more important than others. Quality as such is unreal for both; it is mere essence or eternal object. These changeless characteristics are what they are: they have fixed relations to each other; and Whitehead's description of colors bears much similarity to Lotze's analysis of notes in a scalar hierarchy. What matters is that the world embodies qualities, and is not the soundless, colorless, odorless hurrying of atoms that Newton left for us to contemplate. Both Lotze and Whitehead are sons of the romantic revolution that rediscovered nature.

There is no one perfect order of the cosmos; rather the world is many orders together, with one ground of order. "The notion of one perfection of order, which is (I believe) Plato's doctrine, must go the way of the one possible geometry. The universe is more various, more Hegelian." [168] Both Lotze and Whitehead react similarly to Leibniz's pre-established harmony. Although everything may have a purpose, there is real conflict and frustration. Not all aims can be accomplished. The fulfillment of one is the frustration of the other. Hence, there is inevitable loss of value. It is far from the best of all possible worlds, and God cannot contemplate the world with equanimity. Indeed, according to both, God suffers with the world.

Both Lotze and Whitehead have a similar rejection of the doctrine of divine creation and omnipotence. Both resist paying God the metaphysical compliment of ascribing to him all power, for each wants to guard the freedom and value of the many agents which together make up the community that the world is. Both are immanentists in theology rather than transcendentalists. God procures the value of the world by providing possibilities and care for the achievement, not by forcing a law upon nature and man, and commanding obedience. In neither do we find any necessity, therefore, for vengeance, hell, rewards, and punishment in an afterlife.

How can God be both eternal, as required by being the ground of value without beginning or end, and also the ever-present participant in the process? There is either the same welcome solution or the same offensive nonsense. Would Lotze accept Whitehead's doctrine of "an eternal actual entity whose active character" is expressed through providing possibilities? [169] I believe so, and Harald Høffding points out that Lotze's God is "a timeless happening and working." [170] Lotze's God is also not *before* all creation but *with* all creation. The difference between Lotze and Whitehead may be that Whitehead introduced change into God, whereas Lotze refrained from drawing this conclusion. No one has heretofore noticed that the titles of the last chapters of *Microcosmus* and *Process and Reality* bear the same words, "God and the World." Of course there is little originality in such a conjunction, and it comes naturally to any scientist concerned with the object of worship, as interpreted within limits of rational metaphysics. But the content of their theism is strikingly similar and deserves study to see whether a better formulation cannot be reached by allowing one to correct the other. Has either reached a view more coherent with the other metaphysical positions taken? This summary of two systems is lamentably inadequate. It is meant only to be suggestive, for even chapter-long summaries of either Lotze or Whitehead are tours-de-force.

Now we may conclude by commenting on our indebtedness to Santayana as a critic of process philosophy, and with a comment on a re-estimation of Lotze's importance as a philosopher.

Just as I concluded earlier that James had caught Lotze in a fallacy and had exposed the monistic arguments as untenable, so now I wish to call attention to the value of Santayana as a philosophic critic. What undoubtedly puts off contemporary readers, and strikes them as monstrous, is the excessive optimism in Lotze. He really seems to think that there is a rational solution "between the demands of our emotional nature and the results of human science." Does he really think that metaphysics provides a principle that all requirements of religious faith are met by the physical cosmos? He really seems to continue the quaint traditional belief that the world was made for man's pleasure and satisfaction! Santayana did what a sharp critic should do: pick out the weakest part of a man's system. In "Lotze's Moral Idealism" Santayana shows the consequences of Lotze's "moralism." Lotze sometimes decided on the basis of value what must be the factual case. If Darwinism did not conduce to man's belief in freedom and perfectibility, then it must be false. This is a consequence of Lotze's ill-considered effort to base metaphysics on ethics. Santayana rebukes "the tone of poetry and pious eloquence. And we certainly have no desire to make the inmost nature of things submit to our definitions and formulations." [171] The last page is Santayana's final estimate of Lotze's place in history, that Lotze's philosophy has little contemporary relevance, even to the world of 1890, and far less now after the shocks of the twentieth century:

. . . there is some presumption in calling our personal or even national preconceptions the demands of the human conscience; and there is some danger in talking as if theories had any essential value other than truth. It is unworthy of philosophy to regard affection as evidence, or to contrive a compromise between sentiment and fact. Its business is rather to transform sentiment until it is in harmony with fact, to naturalise the soul in the realm of reality. Lotze may be quite right when he says the conflict between science and sentiment is perennial, but it is fought on ever-changing ground. Had moral impulse in all ages called for the same theories, they surely would have been established and made instinctive long ago, just as belief in other men's consciousness is established and instinctive. The truth is that sentiment clings to whatever beliefs are familiar, and, therefore, are associated with habitual motives and emotions. Some beliefs are certainly in themselves more sublime or flattering than others; but this sublimity or suavity will seem oppressive and degrading to those unaccustomed to them, while they seem inspiring to those accustomed to regard them as sanctions and supports. The case is like that of patriotism: one country is undeniably more beautiful and civilized than another, and yet every man's 'moral demand' is for his own. And this is no natural limitation, no excusable folly: it is the expression of a natural piety and joyful resignation by which a man conforms to the inevitable conditions of his life. The conflict Lotze tells us of is not essentially a conflict between theories morally necessary and theories morally repugnant, but one between familiar theories, sanctified by innumerable associations, and unfamiliar theories recommended by new evidence. The ideas that are morally impossible to-day may be morally necessary to-morrow. Lotze has too much ignored this possibility. Yet the problem he set out to solve could itself arise only by virtue of this transformation of feeling. If our feeling of what naturally should be differs from our sense of what actually is, it is only because we live in an age of transition; the mind has emigrated, but the heart has remained in the 'ol country.' Lotze's philosophy is an admirable expression of this state of things; his solution is ingenious and suggestive in many ways, and has its reality and importance for us now. Only it lacks universality, it lacks the radical quality of nature's own slow but inevitable solution. This solution, Goethe tells us, is renunciation—a renunciation, however, that is not pure loss, but the condition of the only possible and permanent gain.[172]

Santayana's criticism is based primarily on his well-known view that modern philosophies are theologies attenuated rather than sciences amplified.[173] This shows both Santayana's strength in moral philosophy and religion and his weakness on the scientific side. On one hand Santayana sees the pervading difficulty of almost any process philosophy. Can it make clear how there can be a real individual without a principle of individuation such as material substance provides? The self in Lotze and in Whitehead is reduced to a series of experiences. Do aim and recollection provide bonds enough to establish independent individuality? If, in Santayana's words, there is only "one event after another," what provides an "unchangeable kernel of reality" (below, p. 189)?

Santayana's weakness as a critic is in reducing metaphysical statements to professions of faith, which are, for him, expressions of opinion. As he details the doctrines I took to be essential to process philosophy, he prefaced them by saying "Lotze feels" or "Lotze wishes." Santayana missed reading the system logically; that is, in a question, if an event is so-and-so, what kind of event must God be? Santayana reads motives, as did James, and appreciates vivid expression. But such handling is psychological. It follows from Santayana's interpretation that "the only philosophy that remains for Lotze is some form of phenomenalism; the reality must inhere in the world of change" (below, p. 157).

Santayana's weakness also is in taking scientific conclusions as metaphysical principles. Atoms, for example, are "the counters with which nature actually plays" (below, p. 166) —quite inconsistent with his own statement that the atom's "indivisibility is only a synonym of its definition" (below, p. 166). Lotze was far ahead of his time in functioning philosophically as a critic of scientific abstractions. Santayana thinks atomism, for example, is a matter of common sense and even of experience, and not an hypothesis about entities (below, pp. 165, 170–171). Santayana appeals also to "the primary constitutional necessity of things" as a basis for his belief, a pure piece of dogmatism (below, p. 174).

A nice paradox emerges from considering Santayana's criticism of Lotze: the younger man represents the old view. Santayana presents the orthodox reaction against the heresy of process philosophy. Where Lotze would say with Whitehead that "Every existence is an event," Santayana would say that "events are modes of substances." [174]

Lotze has not caught the attention of students of American philosophy, as I believe he should. The distinguished historian of American philosophy, Max H. Fisch, looks at European philosophers after Hegel and finds only Croce who is not one of the epigoni; and of the philosophers between them, John Stuart Mill's reputation has suffered least with the passage of time. Perhaps it is time to examine whether the judgment of men at the turn of the century was quite so wrong: Lotze was then ranked almost equal to Hegel. Among the fourteen "major themes and tendencies" marking the classic age of American philosophy, Lotze is a strong representative of nearly every trait. [175] This has been ignored, for there has scarcely been one article on him in American journals for more than a generation.

Was Santayana right in saying that Lotze's philosophy was stillborn? This seems rather wrong: Lotze's type of philosophy developed and flourished, and prospers today as much as any metaphysics. One critic with more charity and insight calls him a tragic figure because he had all the talents, training, and energy of a great philosopher, yet lived at the wrong time. Had he followed a Plato, says Kraushaar, he could have been an Aristotle. But I would answer Kraushaar by saying that Lotze had the greatness to see the possibilities of process philosophy before Whitehead. I am, therefore, in conclusion, not satisfied either with Haldane's judgment that he didn't make it as a philosopher, or with Moore's judgment that he was "often very confused." A great benefit of Santayana's book is that it forces us to consider the possibility that Lotze does have greater importance than he is commonly allowed, and that Lotze does have great contemporary relevance.

NOTES

I. SANTAYANA AND LOTZE

1. Professor Anne C. Bolgan corrected the text and prepared the bibliography, the index, and the notes for Faber and Faber of London.
2. George T. Ladd, "Preface" to Lotze, *Outlines of the Philosophy of Religion,* translated by Ladd for Ginn, Heath & Co., Boston, 1885, pp. vi–vii.
3. George Santayana, *The Last Puritan: A Memoir in the Form of a Novel,* Scribner's, New York, 1936, p. 83.
4. Ibid., p. 86.
5. Santayana, "Lotze's Moral Idealism," *Mind,* Vol. 20, No. 57, January 1890, pp. 191–212.

II. LOTZE AS CRITIC OF HIS PREDECESSORS

6. "L'infini actuel est-il contradictoire?" *Revue Philosophique,* 1880.
7. "Philosophy in the Last Forty Years," *The Contemporary Review,* January 1880, pp. 134–154.
8. *Streitschriften,* p. 5.
9. *Metaphysic,* translation ed. by B. Bosanquet, 2d ed., 1887, Vol. 1, p. 16. Recently in *The Origins of American Humanistic Scholars* (Prentice Hall, Englewood Cliffs, New Jersey, 1964, p. 159), Robert H. Knapp wrote of logicians as "carpenters who forever sharpen their tools and never cut a board."
10. *The Contemporary Review,* Fiftieth Year, January 1880, pp. 134–154, reprinted in *Kleine Schriften,* ed. by David Peipers, Vol. 3, Part 2, S. Hirzel, Leipzig, 1891, pp. 451–475.
11. *Streitschriften,* p. 6.
12. "Philosophy in the Last Forty Years," p. 454.
13. *Geschichte der Aesthetik in Deutschland,* 1868, reprinted 1913, pp. 11–12.
14. Ibid., pp. 11–12, 17.

15. "Philosophy in the Last Forty Years," p. 453.
16. Ibid., p. 451.
17. Ibid.
18. Ibid., p. 452.
19. Ibid., pp. 466–467; a more complete account of this fallacy appears in *Logic,* translation ed. by B. Bosanquet, 2d ed., 1888, Vol. 2, pp. 12–14.
20. *Logic,* 2d ed., 1888, Vol. 2, p. 3.
21. Ibid., p. 14.
22. *Microcosmus,* trans. by Elizabeth Hamilton and E. E. Constance Jones, Vol. 2, pp. 649–650.
23. F. A. Lange, *The History of Materialism,* Humanities Press, New York, 1950, Vol. 2, p. 285.
24. *Logic,* Vol. 2, p. 5.
25. *Metaphysic,* 2d ed., Vol. 1, pp. 21–22.
26. Ibid., p. 22.

III. LOTZE'S SYSTEM: A THEORY OF ORDER

27. Stephen C. Pepper, *World Hypotheses: A Study in Evidence,* University of California, Berkeley, 1942.
28. *Metaphysic,* 2d ed., Vol. 1, p. 92.
29. *Microcosmus,* Vol. 2, p. 614.
30. Ibid., p. 617.
31. *Metaphysic,* 2d ed., Vol. 1, pp. 96–97.
32. Alfred North Whitehead, *Science and the Modern World,* Macmillan, New York, 1926, p. 196.
33. *Outlines of Logic and of Encyclopaedia of Philosophy,* trans. by G. T. Ladd, pp. 145–147; last paragraph divided by present author.
34. Whitehead, *Process and Reality,* Macmillan, New York, 1929, p. 4.
35. Ibid., p. viii.
36. *Microcosmus,* Vol. 1, p. 380.
37. *Metaphysic,* 1st ed., 1884, p. 14.
38. *Metaphysic,* 2d ed., Vol. 1, p. 18.
39. Ibid., p. 19.
40. Ibid., p. 20.
41. *Encyclopaedia of Philosophy,* p. 150.
42. Ibid., 152.
43. Ibid., pp. 159–160.
44. Ibid., pp. 163–164.
45. Ibid., pp. 167–169.
46. Ibid., pp. 172–173 (for all quotes in paragraph).

47. Ibid., p. 174.
48. Ibid.
49. *Microcosmus,* Vol. 1, pp. 427–428 (for all quotes in paragraph).
50. Ibid., p. 432.
51. Ibid., p. 429 (for all quotes in paragraph).
52. Ibid., pp. 429–430.
53. Ibid., p. 430.
54. Ibid.
55. Ibid.
56. Ibid., p. 441.
57. Ibid., p. 431.
58. Ibid.
59. *Metaphysic,* 2d ed., Vol. 2, pp. 145–150.
60. *Microcosmus,* Vol. 1, p. 380.
61. Ibid., Vol. 2, pp. 587–588.
62. *Outlines of Metaphysic,* pp. 25–34.
63. Ibid., p. 35.
64. Ibid., p. 37.
65. Ibid., p. 16.
66. Ibid., pp. 18–19.
67. Ibid., p. 19.
68. Ibid., pp. 43–44.
69. Ibid., p. 32.
70. Evans E. Thomas, *Lotze's Theory of Reality,* p. xv; cf. Erdmann's, Windelband's, and Ueberweg's histories.
71. *Outlines of Metaphysic,* p. 47.
72. Ibid., pp. 48–49.
73. Ibid., pp. 65–67.
74. Ibid., pp. 71–72.
75. *Metaphysic,* 2d ed., Vol. 1, p. 193.
76. *Outlines of Metaphysic,* p. 81.
77. Ibid.
78. Ibid., pp. 81–82.
79. Ibid., p. 82.
80. Ibid., p. 83.
81. Ibid., p. 84.
82. Ibid., pp. 84–85.
83. Ibid., p. 106.
84. Ibid., p. 108.
85. Ibid., p. 113.
86. Ibid., p. 115.
87. Ibid., p. 116.

88. Ibid., p. 117.
89. Ibid., p. 118, 119.
90. Ibid., pp. 119–120.
91. Ibid., pp. 120–121.
92. Ibid., p. 126.
93. Ibid., p. 138.
94. Ibid., p. 139.
95. Ibid., p. 152.
96. William James, *A Pluralistic Universe*, pp. 54–55.
97. Ibid., pp. 57–58.
98. Ibid., pp. 58–59.
99. *Logic*, Vol. 2, p. 5.
100. James, *A Pluralistic Universe*, p. 60.
101. F. C. S. Schiller, "Lotze's Monism," *The Philosophical Review*, May 1896, as reprinted in *Humanism: Philosophical Essays*, 2d ed., Macmillan, London, 1912, p. 62.
102. *Metaphysic*, 2d ed., Vol. 2, pp. 318–319.

IV. LOTZE'S INFLUENCE ON ANGLO-AMERICAN PHILOSOPHY

103. Appleton's *New Practical Cyclopedia*, New York, 1910, Vol. 4, p. 111.
104. John Passmore, *A Hundred Years of Philosophy*, p. 49.
105. Otto F. Kraushaar, "What James's Philosophical Orientation Owed to Lotze," *Philosophical Review*, Vol. 47, 1938, p. 517.
106. Sir Frederick Maurice, *Haldane: The Life of Viscount Haldane of Cloan*, pp. 18–19. Sir Frederick consistently misspells Lotze "Lötze."
107. Ibid., p. 21.
108. Viscount Richard Burdon Haldane, *Universities and National Life*, pp. 25–27.
109. Borden Parker Bowne, *Metaphysics: A Study in First Principles*, Harper and Brothers, New York, 1882.
110. Jean Wahl, *Pluralist Philosophies of England and America*, p. 319; on Lotze, see pp. 50–55. The original was *Les Philosophies Pluralistes d'Angleterre et d'Amerique*.
111. Isabel Smith Gates, *The Life of George Augustus Gates*, pp. 5–6; John S. Nollen, *Grinnell College*. State Historical Society of Iowa, Iowa City, 1953, pp. 84–85.
112. G. F. Barbour, *The Balfour Lectures on Realism*, A. Seth Pringle-Pattison, with a Memoir of the Author, William Blackwood and Sons, Edinburgh and London, 1933, p. 29.
113. Ibid., p. 30, with a quotation from Seth's review of Henry

Jones's *Philosophy of Lotze,* 1895, reprinted in *The Philosophical Radicals,* William Blackwood and Sons, Edinburgh and London, 1907, p. 150.

114. See "An Unborn Idealism," in G. P. Adams and W. P. Montague, eds., *Contemporary American Philosophy,* p. 395.

115. Ralph Barton Perry, *The Thought and Character of William James,* p. 766.

116. On Lotze's influence on Howison, see Gustav E. Müller, *Amerikanische Philosophie,* p. 172.

117. Meyrick H. Carré, *Phases of Thought in England,* p. 363.

118. Rudolf Metz, *A Hundred Years of British Philosophy,* J. H. Muirhead, ed., J. W. Harvey, T. E. Jessop, and Henry Sturt, trans., Allen and Unwin, London, 1938.

119. John Theodore Merz, *History of European Thought in the Nineteenth Century,* William Blackwood, London, 3d ed., 1907–1914.

120. A Eastwood, "Lotze's Antithesis Between Thought and Things," in two parts, 1892.

121. Olwen Ward Campbell, "Memoir" in James Ward's *Essays in Philosophy,* p. 30.

122. Ibid., p. 32.

123. Ibid., p. 31.

124. James Ward, *Essays in Philosophy,* pp. 174–176.

125. Alban G. Widgery, *A Philosopher's Pilgrimage,* Allen and Unwin, London, 1961, pp. 30–31, parentheses mine.

126. Ibid., p. 70.

127. Paul Arthur Schilpp, *The Philosophy of G. E. Moore,* p. 17.

128. Bertrand Russell, *A Critical Exposition of the Philosophy of Leibniz,* Allen and Unwin, London, 1937, pp. 118, 135–136, 138.

129. Schilpp, *The Philosophy of Bertrand Russell,* pp. 10, 171–173, 263, etc.

130. Schilpp, *The Philosophy of C. D. Broad,* p. 50.

131. Bernard Bosanquet, ed., in Lotze, *Logic,* 2d ed., 1888, p. v.

132. F. C. Conybeare, ed., Lotze, *Outlines of a Philosophy of Religion,* Swan Sonnenschein, London, 1892, p. xviii.

133. Kraushaar, "Lotze's Influence on the Pragmatism and Practical Philosophy of William James," *Journal of the History of Ideas,* Vol. 1, 1940, p. 457; Philippe Devaux, *Lotze et son influence sur la philosophie anglo-saxonne,* Maurice Lamartin, Bruxelles, 1932, refers to Lotze's philosophy as idealism modified to fit democracy and industrial civilization.

134. Robert Adamson, review, "Hermann Lotze's *Metaphysic* translated by B. Bosanquet and others," *Mind,* Vol. 10, 1885, pp. 574–575.

135. A. Eastwood, "Lotze's Antithesis Between Thought and Things," pp. 315–316.

136. Agnes Cuming, "Lotze, Bradley, and Bosanquet," pp. 168–169.

137. Ibid., p. 164.

138. See letter of Peirce to Dewey on "making everything turn on Lotze," *Collected Papers of Charles Sanders Peirce*, Harvard University Press, Cambridge, 1958, Vol. 8, Chapter 3, 8.244, p. 184.

139. Passmore, *A Hundred Years of Philosophy*, Chapter VII, "Some Critics of Formal Logic," pp. 158–174.

140. Santayana, *Persons and Places*, Vol. 2, *The Middle Span*, pp. 152–153.

141. Josiah Royce, *The Religious Aspect of Philosophy*, Houghton Mifflin, Boston, 1885, p. v and Chapter XI.

142. Vincent Buranelli, *Josiah Royce*, p. 59.

143. Ibid., "Autobiographical Sketch," pp. 128–129.

144. Ibid., pp. 60–61.

145. Perry, *The Thought and Character of William James*, Vol. I, pp. 586–587.

146. Ibid., p. 586n, and Kraushaar, "Lotze's Influence on the Psychology of William James," *The Psychological Review*, Vol. 43, 1936, p. 238.

147. Kraushaar, "Lotze's Influence on the Pragmatism and Practical Philosophy of William James," p. 442.

148. Kraushaar, "Lotze's Influence on the Psychology of William James," pp. 253, 256 (quoting from *Microcosmus*, Vol. 1, p. 256).

149. Kraushaar, "What James's Philosophical Orientation Owed to Lotze," pp. 517–526. (The quote is from *Metaphysic*, Vol. 1, p. 115.)

150. Kraushaar, "Lotze's Influence on the Pragmatism and Practical Philosophy of William James," pp. 439–458; cf. John J. Fisher, "Santayana on James: A Conflict of Views of Philosophy," *American Philosophical Quarterly*, Vol. 2, No. 1, 1965, pp. 67–73: "The philosophical chaos which results from James's generosity is indeed distressing. . . . Santayana saw the chaos as the antithesis of greatness. A great man need not be right, . . . but he must have a firm mind. . . . Mere spontaneous variation might be madness. There must be principle of order." p. 73.

151. Sir Henry Jones and John Henry Muirhead, *The Life and Philosophy of Edward Caird*, Maclehose, Jackson, Glasgow, 1921, p. 191, letter of 28 August 1893 to Jones, then two years from publication of *A Critical Account of the Philosophy of Lotze: The Doctrine of Thought* (Macmillan, New York, 1895).

152. Georg Misch, "Einleitung des Herausgebers," in *Logik*, Felix

Meiner, Leipzig, 1912, p. xcii; Devaux, *Lotze et son influence sur la philosophie anglo-saxonne*, p. 23.

153. Harald Høffding, "Die Lotzes Lehren über Zeit und Raum und R. Geijers Beurtheilung derselben," *Philosophische Monatshefte*, Vol. 24, 1888, pp. 422–440.

154. Friedrich Paulsen, *An Autobiography*, p. 225; V. V. Zenkovsky, *A History of Russian Philosophy*, Vol. 1, p. 200.

155. Fritz-Joachim von Rintelen, "Wertphilosophie," *Die Philosophie im 20. Jahrhundert*, p. 443.

156. John Baillie, *The Interpretation of Religion*, pp. 278–287.

157. Devaux, *Lotze et son influence sur la philosophie anglo-saxonne*, pp. 16n, 42–47.

v. LOTZE'S RELEVANCE TO CONTEMPORARY PHILOSOPHY

158. Richard Falckenberg, "Hermann Lotze, sein Verhältnis zu Kant und Hegel und zu den Problemen der Gegenwart," p. 37.

159. Whitehead, *Process and Reality*, p. vii.

160. Ward, *Essays in Philosophy*, pp. 174–176.

161. Devaux, *Lotze et son influence sur la philosophie anglo-saxonne*.

162. Victor Lowe, in Max H. Fisch, *Classic American Philosophers*, p. 399.

163. Whitehead, *Process and Reality*, p. 19, quoted in Fisch, *Classic American Philosophers*, p. 446.

164. Lowe, in Fisch, *Classic American Philosophers*, pp. 399–400.

165. *Outlines of Logic and of Encyclopaedia of Philosophy*, p. 12.

166. Lowe, in Fisch, *Classic American Philosophers*, p. 399.

167. Ibid., p. 403.

168. Ibid., p. 408, quotation from Whitehead, *Essays in Science and Philosophy*, p. 118.

169. Lowe, in Fisch, *Classic American Philosophers*, p. 407.

170. Harald Høffding, *History of Modern Philosophy*, 1924, Vol. 2, p. 593.

171. Santayana, "Lotze's Moral Idealism," p. 207.

172. Ibid., p. 212.

173. Santayana, "Living Without Thinking," *The Forum*, Vol. 68, 1922, p. 732.

174. Max H. Fisch, *The Classic Period in American Philosophy*, p. 22.

175. Ibid., pp. 19–39.

APPENDIX: Santayana's Reading of Lotze's *Logik* and
Metaphysik Revealed in Marginalia

ONLY RECENTLY, AFTER LONG SEARCH, the editor found some of
the books of Lotze used by Santayana in writing *Lotze's System
of Philosophy*. Because of a hundred or two hundred comments
written on the pages by Santayana, we are now in far better
position to judge Santayana's relation to Lotze's *System der
Philosophie*. If Santayana remembered correctly when he wrote
of having "procured the complete works of Lotze," there may
well be more than the *Logik* and *Metaphysik* to consult.*

Although Santayana is a close and careful reader, asking for
definitions, spotting fallacies, and questioning the consistency
of his author, he is highly selective. One can surmise from chapters unannotated what Santayana passed by as uninteresting to
him; this Lotze advised the reader to do. In the *Logik* almost
four hundred pages on formal logic (from page 91 to page 486)
have not a single question, or even scoring in the margin. Consistent with selectivity is independence of judgment. Santayana
had read Plato, Hume, and Kant, and he frequently questions
the accuracy and adequacy of Lotze's historical scholarship.
Doubtless here Santayana was much in Royce's debt. Santayana
never claimed to be a scholar: in his thesis he shows no use
of commentators on Lotze and refers to but one learned article

---

* Thanks are due to Professor Rudolph H. Weingartner of Vassar College
who remembered them as treasures in possession of Professor Jacob Loewenberg. The latter had presented them to Wells College, Aurora, New York,
where they are part of the Loewenberg Library of Philosophy.

bearing on his author. However, the James-like wit of seeing alternatives makes reading his marginal notes in the Lotze books a delight: such and such a question is wrong; it should be so and so; this judgment has a hidden assumption; such and such may be better resolved by saying the contrary. Santayana was clearly struggling between alternative points of view, as Lotze was; and in the marginalia, rather than in the dissertation, we can see clearly certain rival theories pulling him this way and that: contradictory perspectives that he could neither dismiss nor reconcile.

Just as Lotze denies that the mind comes equipped with a kit of logical tools ready to be used on whatever is sensed, so Santayana clearly did not come to his reading with one ready-made perspective which controlled all his responses.[1] We need to determine the philosophic live options between which he was forced to choose.

The most evident, frequent, and intense questioning of the text comes from a perspective influenced by Hume and Kant that might best be called, as Santayana himself calls it, "phenomenalism." With regard to the basic ontological question, what is a thing, Santayana questions Lotze's realism: "Why should not the reality be the total of discrete momentary perceptions?"[2]

When Lotze claims to come to know the inner real ground rather than mere appearance, Santayana counters, "This is perhaps a contradiction in terms: for our knowledge would constitute a phenomenon: the thing in itself is ipso facto *not* what we know—it is only spoken of by strength of analogy: we cannot conceive the order of phenomena except by supposing a substance of some sort. But this reality may be anything: a law, a will, a purpose, a substance, etc." (M12). When Lotze says that there is never a moment in the life of a plant when it is plant in general, the response is, "How do we know that? Hegel would say that the general was definite, and, therefore, could exist. The determinations might be accidental and of external origin, and yet the essence might be concrete. This is what we must think if our knowledge is to grasp the reality of all. Else give me phenomenalism and Hume" (L526).

If Lotze admits that apart from what we observe we may only speculate, Santayana tries to push Lotze into the phenomenalist position (M71). According to Santayana, there is some advantage to a theory of cause that attributes the connection of similar groups of qualities to the observer (M116, 124). Clearly Santayana adopts the purpose of phenomenalism as his own. He rebukes Lotze: "Do you not see that this is a purely phenomenalistic ambition? We wish to find a description for all events" (M120).

When we judge from effects what the cause must be, we are going beyond description. Santayana pits phenomenalism against realism: "This realism is so gross that it seems almost allegorical. What the effected thing does is its recognition of the presence of the cause: hence this effect does not of itself indicate a cause, either in the thing itself or in another thing. The connection of the cause and effect is external and due to the observer" (M124).

The second perspective most evident in Santayana's criticism is what he calls "scepticism." As to definition, Santayana agrees with Lotze, who wrote that scepticism is not "the unconditional denial of all truth." The comment in the margin is: "Scepticism is not a denial of the existence of truth, but a definition of its nature: truth, it says, is subjectively and psychologically necessary opinion" (L486). Explicitly Santayana lacks the Cartesian assurance of Lotze, that God would not deceive us. Santayana comments on the security of this moral idea. "And logically too: for if the world had our moral impulse it might well have our intellectual habit. We might argue the other way and say: the fact that our moral ideal misses the reality makes it probable that our intellectual forms miss it also" (L488).

Lotze states as a ground of scepticism that we can know only the appearances rather than the essence of things—the first truth of every theory of knowledge. Santayana responds: "And this is the fact, not because there are things in themselves but because our knowledge of phenomena is incomplete" (L503).

Santayana displays specific doubts about the capacities of reason to bring us knowledge, to know causal connections, and to grasp the purpose of the cosmos. Santayana takes the irrationalist side in many particular disputes. Probably he is most explicit when dealing with Lotze's efforts to discover reasons for events. "The enemy here is not Hume but the rationalists. For experienced sequences never can fail, logical consequences of course may." Santayana interprets Lotze and frequently indicates agreement: "the world is not a logical process" (M91).

In the dialectic of positions, Santayana apparently did not yet have his doctrine of essences. His phenomenalism might indeed have responded to his scepticism—the immediately presented qualities are not mere opinions, but are exactly what they are and are not subject to doubt.

The third tendency, scarcely less prevalent than phenomenalism and scepticism, is what Santayana had learned from James: the stress on the will and free choice, the psychological factors that rationalists had ignored. Let us call this "voluntarism." Santayana explicitly mentions "the volitional way of looking at things" which characterizes prescriptions in contrast to descriptions. Lotze contrasts this as the impersonal to the personal (L71). When Lotze speaks of things as though related just as we find them, Santayana asks whether we have not chosen out of need to see them in a certain way. For example, Lotze distinguishes a "blos zusammenseiende Summe" from a "zusammengehöriges Ganze." Is there an objective difference between "a sum which coexists" and "a whole which coheres"? "What is the difference?" asks Santayana. "What is usually together belongs together, unless we wish to separate it for some purpose of our own" (L85).

This voluntarism is a deeper strain in Santayana in the sense that he sees consequences from it that affect epistemology, metaphysics, and areas of value. It may serve as the basis of scepticism. When Lotze seeks "certainty" (Gewissheit) of knowledge, Santayana underscores the German word and comments:

"There is a great difference between certain knowledge and habits of thought. We contradict ourselves in trying to build knowledge on subjective habits of mind: we only build *convention* on them. Then by *convention* I speak of a material world, of other beings, of science, of religion. I generally have no knowledge of what I speak of. Knowledge is only about the internal economy of these conventions. It is certain only because it is hypothetical: it is the certain content of an assumption" (M13).

In sharpest contrast to Lotze, who defends the autonomy of the logical order, Santayana consistently reduces the logical to the psychological order. We need, says Lotze, the principles of identity and excluded middle to proceed to make predictions. Santayana responds: "Of course the truth of these logical principles is assumed: the point is to show that by using them we are led to discover their origin. Logic forces us to admit the psychological nature of logic" (L544). When Lotze points to belief in general orderliness of events (Allgemeingesetzlichkeit) as the presupposition of inquiry, Santayana finds the situation quite different. "The starting point is a logical habit which is a psychological fact" (M17).

Santayana uses voluntarism to defend human values. Far from being tertiary qualities or merely subjective, they are the basis of whatever is real for us. Here Santayana could scarcely sound more like James. As Lotze reviews various principles of reality, Santayana reflects: "One is tempted here to think of Schopenhauer, and also Hume, and to put the essence of reality in the relation of ideas to the will: a thing is real that determines our conduct." Lotze was noted for his remark that metaphysics has a basis in ethics. Santayana has a parallel theory: "Philosophy is at bottom theology: The question is about the hierarchy of reality and we may make anything the deepest reality. For how can the objectivity of any idea be proved?" (M217).

Like a pragmatist, Santayana is far from wholly sceptical and consequently arbitrary about the real and the good. "Our habit of relating ideas is supported by nature: it survives." (Here

Santayana refers to "Notebook p. 95," L91.) To what extent can there be agreement between individuals on this basis of pragmatic tests? Perhaps this Notebook shows Santayana's grappling with problems to which he addressed himself in *The Life of Reason.*

There is another strand in Santayana's thinking that has no logical connection with his phenomenalism, his scepticism, and his voluntarism. This is his defense of Plato and Aristotle, more especially the former, whenever Lotze makes a disparaging remark about the ancients. Indeed, whenever Lotze characterizes Platonism, Santayana feels impelled to set him straight. We shall call this perspective "classical realism."

Lotze held that Plato's ideas were abstractions invested with the status of greater reality than changing things because the ideas were permanent and unchanging. In Santayana's reading, this is an abominable misinterpretation of Plato: "His ideas were not abstractions but types, goals of thought, things we mean to speak of when we have thoughts. For what we are talking of is never that which is actually in our minds, but something transcendent that our own thoughts aim at" (M80).

Throughout Lotze's chapter "Die Ideenwelt" (L III, II) Santayana has nothing good to say of Lotze's Plato scholarship. Lotze thinks neither Plato nor Aristotle was clear about what either meant by an idea existing apart from things. Santayana snaps: "That is Lotze's mistake: the question is quite another" (L518). Lotze thought he was siding with Aristotle in criticizing Plato's theory of ideas: they are useless because they provide no beginnings of motion. Here Santayana speaks to Lotze the author as a living protagonist: "Don't you see that this is an objection to the transcendent reality, that does not show why our ideas should have begun to strive after it?" (L520). Lotze thought it necessary to explain Plato's error in hypostatizing universals, but Santayana denies that they have only "hypothetic existence," and discounts the linguistic explanation. Lotze argued that the Greeks had only ὄν or οὐσία in their language to call the ideas. Santayana dismisses this curtly: "Bad" (L515–516).

Lotze had made two very fundamental errors about Plato's ideas. He missed the aspect of the good and the aspect of the real. In Lotze's interpretation, according to Santayana, "there is a problem here entirely overlooked: the transcendence of our meanings, of our goals of thought" (L513). "Plato's ideas are not universals: else where is the difference between him and Aristotle?" (L517). "Here again is a confusion of the abstract, which is posterior to the concrete, with the transcendent which is prior to it and its purpose. Laws of course are abstract: not necessarily ideas" (L519). "Who can tolerate this confusion of the abstract and the ideal?" (L522). Santayana, in spite of his phenomenalism, scepticism, and voluntarism, seemed convinced by the doctrine of the really real (ὄντως ὄν) : "That is a deeper reality than our real things" (L514).

Santayana clearly retains the classical criteria of the real: "eternal, omnipresent, self-existent thing" (M212). The real gulf between Santayana and Lotze, developed in the dissertation, is that Lotze has rejected the derivation of the moved from the unmoved. Motion cannot, says Lotze, come from the motionless. This means a rejection of Aristotle's theology, and on this point Santayana speaks for classical realism: "As if Aristotle's *primum mobile* were a *state* of the world!" (M162). This is much like Santayana's indignant rejection of Bergson's *élan vital* some twenty years later.

Can Santayana coherently be both a Jamesian voluntarist and a classical realist? Reality for the former is actively satisfying needs and producing changes in the world. Reality for the latter is that which is there to be contemplated. There is already a reason why Santayana was later to break with voluntarism; this is his famous epiphenomenalism, that consciousness is independent of behavior. Two notes express this. "Perhaps our inward states, and those of atoms, have nothing to do with our external behavior" (M158). The other is in context of Lotze's theory of materiality: "The theory Lotze rejects is one that makes change apparent only, while the elements that produce the change are not affected. This would make our consciousness ineffective" (M360).

Lotze's philosophy had taken a modestly linguistic turn, and some of the points made by Lotze caught Santayana's attention. Lotze inquires into what "it" might refer to in "it lightens" (L71). Some questions cannot be answered, they are therefore not to be asked (M163–164). Abstractions are to be used with suspicion for we are easily tricked into thinking them real things. What rouses the greatest enthusiasm in Santayana is Lotze's long and thorough inquiry into the meaning of "is" in *S* is *P* and *S* is *S*. The copula of identity, if the only and strict meaning of "is," would make the copula of predication self-contradictory: "this absolute connexion of two concepts *S* and *P,* in which the one is unconditionally the other and yet both stand over against each other as different, is a relation quite impracticable in thought. . . ."[3] To this Santayana responds, "Excellent: is this original with Lotze?" (L75). Years later Santayana did an essay on "Some Meanings of the Word 'Is.' "

Santayana reading Lotze is one metaphysician reading another. When early in the *Logik* Lotze mentions the actuality we perceive as thunder and lightning, Santayana responds: "Yes: it is the not-ourselves, the divine, that which affects us" (L71). Santayana seems to agree that the real issue is indeed that of the one and the many, and therefore we cannot ignore how the parts of a whole are related and constitute an order (L557). The simple predication, *S* is *P,* is both: one is the other yet one stands over against the other. Perhaps it is to the metaphysical insight that Santayana responds in his "excellent" (L75). Lotze's doctrine is that the true subject of a proposition is not the universal. In "Caesar crossed the Rubicon," the subject is "not Caesar lying in his cradle, but he who returned from Gaul." To this reading of a proposition as having one foot in the actual flow of events, Santayana comments, "Important and true."

An ideal has status in reality as "a direction, as a goal of thought." Santayana's sharpest criticism of Lotze is that he has not done justice to the ideal as a realm or mode of being. In spite of the phenomenalism, scepticism, and voluntarism, Santayana is critical of Lotze because he is insufficiently realistic. "The thing in itself," which we speak of "by strength of analogy . . . may be anything: a law, a will, a purpose, a substance, etc." (M12).

Santayana is sympathetic with Lotze's process philosophy, but critical. To the general view of a thing as a law of its regular behavior or as a subject of change Santayana responds, "This is notable. Try to clear up what Lotze means." And Santayana does indeed put the matter succinctly and epigrammatically: "Reality is a history, a thing is a group of states" (M63, 65).

Although in his dissertation Santayana credits Lotze with not contradicting himself, in the text itself Santayana finds inconsistencies in Lotze's pluralism, where the causal relation is "transeunt" between different things, but must be "immanent" within one thing. Santayana also questions the degree to which we may expect nature to conform to our desires and needs. Notably Santayana is more concerned with the order of nature than with human freedom, and Lotze's indeterminism is a stumbling block.

Lotze frequently reaches the end of a chapter with an apology for his long-windedness and lack of positive clear results. Santayana expresses pity for an author who could not do justice to his metaphysical vision. "The beauty of this system is very great, when we stop to poetise on it. Had Lotze had Schopenhauer's eloquence, his philosophy might have won an equal popularity. The exquisite fitness of these infinitely variable relations demanded and guaranteed by the nature of the world is notable: it gives a support and meaning to every phase of existence and both love and isolation could find their function and justification in it. Every system of philosophy is a poem and should be treated and judged as such. But not every philosopher can write his *De rerum natura*" (M142).

Santayana's last word written in Lotze's *Metaphysik* reinforces his concern with the world as both one and many. Lotze wrote that the world is a living idea expressed in words, sentences, and paragraphs; an interconnected web. The elements have their meanings as related to one another, and isolated they are meaningless. "This beautiful example, if pressed, will betray the descriptive and symbolic character of the whole view—for words have no meaning in themselves, but stand for objects and their relations" (M381).

What, finally, makes Santayana's marginalia worth reading along with his dissertation? I should say that Santayana is virtually unmatched in his sympathy with the greatest range of philosophic possibilities. It isn't fair to characterize Santayana as a philosophic acrobat who moves through the air twisting and turning to see things from six or seven different perspectives in rapid succession. He has love for variety in points of view, and his respect for the human spirit is based on a deep regard for each kind of thought maintaining its autonomy. His sense of justice is to defend the right of realists to be realists, idealists idealists, mystics mystics, Leibnizians Leibnizians, and Hindus Hindus. All these types are mentioned as having distinctive points of view, as do the phenomenalists, the sceptics, the voluntarists, and the process philosophers, whose views we have seen sympathetically interpreted by Santayana. He makes his philosophic principle clear. When Lotze is severe with a view as "unfruitful" and "pernicious" (schädisch) Santayana chides him: "Here I see a case of that injustice to others which comes from not accepting their point of view" (M115).

One might cite passages to prove that Santayana's tolerance springs from scepticism: if no one knows reality or can prove his view correct, anyone is free to believe anything. This is not a final just estimate. No one philosophy can express the total of insight and wisdom. To keep from narrowness of vision we need both *a priori* and *a posteriori* philosophers: "We must look to *a priori* philosophers for the philosophic impulse and to *a posteriori* philosophers for philosophic results" (L582). Perhaps different types can be judiciously combined to yield a result more adequate than the components. He has genuine sympathy for a Lotze trying to put his monistic and idealistic conclusions on a pluralistic and realistic basis: "In these two phases lie the idealism as to the content, the realism as to the *locus* and existence, which characterize Lotze" (M78) .

Santayana is the most generous of critics. When Lotze opposes the view of a premundane truth, such as a principle of identity true of all possible worlds, Santayana again rebukes him: "You are herein more dogmatic than those you blame for you believe in absolute possibility of things, they only in their relative possibility. At bottom, however, you are right: only instead of possible worlds, you should speak of different intelligences. For we might experience a different world, even with these same faculties" (M166) .

William James once wrote that "philosophic study means the habit of always seeing an alternative, of not taking the usual for granted, of making conventionalities fluid again, of imagining foreign states of mind. In a word, it means the possession of mental perspective." [4]

It is Santayana, spontaneously reacting to Lotze, who displays, better than in the finished dissertation, the very high degree to which George Santayana achieved the ideal of William James.

NOTES

1. Hermann Lotze, *System des Philosophie, Erster Theil, Drei Bücher der Logik*, Zweite Auflage, p. 24. Lotze's point reminds Santayana of "Royce's 'catch.'" There is no evidence that Santayana used the Oxford translation of Lotze. This was available in the first edition of 1884, and the second of 1887–88. *Logik* will be abbreviated "L."

2. Lotze, *System der Philosophie: Metaphysïk Drei Bücher der Ontologie, Kosmologie, Psychologie*, Zweite Auflage, Verlag von S. Hirzl, Leipzig, 1884, p. 87. Santayana's spelling has "discreet." This book will be referred to as "M."

3. Lotze, *Logic*, Oxford translation of 1884, §54, p. 59.

4. William James, unsigned letter, "The Teaching of Philosophy in Our Colleges," *The Nation*, Vol. 23, No. 586, 1876, p. 178.

LOTZE'S SYSTEM

OF

PHILOSOPHY

[I]

Lotze's problem—

His relation to natural science

THE WORKS OF LOTZE have not received so much attention from philosophic critics as their admitted value demands. A little book by Caspari and another by Pfleiderer, together with a few scattered articles, make up the literature of the subject. (For their articles and pamphlets, see Ueberweg, vol. III.) Yet Lotze's chief works have been translated into French and English, and his name is familiar to all students of philosophy. Some of his psychological theories, notably that of local signs, have been generally accepted, and he is always mentioned as an authority of weight. His style is clear and exquisitely finished, and his amiable and optimistic temper is not such as to upset any class of minds. With all these obvious advantages he remains little known; he has won the respect of all and the attention of few.

The middle ground that Lotze occupied on almost all important questions is perhaps a cause of public indifference. With all his clearness of style, Lotze does not produce the impression of clearness. His opinions are generally qualified and two-sided, and it is hard to classify and label his conclusions. Some labor and attention are requisite before we can discover whether we can agree with Lotze or not; and nothing so much fatigues and discourages the ordinary reader as inability to take sides for or against his author. The pleasures of battle are not offered us by Lotze, yet he imposes upon us all the labors of a campaign. We follow him backwards and forwards, around and

around a problem, and its equivocal solution is hardly an adequate recompense for our fidelity. In other words, Lotze's philosophy is not a result presented to us that we may judge of
the effect: he does not put before us a completed picture, with
all the details in their places and all the vistas carefully pre-
arranged to produce illusion; he rather invites us to assist at
the construction of the work and watch him combine his effects and try his experiments. Thus two circumstances detract
from the pleasure of reading Lotze, the redundancy of material
and argument, and the comparative indistinctness of the conclusion.

Lotze's argumentation is not limited to what is strictly necessary to justify his result. He gives us, in each chapter of his
Logic and Metaphysics, a little treatise on a philosophical topic.
The number of points discussed is out of all proportion with
the clear result we carry away with us. The minuteness of the
argumentation requires us, if we are to criticise it at all, to be
no less minute and detailed; so that to consider the text of one
chapter we should require a chapter of at least equal length.
Naturally anyone having the courage to undertake so elaborate
an investigation would not be willing to be a mere expositor
and critic; what he would write would be his own theory, not
an account of Lotze's. Lotze's works are a storehouse of exquisite
dialectics, of singular value to anyone working out the special
problems they discuss. In this study I cannot hope to speak of
more than one or two such problems: my main purpose is to
consider the final result of Lotze's thought, his general system
of philosophy. Much will necessarily be passed over that is of
great intrinsic interest. Some of Lotze's best work lies in his suggestions on minor points of logical and psychological theory,
and all this, in a general account of his system, has naturally
to be omitted. The judgment we may happen to pass on his
general opinions will not concern the value of these minor but
not insignificant points: thus the theory of local signs, the treatment of the principle of identity, and many other investigations,

have an interest and value in themselves, quite apart from Lotze's theory of the universe.

The apparent indistinctness of this theory has an obvious cause. Lotze intended his work to be one of mediation and reconciliation between the opposing schools of German philosophy and between the conflicting tendencies of our time. There is hardly one received antithesis of opinion in philosophy that Lotze does not in some sense take up into his system and partially amend: we cannot call him unreservedly either a realist or a phenomenalist, a positivist or an idealist, a monist or a pluralist, a pantheist or a theist, an empiricist or a rationalist. He shows some leanings toward socialism (See *Grundzüge der praktischen Philosophie,* pp. 66–75) , yet is not plainly a socialist: he is by temper an optimist, yet abandons the attempt to justify the ways of God to man. So indescribable an attitude would at first sight seem to be necessarily full of contradictions; yet perhaps few systems are so free from contradiction as Lotze's. We need not, to think justly and consistently, enroll ourselves under the banner of any sect; the distinctions that historical schools of opinion have emphasized are not necessarily well taken. A man's thought is not necessarily vague because he can be called neither a simple realist nor a simple idealist; a thinker has no obligation to adopt an antithesis that custom has made familiar. The dilemma of thought may be really at another point; and at any rate our vocabulary should not limit the choice of our opinions. To blame a man for not fitting exactly into any of our conventional categories is little less absurd than to blame him for not being exactly so many feet and inches in height. Truth has as little obligation to conform to philosophic antitheses as nature to conform to English long measure. The difficulty we may feel in classifying Lotze's system is therefore no presumption against its clearness or truth. Yet as a matter of fact its singularity is not the consequence of its new and original nature: it is an eclectic system, and is a most measured and judicious combination of various theories already current, not a new and original conception spontaneously formed in the mind of a genius—the quality of genius we must not expect. Lotze is a critic, a master of adaptation and combination; and he brings into philosophy but one new thing—moderation.

Among the schools of thought that Lotze seeks to combine and reconcile we do not find Christian theology. Natural piety and religious sense are explicitly allowed to exercise influence on our convictions, but the forms in which religious conceptions appear have nothing about them distinctly Christian; the theological current is not perceptible, and our religious demands are felt to be essentially the same as those satisfied by ancient philosophies. A personal but naturalistic God and a hypothetical immortality make up the share of satisfaction allowed to the religious imagination; and these conceptions flow out of the inward nature of Lotze's metaphysics and are not adopted in view of conventional demands. They resemble in form and in foundation the corresponding doctrines in Plato and Aristotle; for the theologian they have the merit of furnishing an independent although partial confirmation of his dogmas. Lotze, like Plato and Aristotle, can win the approbation and sympathy of the orthodox without being, any more than they, an apologist for Christianity. One element of conflict is thus removed from the sphere of Lotze's thought: among the demands of our moral nature and of our religious feelings he does not find any fixed traditional conceptions of God, of human history, or of personal destiny.

A tendency with which Christian theology is often thought to conflict, the tendency of natural science, is, on the other hand, a prominent factor in Lotze's philosophy. The attitude toward science is noteworthy: in this, as in many other respects, Lotze combined the characteristics of opposite schools. Like the positivists he grants to science that finality that German metaphysicians generally deny to it: he does not attempt to find some absolute principle behind the process of nature that gives it a different meaning than it has as an empirical object. His system is not an interpretation of the world of experience, it is rather a description and formulation of this phenomenal world. Philosophy for Lotze does not begin where science ends; the two are coordinate and inseparable. They do not succeed each other as totally different methods of treating the object of knowledge; they check and control each other as complementary parts of one and the same investigation. In this way we see the rank of natural science raised to that of sovereign and final judge of knowledge; and we should be inclined to think Lotze a positivist but for the new aspect of his thought that at once appears.

If metaphysics does not pretend to reinterpret nature after natural science has done all it can, and thus to abandon the empirical and objective point of view for one supposed to be higher,—if metaphysics does not amend science after this science is complete, it proposes to supervise and control scientific investigations while in progress. The results of natural science are to be final, but in reaching those results we are to be mindful of ontological difficulties and of moral and emotional demands. Although not concerned about the traditional doctrines of Christianity, Lotze has certain cherished convictions of his own that empirical theories are forbidden to contradict; and these moral and aesthetic postulates are checks to a purely theoretical and objective conception of things.

The apparent conflict between the demands of a susceptible and poetic disposition and the evidence of scientific study is everywhere the spur to Lotze's thinking. That this conflict is only apparent is his primary postulate, and his final conclusion is the proof that this postulate is legitimate. He does not sum up the results of science and say, "This is the truth; let us see what comfort we can take in it;" nor does he sum up the demands of our inspiration and say, "This is the ideal; let us see how far the reality fulfils it." That might be the method of a man to whom the final reconciliation of feeling and experience was not an axiom. Lotze does not ask in how far this reconciliation is possible; he assumes that it is complete, and then begins his investigations in the hope of finding his assumption corroborated. A consequence of this assumption is that he never leaves the demands of sentiment out of view when he formulates natural laws, nor natural laws when he formulates the demands of sentiment. Hence a certain lack of boldness in the general effect of his system; but this lack of clearness is compensated by the check to illegitimate speculation that this double point of view affords. A man who allowed himself to be carried away by the analogies of science would for example come to the conclusion that all living beings are automata; Lotze, keeping in mind the great repugnance of our imagination to such a conclusion, stops in the formulation of mechanical law where mechanical law ceases to be observed. He does not extend the law by analogy to all events in the physical world. A man, on the other hand, who considered only the demands of feeling would not fail to assert the essential permanence of valuable things; he would believe in a world of unseen things which are eternal to which he and his ideals belonged by nature. Lotze, keeping in mind the universal flux of things, and feeling that nature and our own lives as parts of nature are essentially processes, refuses to indulge in that dream of eternal and changeless being; he conceives of value as an accompaniment of the process, and is willing to see our affections transform themselves with the transformation of their objects. In this way both the dogmas of experience and the claims of aspiration are minimized by constant comparison: yet this mutual control is not conceived to be an external check to the development of either impulse, but rather a means to prevent their misunderstanding themselves. For Lotze begins always with the axiom that the reality must satisfy our emotional demands. Hence any demand that the reality cannot satisfy is at once proved not to be a genuine demand of the spirit, but only an exaggeration of sentimentality. So also any scientific hypothesis that offends our deeper moral instincts is *ipso facto* disproved and classed among those materialistic theories that greatly overreach possible experience. Evidently such a method of mutual correction is sound only if the axiom on which it is founded is true: if haply the laws of nature were irreconcilable with our emotional demands, this method would be in danger of leading to a misrepresentation of both. Nor does Lotze seem to have wholly escaped this danger: yet his characteristic caution and his intimate acquaintance with several branches of physical science keep him comparatively free from the fault to which his method exposes him.

Lotze's education was medical, and from his professional training he derived a mechanical theory of nature that is of primary importance in his system. This mechanical theory shows the preponderating influence of physiological studies; had Lotze's attention been chiefly fixed on astronomy, geology, or natural history, we may doubt whether his conception of mechanism would have been the same. In all Lotze's earlier works, in the article on life and vital force, in his general theuropathy and physiology, in his early metaphysics and medical psychology, and also in his two treatises on aesthetics appears a clear and admirable exposition of this mechanism of nature. Three coordinate principles of explanation are admitted, which remind us of Aristotle's four kinds of causes: only Lotze identifies the formal and the efficient cause, thus giving the theory a more modern shape.

The three principles of explanation that Lotze recognizes are (1) the relation of reason to consequence, (2) the relation of cause to effect, and (3) the relation of end to means.

(1) In the relation of reason to consequence we have the typical form of explanation. The other two grounds of reference do not really furnish explanations, but rather two sets of primary facts to be the units and factors of explanation. When we refer a thing not to a reason but to a cause, when we recognize the given elements active in the world, we explain nothing; we only take note of the presence and character of what lies before us. Likewise, when we regard processes as governed by a purpose, we do not explain them; we simply give a moral value and meaning to them which justifies for us their unexplained existence. But when we refer one thing to another as its logical consequence, we explain it by showing its necessary derivation from the given facts. This principle of necessary deri-

vation is a general name for the laws of nature. Granting a number of accepted processes and general ways of behaving, which the mind expects and considers matters of course, the work of explaining events consists in showing that they occur by virtue of these habits of nature and not as exceptions and anomalies. This, Lotze tells us, is what the scholastics wished to predicate of the world when they said: *Omne ens est verum.* For truth is that order and combination of elements that flows from the primary and everpresent principles and postulates of thought; to say that being is true is therefore to say that it can be expressed and comprehended according to those principles and postulates of intelligence. If every new thing that we met had to be understood on fundamentally new principles; if a new logic, a new set of expectations and presuppositions had to take possession of our minds before we could regard the new phenomena as natural, then the world would be untrue,—i.e. it would be unintelligible and have no consistency. There would be no passing from one thing to another; every analogy would be misleading. But the opposite is the case: the world is true and faithful to its own constitution. The logic and presuppositions that it sanctions here and now it sanctions everywhere and always by allowing us to apply them with success and practical profit. This truth and faithfulness of the world is what makes experience possible. For evidently in that fragmentary and disjointed dream that we should have, did new principles and laws appear at every turn, we should learn nothing valid; we should remember, perhaps, a series of visions and magical transformations, but we should not know what to expect, nor know whether we should awake in the land of Lilliput or in a space of fifteen dimensions. The fact that we *can* acquire experience, the fact that our habits of action and thought are maintained and encouraged by our discoveries, and not checked and constantly reversed: this fact that knowledge of the world is possible rests on the truth and consistency of things. *Omne ens est verum:* all nature is intelligible.

On the basis of this postulate Lotze goes on to show that the phenomena of life must proceed according to the same laws that would govern the motions of the material elements apart from any life. If the laws of physical attraction and chemical reaction that are elsewhere observed failed to hold where matter entered the living body, then there would be no consistency in the behavior of matter. We need not know what in chemistry we do not know, viz. how the parts combined manage to produce the actual result; but what we must demand is that this result should always appear under like circumstances. The effect must remain proportional to the causes, and must be repeated when the causes recur. Apart from this postulate science becomes impossible, for we can have experience only in so far as we can discover law.

(2) But a law is a relation that obtains between things already given, it is not a ground for the existence of the realities themselves. Our first or logical method of explanation treats effects as consequences of given premises; it shows that the law of development, the law of derivation is everywhere the same; but it takes for granted the premises, the conditions on which the possibility of the development depends. The second method of explanation consists in referring effects to the existence of these premises. For while the nature of the results follows according to a general law from the presence of the conditions, the presence of the conditions follows from no law and is the fact that is really responsible for the existence of the result. Nothing is accounted for by a law alone, for law is not a cause but a method of operation of causes, a way in which results are brought about. The decision whether an event is to occur or not never rests with the law. The law is inefficient and only asserts that if certain conditions are realized certain consequences will follow; what is efficient is the constellation of causes which, exercising their influence and combining their effects according to law, produce the expected result. If we know the presence of the conditions, the law will tell us what result to expect, but if we know the result we must not be satisfied with saying that it was brought about according to general laws; we

must go on to say that, since the result was brought about according to general laws, and general laws are forms of association of effects with their causes, these causes must have been present and offered an opportunity for the laws to manifest themselves. The causes of events are therefore not the laws of nature but the things in nature, the facts and conditions extant from which consequences follow according to general laws.

(3) The series of causes is infinite, and the world regarded as the result of given realities interacting according to general laws is an incomplete whole. Even if we knew the entire history of things we should still ask for a justification of it. We should demand that this fact should have the sanction of some authority; that it should not impose itself upon us without a good reason. A mere description of the world would not contain this justification. A purpose is the content of a judgment, not of an idea; it is not there by virtue of the presence of things but by virtue of a value attributed to them. The purpose is never a real thing, or a part of the object realized; for so long as the purpose remains unfulfilled, it is something that ought to be but is not; and when fulfilled it is not a thing but a relation, an action, a passion of the things. The purpose must not therefore be regarded as an efficient cause of the process. A purpose cannot be the ground of existence, but only a demand that what already exists should be a means to an end, and should be directed to an ideal result. The realization of a purpose, says Lotze, is never the work of the purpose itself. The result must follow from the given reality according to general laws, and the purpose must be realized by their agency, while it remains in itself inefficient. And evidently, since the course of things is to be influenced only by the given realities and their general laws of combination, the fulfilment of the purpose must be involved in the originally existent reality and in the ever valid laws. The whole of nature must therefore subserve a purpose, while no part of it can be exempted from obedience to the law. There is a fundamental error in the practice of regarding general laws as efficient in one part of nature and purposes as efficient in another part. A law would not

be a law unless it were universally valid, unless the premisses that it makes the basis of a conclusion did in fact involve that conclusion. And every event in nature must in like manner stand in some relation to a general purpose, for that irrationality and lack of justification which would attach to nature if it had no purpose at all would attach to any of its parts that did not subserve its general purpose. But the law may be more evident to us in some parts of the world and the purpose in others, so that it may be convenient to classify the facts now according to one, now according to the other principle of explanation. The purposes of nature, however, are not clearly known; in using them in science we are exposed to mistake an accidental for an essential relation. For in regard to the universal purpose many things are accidental. Natural elements, although they fulfil a purpose, are not produced by that purpose; in every machine there is some friction, some vindication on the part of the means of their independent existence and origin. The elements of nature, although all useful to her ends, are not everywhere and in every respect useful. In fulfilling their function they introduce disturbances and obstacles, and they stand in more relations to one another than the sense of the world absolutely requires. We may therefore mistake one of these accidental relations for an essential and significant one; the safer way is to classify objects and events according to universal laws, and to use aims as means of classification only when they are evident, and the mechanical law of these same objects and events is not easily discovered.

Now it is easy to see how entirely satisfactory this triple principle of expectation is from the medical point of view. A mechanism of action in a machine that is already there is all that medicine wishes to discover; it is not concerned about the origin of the organism that it studies. And the third principle of explanation, the principle of final causes, is more congenial to a practical and humane science like medicine, that itself exists for a purpose, and seeks to aid nature in fulfilling her own, than it might be to purely speculative and contemplative sciences like astronomy or natural history. It is much easier for a physiologist to speak of the "evident purpose" of bodily organs than for a geologist to speak of the purpose of stratification. Yet however unwilling certain sciences may be to consider final causes, all must admit Lotze's principle that natural law does not account for the presence of the facts to which it applies. This principle is applicable to historical sciences no less than to physics and physiology. History does not explain human nature nor the physical conditions in which society lives. Geology does not explain the presence of the materials of the earth, nor the heat and gravitation that keep them in motion. And even the most complete theory of evolution would have to assume the given matter and motion of the world. Thus if we consider the nebular hypothesis, we see at once that gravitation, which is to account for the subsequent motions of this mass, does not explain the presence of a single atom of the nebula nor its position. That the number of atoms is what it is and that they are disposed as they are in space are both original data quite independent of the laws of motion. Lotze's principle is therefore in strictness no limitation of the function of any science.

At the same time one cannot help feeling that, under the form of this unassailable principle, Lotze expresses his aversion to evolutionary hypotheses. The creation, he tells us, is an object for mystical and religious, not for scientific, treatment. To be sure, the evolutionary theories current about 1840, when these earlier works of Lotze were written, were rather theosophical than empirical. There was a certain naturalness, therefore, in denying the scientific value of such speculations. Yet empirical theories of evolution, when they appeared, proved to be more distasteful to Lotze than idealistic cosmogonies. For these have a motive and answer a question to which Lotze is not indifferent: they attempt to formulate the ideal significance of the world. But an empirical evolution is something not required either by exact science or by the religious imagination. For the laws observed in the developed world are quite primary and general enough for science; while the answer to our question about the meaning and justification of things is by no means contained in a materialistic law of evolution, which only describes a given process and tells us nothing to justify it ideally or to account for the presence of the conditions that make it applicable.

To leave something unexplained, however, is the common lot of all science and philosophy; Lotze cannot make it a particular reproach of evolutionary theories. The value of science, after all, does not lie in any tendency to solve the fundamental riddle of things. What science must always leave unexplained remains as deeply and hopelessly inexplicable as things could ever be to savages or wise men. In so far as rationality is concerned men were as well off when the world was a flat arena walled in by clouds and vaulted over by the revolving heavens. In truth they were better off, for living trees and mountains and rivers are more comprehensible objects than dead stones. The discovery that the world is infinite has made it so intolerably irrational that we can hardly believe it is a real thing. Our gain has not been at all in rationality, but in practical resource. So Bacon hoped it might be when he wrote the *New Atlantis* and when he said, *Knowledge is power.* Both practically and theoretically we can handle nature as the ancients could not; we can travel with ease all over one planet and calculate how long it would take us to travel to any of the others. And the same kind of progress would continue if we could reduce still more the number of observed laws and inexplicable facts.

Yet Lotze betrays a desire to retain a very complex system of unexplained objects as the starting point of natural science. He admits the possibility of evolution in general, but seems to deprecate any attempt to show that it is real in particular instances. Darwinism and kindred doctrines he regards as hasty and impendent; he ignores these theories as built on an inadequate basis of fact. It is impossible, however, to believe that his dislike of them is founded entirely on a scientific scruple; undoubtedly his anxiety to reconcile the idealistic and the scientific temper led him to turn away from the moral difficulties that such theories suggest. For an alliance between general laws and moral purposes is much more easily conceived when these laws do not involve a Penelope's task and the dissolution of everything evolved. Lotze blamed the older metaphysicians for regarding types as fixed, and abstract ideas as realities; he is willing to admit gradual variation; but he is most unwilling to admit that sort of variation which observation leads us to expect. It was the law of things itself that Lotze hoped might be variable, so as to admit of more perfect life. But he shrank from admitting variations according to a given and apparently eternal law, that shows all life to be in a state of unstable equilibrium, requiring a complex of conditions so immensely intricate that its appearance in nature is a matter of extreme improbability. He would have welcomed an evolution that pointed out an essential expansiveness and progression in things, that allowed us to conceive the cosmic process as a melody with ever new meaning and augmented beauty. But the evolution that modern science has led many to believe in is only an incidental evolution, followed by dissolution. It is the evolution that ancient materialism had already conceived, and which is inevitably suggested by any purely objective study of the world:

> Nam certe fluere ac decedere corpora rebus
> multa, manus dandum est: sed plura accedere debent
> donec alescendi summum tetigere cacumen.
> inde minutatim vires et robur adultum
> frangit, et in partem pejorem liquitur aetas . . .
> sic igitur magni quoque circa moenia mundi
> expugnata dabunt labem putresque ruinas.*
>
> Lucr. II, ll. 1128–1132, 1148–1149

Such evolution Lotze regards as a wilful exaggeration of materialism and impiety. He prefers to regard the given types of animals and plants, and the given arrangement of the heavenly bodies, as facts irreducible by empirical analysis. The reasons for their being such as they are are to be sought, not in any law of

---

* For it must be granted that many particles of things fly off and are gone: but even more should be added on until they reach the highest peak of growth. After that, age by minute degrees breaks down mature strength and vigor, and melts into an inferior state. . . . So therefore the walls of great heaven will be stormed all round and will collapse into crumbling ruin.

evolution empirically discovered, but in the sense and moral purpose of the world, that must have demanded them as a stage and stepping stone in its progressive manifestation.

Of the specific theories of the evolutionary school Lotze has little to say and his rejection of them, were it founded on specific technical objections, would not have much importance in his general system. But allied to this reserve in regard to evolution, we find an explicit objection to the principle of mechanical unity —Lotze contends, as we have seen, that every event in the world has a mechanical explanation, but he conceives this explanation to vary in different spheres; mechanism can be psychical as well as physical, and physical mechanism has many forms and principles, such as gravitation, magnetism, chemical affinity and electricity. These he conceives as irreducible and fundamental; we must give up the attempt to reduce all causation to one type. In this general form Lotze's objection to certain modern theories ceases to be a friendly and scientific one; it becomes an objection to the ideal of science. He asks us to give up the postulate of the empirical intelligibility of things, to comprehend means to reduce to one type, to see in the unfamiliar a case of the familiar. And Lotze, in spite of his objection to reducing all events to one type, must himself reduce them to a small number of types; else all science would be annulled. The same method that has led us to reduce the multitude of phenomena to these few types might lead us to reduce these to one; and the same satisfaction that we find in the progress we have made we should find in further progress. What test can Lotze have to decide where the simplification of natural processes should stop? Here we have a case in which Lotze's system of checks seems to work unfavorably: the check is external and arbitrary, and we cannot feel that it prevents conflict; on the contrary, it exemplifies the conflict.

The reason why Lotze demands the concession of the unity of empirical science is an aesthetic one. He does not wish the world to become monotonous. If all events were of one type, nature would be the ceaseless and infinite repetition of one and the same art. All the variety we find in the world would be the result of a process in reality always the same; the variety of reasons for things would disappear. Lotze is quite right; the reason for everything would then be the same sort of reason; always the cause of events would be of one type. And that is the ideal of science; to give it up is to surrender the scientific impulse. There would then be a great monotony in the reason for the variety of things; but the variety of things would remain. In feeling that the world would be impoverished by unity of principle, Lotze seems to share a popular illusion. The opposition to new theories is often founded on a belief in the ability of a theory to change the facts on which it rests. It is not the old theory that is to be replaced but the facts themselves that are to disappear. In so far, of course, as the theory itself is the object of affection, this dislike to see it superseded is natural and legitimate; but it is unreasonable when the old theory has no value except that which it borrows from the facts, a value that evidently the new theory, if accepted, will also possess, since it is not the personal property of the theory, so to speak, but the appanage of its office. And this is the case in the question before us. The variety of nature does not derive its aesthetic value from the multitude of physical laws; but each principle of explanation requires dignity in proportion to the value of the phenomena it explains. Theories are like money that has the value of the things it can buy. And the variety of the world would retain all its interest and charm if we could express the principle of its causation in one phrase instead of in a hundred. The only change would be in the theory itself; but simplicity and comprehensiveness are the virtues of theories. The world as an object of experience would be no less picturesque for having a simple explanation, and the beauty of the explanation would be all the greater if it were simple and universally true. The renunciation of the unity of empirical science that Lotze demands seems therefore to be uncalled for; such unity does not involve a loss of beauty in the world. In this respect scientific and aesthetic ideals do not conflict; we are not driven to any revision and partial surrender of these ideals in the interests of peace.

There is another principle, of much greater importance than the typical unity of science, that Lotze gives up: the principle of the conservation of energy. The unity of science is only a natural scientific ideal, but the conservation of energy is an indispensable scientific assumption. Lotze, indeed, admits its utility; he approves of it as a means of investigation; but he denies its objective and ultimate validity. His reasons for this denial are two: one—the desire to admit action and reaction between body and mind; and the other the desire to admit new forces, new beginnings dropping into the course of events and changing their direction. These two conceptions are too important in Lotze's system to be treated here; we shall consider them at length later on. In this place it is enough to point out in what sense and under what limitations Lotze accepts a mechanical theory of nature. He admits the existence of laws, laws that necessarily and invariably are obeyed when the data to which they apply appear. But these data are not invariably in turn accounted for by regular derivation from previous conditions; just as in the end we should have to admit an underivable set of facts as constituting the nature of the given reality, so at any point in the development of this reality underivable elements may appear. But when once created these new elements enter into the domain of general laws, their influence in the further course of nature is determined by those laws; only their own appearance is undetermined. Thus instead of a principle of sufficient reason we have one of adequate effect, instead of a necessary cause we have an inevitable consequence of every fact in the world—if the consequences of any fact are fixed they can be fixed only by a law that makes that fact at the same time the sufficient reason for those consequences. The reservation of the possibility of a new and unaccountable fact appearing at any time does not practically affect the method of investigation; the hypotheses of science can continue to be framed as before; the only thing given up is the hope that these hypotheses may ever be adequate to the reality and cover the process of nature without leaving a remainder. This is no great renunciation; for that consummation of science, even if devoutly to be wished, is by no one really expected. Granting therefore that we have adequate moral motives for denying the conservation of energy, we cannot regard its surrender as of great consequence to science, if, like Lotze, we substitute for it a principle of hypothetical mechanism. If the consequences of data are fixed, it matters little if we can know these data only as accomplished facts. The theory of science is necessarily hypothetical; for the proof that it describes the reality we must constantly appeal to the perception of the moment. We therefore in no way invalidate the theory when we say that this continual appeal to the fact is necessary not only to show us that there is a reality to which the theory applies, but also what this reality is, and what basis it offers for the application of the theory.

Besides his mechanical theory Lotze has another point of contact with natural science. He is a realist in his method. He does not fly from positivistic arguments into the impregnable fortress of subjective idealism; he does not seek to invalidate all evidence by appeals to the neglected Ego. He does not constantly tell us of the necessity of going back to Kant and Hegel and of acknowledging the fact that thought produces its objects and that nothing has significance except to the reason of the absolute. Lotze is content to found his philosophy on realism. The chain of arguments will concern us later by which he passes from this realistic starting point to an idealistic conclusion; but he makes this great initial concession to positivism that he admits its point of view. We are not to discuss, he says, how the reality is made, but what it is now that we stand before it. We shall not deny the reality of things on the ground that their being is exhausted by representation, that our knowledge or images of a thing makes up all of that thing that concerns us; but we shall follow that primary impulse of our cognitive nature that leads us to speak of things at all; we shall examine what we may believe in, what has such a nature as to admit of existence. And moreover this object is to be conceived as an aggregate of parts; we speak of many things, not of one. Hence our philosophy will have the same starting point as natural science; it will deal with the same things, although of course with a different purpose.

This objective and realistic point of view makes Lotze's philosophy approachable to common sense, and herein lies his greatest concession to natural science. The point of view is objective, it regards phenomena as things, studies them in themselves, considers their relations and qualities, the principle of their variations. There is no revolutionary idealistic turn given to everything at the beginning; the Copernican revolution that Kant accomplished is not condemned, but it is ignored. This may be done, Lotze tells us, on the same principle on which we still continue to talk of the rising and the setting sun. It might fairly be urged that in astronomy we should not do so; and no more should we in philosophy continue to speak of objective things without reference to the forms of human intelligence. But Lotze believes that the Kantian foundation of idealism in a criticism of our faculties is necessarily subsequent to an ontological treatment of the objects these faculties discover to us; our intelligence is not the first objective our intelligence must consider. In this removal of the Kantian philosophy to the end of our system, instead of maintaining it at the beginning as Kant himself requires, consists the realism, the positivism of Lotze. In his conclusion he is an idealist of the Kantian school; but he removes these idealistic conceptions from their place as the guardians of philosophy to a more honorable but less influential station at the end of his speculations. The criticism of the objects of knowledge as they appear to us leads him to accept Kant's principal conclusions, but he abandons Kant's argument and in a great measure Kant's point of view.

We find then that Lotze's combination of modern science and modern philosophy consists in adopting the premises of science, even in philosophy, but in requiring the surrender of scientific principles and conclusions in favor of a philosophic system. He is not willing to let science proceed undisturbed and come to its own independent conclusions with the intention of judging afterwards their philosophic value; he wishes to keep in mind philosophic problems in the midst of purely scientific investigations. He will not hear, for instance, of a parallelism of mind and matter, of an automatism of life; he has moral and aesthetic objections to such hypotheses. He will not hear even of the conservation of energy; that would, he thinks, deprive nature of all vitality. Yet in thus subjecting science to a metaphysical and aesthetic censorship, he brings metaphysics down to the scientific level; the interference is therefore not that of a foreign power, as would be the interference of theology; it is rather the warning of a friendly and fraternal faculty, with identical rights and purposes. Lotze's philosophy seeks to be a rationalized natural science, a science made clear and logically sound; it does not seek to be an interpretation of science or a translation of the empirical facts and laws into the language of theosophy.

Lotze's attitude toward natural science is, then, that of a modified positivism; but we know that even this modified positivism is not to be final. Lotze wishes his philosophy to supply that scientific unity which he refused to let science acquire of itself; his system is intended "to join the separate fields of our certain knowledge into a theory of the world capable of completeness." (*Logik*, "Vorwort.") Instead of a single type of event to which all events may be reduced we have the poetic unity of a work of art in which each part is not the repetition but the complement of the rest. The problem of philosophy is the same as that of science, the data are the same, and the object in both cases is the unification and intelligibility of the world; but the hypothesis that is to furnish this unification is for Lotze a moral hypothesis: instead of assuming that the process of nature is everywhere similar, he assumes that the process of nature has everywhere one purpose, one meaning, but subserves and expresses these in various ways. The intelligibility to be brought into the world is not intellectual but moral; we are to have not a working but a living hypothesis. Thus with the same material, from the same starting point as natural science, philosophy is to reach a semi-religious conclusion. By the authority of this moral postulate Lotze is able to check the spontaneous movement of science, at the same time, as he believes, really serving a scientific purpose. Lotze's philosophy in its initial stage may be defined as natural science constructed on moral postulates. He accepts that objective and realistic standpoint that so often seems to involve materialism; but he rejects conservation of energy in favor of expansion and radical correction of natural development; he rejects automatism in favor of mental efficiency; he rejects uniformity of type in favor of aesthetic variety and diversity. In this way we arrive at that conception of things which Lotze himself, at the end of his earlier work on metaphysics, calls moral idealism. We have an objective world of animate and inanimate things, but the law of this world is not physical; it is a moral law, producing moral and aesthetic goods, for the sake of which the physical and mental world alone exists.

[II]

Lotze and the Kantian philosophy

THE CRITICAL PHILOSOPHY, as Kant bequeathed it to the world, was a complex and not wholly consistent system. In regard to this philosophy, as in regard to so much else, Lotze holds a double yet perfectly tenable position. The best known element of Kant's thought, and that which especially deserves to be called the critical element, is the doctrine that the structure and laws of our mind determine the sort of experience we can have, but give us no clue to the nature of any reality that may be beyond our experience. This leading Kantian doctrine Lotze admits as self-evident; but its very self-evidence seems to him to take away its importance. For although evidently we cannot have any ideas that our mental constitution is incapable of producing, the fact that these ideas are products of our faculties does not prove that they do not correspond, as they pretend, to an external and independent reality. The belief in an objective world similar to our idea of it is therefore not compromised by the Kantian philosophy; we simply are made aware that our knowledge does not produce these external objects, if they exist, but merely knows them,—has ideas and images that it regards as signs and representations of these external objects. Lotze thus accepts the letter of Kant's doctrine; he admits that our ideas are primarily products of our psychical activity and only secondarily, if at all, representations of an outward reality; but he rejects the spirit and intention of this very doctrine. For he does not cease to investigate this hypothetical reality in order to consider the internal economy of these ideas, and the implications of our postulate that they know one another and stand in mutual relations. Lotze continued to speak of the represented external things; he retains, as we have seen, the point of view of science. And his consideration of the nature and constitution of the world is based on an analysis of our ideas as self-existent objects; his criticism is ontological and regards the possibility that certain things should be; it is not epistemological, nor regards the possibility that certain things should be known. In this respect, therefore, his philosophy is just what it might have been had Kant never lived, or were he not himself a Kantian. Many of the conclusions that Lotze shares with Kant, he places on entirely different arguments; so that the apparent and external agreement between them is much greater than the inward and intimate agreement between their methods and presuppositions. A consequence of this outward agreement and inward lack of sympathy is that Lotze seldom mentions Kant or discusses anything in the shape in which Kant put it; for nothing is more unattractive to us than a man who does as we do, but for a different motive. Lotze prefers to borrow his problems from Leibnitz, or Herbart, or Hegel; he does not always agree with their conclusions, but he is more in sympathy with their procedure.

Kant, as is well known, escapes from his phenomenalism and enters the world of objective reality by means of the postulates of the practical reason. These are the only evidences he finds of the necessary constitution of being. And we have seen that Lotze, although a realist, makes the governing principle of the reality a moral law; here we have a new point of contact between Kant and Lotze. But Lotze, neglecting as he does the phenomenalistic side of Kant's system, thinks of this historical world, the world of his *Microcosmus,* as the reality that satisfies our moral postulates. Kant never conceived of such a thing; he was deeply religious and somewhat pessimistic, and the main value the moral postulates had in his eyes was that they suggested the belief in a world fundamentally different from the phenomenal, a realm of spirits with a hierarchy of aims that he never would have

dreamed of discovering in the empirical reality. The values that
moral postulates demand Kant never sought in the phenomenal
world; his deep sense that they were not to be found there was
what made him look upon the moral postulates as guides to the
transcendent world; we have the moral conviction that the reality
must possess these values; we have the ocular proof that the
phenomenal world does not possess them; therefore we know
this, but only this, of the transcendent reality, that in it lie the
values that our moral nature demands but that our mortal life
cannot discover. For Kant practical reason could postulate
transcendent truths; it could assure us of God, of freedom, and
of immortality. But for Lotze practical reason, or the postulate
of moral worth, involves all sorts of truths. It can, as we have
seen, correct our empirical knowledge, throw out scientific hypotheses, and in short superintend all our intellectual life. For
Kant transcendently valid knowledge could never revise the laws
of the phenomenal world; it could only give us a point of view
from which to regard the whole world of experience. Thus in
the case of freedom both Kant and Lotze appeal to the moral
postulate; but Kant never thinks of denying the empirical laws
of antecedence and consequence. He would never, for a moral
reason, have condemned the doctrine of evolution, or the conservation of energy, or the automatism of motion. He would
only have pointed out that these were phenomenal laws, applicable to this world of experience. The demands of our moral
nature have free scope in the infinite remainder of reality;
somewhere in that transcendent sphere they must find their
satisfaction; they must not interfere with our candid and disin-
terested observation of phenomena. Thus, if freedom is a postulate of moral reason, it must not on that account be permitted
to introduce disorder and unintelligibility into the empirical
world; yet we may believe that in reference to other realities, and
regarding our lives *sub specie aeternitatis,* we are free. And as
the whole world of matter is for Kant internal to the soul and
its product, it is enough satisfaction for the demand for moral
independence to know that the ground for the primary direction

of the will is nothing but the will itself. The plane of reality in which moral facts belong is not the same as the plane of physical objective facts; the objective world is a product of our imagination; it is not the cause of our inward nature but its effect and consequence. All this may or may not be satisfactory; we may even doubt whether freedom is a moral postulate at all. But undoubtedly Kant's whole conception is kept within the bounds of his first principles, and does not contradict that critical philosophy that seeks to give to experience what belongs to experience and to faith what belongs to faith.

Wholly different is Lotze's attitude. His realism in the first place forbids his treating empirical facts as on a different plane of reality from moral facts. Then his moral postulate, becoming his guide not only in morals but also in science, affects his theories of experience as much as his theories of transcendent things. Hence we may say that the greatly increased scope of the moral postulate in Lotze completes for him that revision of the *Critique of Pure Reason* which the *Critique of Practical Reason* began. But while in Kant the moral postulate furnishes only an addition to his critical results, in Lotze it furnishes an exception and disproof. The validity of our scientific conclusions, if consonant with our moral demands, is final for Lotze. And no scientific conclusions are possible for him that are not consonant with such demands, for moral hypotheses have taken the place for him of purely phenomenalistic theories. Thus instead of the Kantian separation and coordination of moral and phenomenal laws, we have in Lotze a combination of both and a subordination of one to the other. The admission that our faculties limit and form our knowledge loses its importance when we learn that this knowledge may have transcendent validity. The function of moral postulates also loses its limitations when we learn that the real and the phenomenal world are continuous and homogeneous, so that the phenomenal world also must satisfy those postulates. In general we may say that Lotze softens the sharp outlines of the critical philosophy; he represents the authority of reason as less limited in range, but at the same time as less authoritative in its widened sphere. Lotze is more cautious than Kant in dealing with empirical laws; he never would have written a *Natural History of the Heavens*. He is more hopeful and bold in metaphysical speculation; he has elaborate discussions of the nature of efficient cause, of the soul, and of the cosmic life. But while thus retreating somewhat from Kant's position, Lotze does not abandon wholly any element of Kant's doctrine. He distributes the emphasis differently and more evenly than Kant did among these various doctrines; thus the neglected things in themselves are brought into prominence, the subjectivity of time and space are fully discussed, as in Kant, but the relation of judgments to their objects sinks from a metaphysical to a logical question. The moral postulates, as we have seen, extend their authority; but they no longer secure those old-fashioned and Christian goods, God, freedom, and immortality, but the harmony of the cosmic life, and the moral and aesthetic value of human history.

Lotze, by retaining all these Kantian elements in a modified form, stands in one sense nearer Kant than either of the two Kantian schools with which we may now go on to compare him. He forms with Herbart a third school of Kantian philosophy, one that interprets Kant in the sense of Leibnitz and the earlier rationalists, and keeps nearer to the traditions of popular philosophy than the Platonizing or the sceptical Kantian school.

Two important considerations separate Lotze from the post-Kantian idealists, first his method, which is realistic and empirical, and second, his decided revolt against formalism. The *a priori* element in Kant is what first attracted the attention of his followers. The limitation of this *a priori* to the field of possible experience could easily be ignored; by an apparently modest and judicious surrender of the pretension to know anything beyond that field, we may be led to the truly pretentious and dogmatic identification of our possible experience with the sum total of reality. The transcendent elements in Kant's system were the material things in themselves on the one hand and the supernatural realms of God and immortality on the other. As lying between these two transcendent realities, the phenomenal world, constructed according to the a priori forms of perception and judgment, remained subjective and fragmentary; to claim knowledge of it a priori was not to place man at the center of the universe, nor to identify his forms of thought with the forms of universal being. But both these transcendental elements were eliminated by Kant's followers. The material things in themselves were useless and obsolete; Kant retained them only through a sort of mental inertia, through an insufficient application of his own critical principles. And the transcendent God, freedom, and heaven were also illegitimate adjuncts to his theory; they were concessions made to traditional piety. The moral postulates, like the forms of thought, refer only to the world of possible experience and its laws; no other world concerns us, no other exists. The Kantian philosophy thus became a system of the conditions and necessary laws of experience, or (what is the same thing) of reality; and the *a priori* functions that Kant regarded as human faculties, his followers transformed into cosmological principles.

Exclusive insistence on the moral postulates led Fichte to inaugurate the Kantian school of absolute idealism. His object is to deduce the forms of thought and the conditions of life from a single moral task, a single practical problem, of which they should be the terms. This primal fact or rather duty must be found by inspiration, by insight; as Lotze says (*Geschichte der deutschen Philosophie seit Kant,* Fichte.) it must be guessed at (*errathen*) and the felicity of this guess must be tested by the consequences it involves. Now Lotze is not incredulous about the existence of such a first principle; the same idea pervades a great part of his thought, as, for instance, his aesthetics. But he is incredulous about the possibility of discovering that principle. We should first have to reach the centre and core of the universe. And Lotze also deprecates a method that would deduce everything from a given principle. In this Lotze's scientific sense separates him from the post-Kantians. He feels that we must collect the facts in the various provinces of our experience, try different hypotheses, and only gradually and cautiously, by means of a long historical accumulation of knowledge, reach generally valid results. He believes in starting with common sense and with the ordinary aspects of things. In the matter of method he is therefore entirely removed from the deductive rationalism founded on divination which characterizes the post-Kantians. For besides the intrinsic uncertainty of such a first principle, Lotze deplores the frequent misrepresentation of facts and fanciful coupling of events that such a method almost inevitably involves. The temptation is irresistible, when one has already the secret of things in one's possession, to avoid difficulties in the evidence and to read one's doctrine into the facts. But this danger is unfortunately not confined to absolute idealism. Every man who has made up his mind is in the same position. Every theory of things that is complete compels those who believe in it to see its illustration in all experience. And we can object to such a tendency only if we doubt the truth of that first principle or highest theory; if it is really true, the predisposition we have to see confirmations of it everywhere will be nothing but the predisposition to discover truth which belongs to intelligence. Those who are ignorant or stupid often wonder at the facility and assurance with which scholars handle a subject; who has not sometimes felt a suspicion that all the stories told by astronomers, geologists, and philologists may be hasty fictions? Yet where knowledge is real and bears the test of experiment and sceptical scrutiny, this distrust is a proof of ignorance. Knowledge produces a legitimate prejudice, and easy recognition of the typical in any new fact is the fruit of study. All experience constitutes a presumption about future experience; and every conception that lives becomes a preconception. But for this fact all progress in wisdom would be impossible. So that what Lotze really means when he deplores the bias given by a priori principles to our investigations and perceptions is that these a priori principles should have been false. For had they been true that bias would have been what those subject to it believed it to be—a guide to truth, in itself worth an education and a lifetime of experience.

Lotze's attitude toward absolute idealism is, however, not wholly negative. He does not venture to use a conception of the inward sense or moral function of nature as a guide in philosophy; but he does use such a conception as a check to other theories. Lotze feels that the general sense of a principle like Fichte's, that the universe is essentially a theatre of moral action, may be deeply sound and true, yet, in the vague form in which we may assert it to be true, may be worthless as a practical guide to investigation. At the same time such a principle may suffice to condemn any theory of things that takes away the moral significance of life; a philosophy that did not present the world as the theatre of moral action would be an inadequate philosophy, although our assurance that the world is a theatre of moral action cannot lead us to detailed and exact knowledge of the constitution of the world. In harmony with the spirit in which Lotze treats final causes in general, he regards these moral postulates or absolute principles as functions that nature must possess, as standards to which she must conform, as demands she must satisfy; he does not regard them as efficient powers by which she is brought into being. Nor does he even regard them as ruling principles by which nature must be understood, as starting points for our description of the world. While he admits the significance, then, of the idealistic treatment of nature in so far as it dwells on the moral function and fundamental rationality of the cosmic process, Lotze entirely renounces the idealistic method of construction. He wishes to gather his philosophy from empirical sources, and hopes to find that, when thus described, the course of nature actually fulfils our idealistic demands, and is found to express a moral principle. In regard to Kant's formalism and especially in regard to Hegel's, Lotze expresses himself with unusual energy. Hegel, he tells us, (*Microcosmus* II. p. 43) saw in the preservation of the absolute Idea not a means to the production of other goods but an end in itself. But only the "most nonsensical form of mysticism" believes in purposes the content and realization of which no one is aware, or in goods that no one enjoys. "What is to be a good has the only and necessary locus of its existence in the living feeling of some spiritual being." "So long as we have breath we will fight against the starved yet so terrible superstition that, lost entirely in worship of facts and forms, forgets the significant aims of real, warm-hearted life, or overlooks them with incomprehensible negligence, in order to seek the deepest meaning of the world in the contemplation of the formula of evolution."

Lotze everywhere seeks to reduce relations between things to affections of the things themselves. Hence his aversion to a system that tends to reduce things to the relations between them. But this theoretical aversion is increased when the value of the world is found, not in the happiness it produces, but in the regularity of the law that produces both happiness and misery. The value of regularity, of uniformity, does not seem to Lotze to be intrinsic; if law has a value it is derived from the happiness that its observance brings about. He has no *a priori* attachment to the uniformity of nature; he has, as we have seen, an *a priori* repugnance to uniformity of type in events. We shall have occasion in the sequel to consider how far Lotze is able to escape formalism; how far relations between things can really be reduced to affections of the things themselves. But we can here observe how great a moral chasm separates the human and hedonistic standard of worth recognised by Lotze from the cruel theological optimism of a thoroughly pantheistic philosophy. Lotze will speak of the unity of the cosmic process and of the purpose of nature; but this unity will never constitute for him the value and justification of what comes under it; rather it will be the condition and means of producing conscious and happy life. The essentially momentary, although often repeated and sustained, happiness of living beings is what alone gives value to the scheme of things; such aesthetic or mathematical beauties as this scheme may possess have themselves value and existence only in emotion.

This rebellion against formalism undoubtedly puts Lotze on the side of common sense and humane feeling as distinguished from sophistical attempts to show that the good in the world is not what makes the world good, but that the value of the good comes from its necessary function in the universe. But the subject is not so simple as this unusual decision and clearness on

Lotze's part might lead us to suppose. For granting that value belongs to feeling, yet we observe that the production of this valuable feeling depends on certain material conditions. Suppose we call these conditions the instruments of good. Now nothing prevents our discovering an analogy between the instruments of good that produce our happiness and the universe as a whole; there may be some similarity of structure, some formal unity, between the universe and that part of it we know to be an instrument of good. Suppose, for instance, the instrument of good in our case were a certain regularity or rhythm of our life; did we discover a similar regularity and rhythm in all nature we should be legitimately led to regard all nature as an instrument of good. And in view of such a vast extension of the field where values might appear, we should naturally cease to speak of our own feelings as the seat of value; we should regard the value of the world as coextensive with that analogy which allows us to regard nature as an instrument of good. The form of nature, the type of events, would thus become the mark and condition of excellence; to discover a particular type would be to discover the worth of what conformed to it. And indeed if we are to estimate the value of the world in any other sense than its influence on our momentary moods, we must base our estimate on some such formal condition. We must select some typical process, some scheme of development, and attribute intrinsic value to all that exemplifies it. Our reason for selecting one typical process rather than another must always remain, however, a human and subjective reason; it might be the type of event that in our bodies produces pleasure, or it might be some type speculatively comprehensible and pleasing. And in estimating the value of nature or in attributing intrinsic worth to any of its parts, we must necessarily be guided by some rather obscure and doubtful analogy of this sort; the worship of forms which Lotze condemns is therefore more excusable and natural than he seems to consider it. The happiness which according to him the world produces and which constitutes its value can be discovered only by applying to nature a vague analogy drawn from human emotion; the happiness that really gives this value to the world is not mine or yours, but the divine happiness, in which you or I may have some part; and evidently the existence of this divine happiness is known only by bold conjecture. The difference is not great between a person who, like Hegel, finds the value of the world in the Idea it expresses, and one who, like Lotze, finds it in the divine happiness it produces. For that it produces divine happiness we infer from its obeying some law, from its fulfilling some idea; and the only addition Lotze makes to Hegel's theory is to materialize it a little by regarding the expression of the universal Idea as a source of universal delight. The implication of a soul or spirit in which this Idea or happiness should reside is the same in both; only while spirit for Hegel implies only the presence of the Idea and its action, for Lotze it implies also an accompanying emotion. Lotze exaggerates the importance of this variation; he seems here, as in many other places, to feel that there is a great difference between an idea and a soul having that idea. But if the idea is objective, as Hegel undoubtedly conceived it to be, the difference between the two expressions vanishes upon analysis.

Certain elements of Kant's philosophy gave rise, as we have just seen, to German idealism; other elements have led, in our own day especially, to sceptical and materialistic systems that bring the critical philosophy into practical agreement with positivism, or the philosophy that regards natural science as final. The transcendent elements in Kant were of two sorts: first the material things in themselves, second, the objects postulated by our moral feeling. The idealists renounced the things in themselves as needless; the sceptics on the contrary feel the need of them; they insist that the phenomenal world of time, space, and the categories is a subjective and human world; that therefore the reality lies beyond it. At the same time they acknowledge that the demand for this objective reality is a subjective and human demand, and that the hypothesis of such a reality, although indispensable to our thinking, has nothing in its favor but its naturalness. A similar point of view, however, sees in the moral postulates no evidence for the existence of their objects; to substitute these moral objects for things in themselves is therefore illegitimate. We have knowledge only of the phenomenal world; our postulates, intellectual and moral, are simply expressions of the fact that this world is given to us as phenomenal, as derivative, not as real and self-justified. But what kind of reality or justification is to be supplied we do not know; that lies beyond the scope of our *a priori* faculties. In view of the impossibility of transcending experience, this form of the critical philosophy is in practical agreement with positivism; phenomenalism is nothing but a wistful materialism. When all our spontaneous assumptions are criticised and exposed we fall back in practice on the most inevitable of them; some working hypothesis, some conventional expression for the reality, we must employ; and if we are convinced that all are equally doubtful assumptions, full of logical difficulties, we shall undoubtedly employ that which usage and necessity most impose upon us; we shall be materialists. The world of matter and of history is the world of language and human society; its final and absolute reality is ordinarily assumed even by believers in other deeper entities. And if criticism has discovered to us the equal arbitrariness of all metaphysical conceptions, we shall retain those that we cannot surrender, and that make our thought and conversation intelligible to the world.

What Lotze's attitude toward such a system would be we may conjecture from his attitude toward natural science; he is, however, extremely reticent in regard to the sceptical arguments of phenomenalism. His treatment of these questions is summary; he reserves his detailed and elaborate arguments for subjects properly metaphysical; the question of the validity of such discussions is itself little discussed. He acknowledges that directly given we have only phenomena and moral postulates; but these practical postulates are assurances of the existence of what they demand; we know by their authority that the world is both intelligible and valuable. And, this being so, phenomena have a transcendent significance; for they cannot arise for nothing. Although they may not be pictures of the true reality, they are evidences and effects of it; we may therefore study them to discover what message they really bring. This message will be true, because our reason has transcendent validity and that which we must believe is necessarily true and would hold even if we knew nothing of it. Lotze is a rationalist, and he turns invariably from phenomenalistic conceptions with a feeling that they are intellectually possible, but too trivial and impotent to deserve attention. The modern school of sceptical Kantians did not exist in Germany when Lotze formed his system; for his system was formed early and not greatly modified in later years. A somewhat analogous place—analogous because of its scientific tendency and its distaste for Hegelianism—was then occupied by Herbart and his school. It was in reference to this school that Lotze chose his arguments; his philosophy is offered as a substitute for Herbart's; it is essentially different and better, yet springs from the same influences and answers the same demand.

To Herbart belongs the leadership of the reaction against the Hegelian idealism. Schopenhauer's invectives remained long unread; and, as often happens, the ferocity of Schopenhauer's attack springs perhaps from a certain rivalry. It is a family quarrel, for Schopenhauer, in spite of his heretical worldliness and maliciousness, is at bottom a discoverer of the secret of the universe, like Fichte and Hegel. And Lotze himself is rather an apologist for the idealists than their opponent; he is, as it were, a Herbartian that meets the Hegelians half way, and wishes his own friends to recognise the element of truth in the doctrines of their opponents. This element of truth is for Lotze the belief in the moral significance and rationality of the world. But Herbart renounces Hegelianism entirely; first, by adopting a method of gradual investigation, instead of the deductive construction of the idealists, then by returning to an objective application of pure logic, and finally by separating the theoretical and practical parts of philosophy. Lotze follows Herbart in the first two particulars; in regard to the last he verbally commends him; but, judging from his own practice, we must interpret this praise as applying only to Herbart's method of procedure and exposition, and not at all to his principle that moral considerations should be banished from speculative philosophy. The dangerous habit, introduced by Kant, of using moral postulates as criteria of objective truth is by Herbart consistently laid aside. Herbart treats morals as a branch of aesthetics; and this classification, if otherwise inaccurate, has one great merit: it prevents any juggling with abstract ideas, half moral half metaphysical, whereby a desire is treated as evidence, and an ideal is given the validity of a truth. According to the proper and general use of terms, ethics is not a part of aesthetics. But much less is it a part of logic or a clue to the discovery of valid truth. Lotze tells us, at the end of his earlier *Metaphysics,* that metaphysics has its beginning not in itself but in ethics; and he means that the final explanation that philosophy can give of things is a moral explanation; it will justify the world by making us see, not its necessity, but its value. To such an ultimate moralism Herbart might have had no great objection; what he deprecated was the actual deduction of metaphysical doctrines from moral postulates; in this sense ethics does not merely justify nature as discovered to us by experience and reflection, but is treated as an instrument of discovery, like a sixth sense, by which the objective nature of things is revealed to us. The first and typical example of this extraordinary abuse of moral feelings is found in Kant's famous cry: "Thou shouldst, therefore thou canst!" If this is false as applied to human conduct much worse is the same method as applied to philosophy in general. Our preference, our moral impulse, expressed by this "should be" or "ought to be" is after all one fact among others. To make it a law for its fellow facts in nature is to expose oneself to constant disproof from experience; our desires promise their own fulfilment, and it is natural to trust their promise. But if experience teaches the individual or the race anything, it is that desires cannot fulfil what they promise. They may remain a ground for hope, they may remain the standard by which we judge the value of the reality when it appears and the ideal by which we direct our conduct; i.e. they may remain the principle of ethics. But to make them the principle of meta-physics or even of natural science is to exceed the recklessness of the most childlike theology. Lotze, with customary prudence, re-frains from carrying out his own principle to its remote conse-quences; the things he ventures to assert on the authority of moral preference are few, obscure, and hard to decide empiri-cally. As he does not propose to employ these doctrines as guides to discovery, their vagueness is no objection; it is even a merit for expressions that are intended not so much to convey an idea as to pacify a demand and allay a fear. Thus the maxim "the world is because it ought to be" is intellectually most obscure and equivocal; the relation expressed by the "because" and the relation expressed by the "ought" are both extremely difficult, not to say unintelligible. Yet the phrase "the world is because it ought to be" has an emotional value; it suggests a mood, a hope, a final peace; we do not care to know in what way its truth af-fects our experience or the inward constitution of the universe. But harmless as Lotze's moralism is, when kept on such ground, it becomes more questionable when it assumes a censorship of scientific theories; and the same principle, in less prudent and learned hands, might lead to many errors.

Herbart, while renouncing the transcendental significance of moral postulates, insists on the other transcendent element of Kant's system. Kant had always retained the things in themselves, but made them unknowable; they had become either super-fluous altogether or at least an unjustifiably distinct expression for a postulate of the imagination. How can we know their plurality? The categories of unity and plurality must not, accord-ing to Kant's fundamental principles, be applied to anything but objects of experience. This fundamental critical doctrine has been eluded or ignored both by Kant and by most of his followers; Herbart, however, denies it flatly and in its place de-fends the ancient belief in the transcendent validity of our intel-lectual forms. Every phenomenon is a witness to a real thing, every appearance is an effect of a reality that appears. We may not, indeed, have images of things as they are in themselves; our imagination is subjective. But we know these things in themselves; our intelligence can determine their nature, and our reflection can discover to us some qualities they must have. For instance, we know their plurality, their simplicity, their indestructibility. The evidence of their plurality is simply the plurality of the phenomena that represent them. But the influence that phenomena seem to exert over one another, their apparent incompatibility and mutual exclusiveness, cannot be extended to the things in themselves; for it belongs to the definition of things in themselves to be self-sufficing, to exist by and for themselves, without borrowing their being from any other thing. Evidently somewhere in nature must be a perfectly independent and self-sufficing ground of being; but we have found this ground to be a plurality of things; each of them consequently must be quite independent not only of the knowledge we have of it, but also of the existence of the others. This doctrine is clear as applied to material atoms forming a universe in space. But the difficulty begins when we ask in what sense they form one world. If they are really independent and indestructible they would form each a world by itself. Suppose our world were a sphere such as the ancients conceived, and that the heavens were inclosed in a globe of steel, entirely inelastic, entirely indestructible. Whatever other such worlds moved about in outer space, if their relations and shocks did not affect them internally at all, evidently each of these worlds would be exactly as if none other existed. Only an observer stationed outside of all could perceive their relations or notice when they approached or struck one another. But to them, or to any observer within any of them, such external relations would be imperceptible, nor would any ground exist to suspect their existence. The possibility always remains that our cosmos, such as science, philosophy, and theology may agree to represent it, is nothing but an independent atom, surrounded by an infinity of unattainable and inconceivable realities. But such a possibility does not concern us. The independent realities we seek are not beyond our world; they are to be component parts of our universe, and are to lie within the field of our observation. Hence it is evident that our point of view, our sphere of susceptibility, cannot be internal to any of these independent things; we must embrace them all, and be affected by all, since they all enter into the world we have before our minds. But Herbart, subject in this to the influence of Leibnitz, wishes to regard the soul as itself one of these absolute and independent things. And hence the obscurities and difficulties of his system arise.

Our ideas are, we know, effects and representations of the external reality; they are at the same time modifications of an independent entity, one atom of that reality, called the soul. Hence it is evident that real things must be made not quite absolute and independent, since in each may arise representations of the others, and each may know some things about the others, especially its relations to them. Now this involves some communication, some mutual influence between the elements of reality. The ground of this mutual susceptibility Herbart calls contiguity—"das Zusammen." This contiguity is the occasion for the rise of reactions in each monad that have reference to the nature and situation of other monads. In some monads in souls, this reaction takes the form of ideas. Ideas are called the acts of self-preservation of the soul, not because they preserve and continue the life of the soul, but because they arise when the soul rebounds, as it were, from its collisions with other monads. The soul, like all monads, is indestructible; ideas are not essential to its existence; but they arise when, coming in contact with other atoms, it proves its indestructibility by remaining unaffected by the threatened disturbance. Ideas are not properly internal to the monad called the soul; they are representations, existing as it were in the void of the shocks and collisions of one material atom. This atom is not so much the seat of ideas as their object; they describe its fortunes, but are not themselves events in it.

Here we have a conception not only interesting in itself, but important for us on account of the light it throws on Lotze's ambiguous doctrine of the soul. For Herbart the soul was a substance, an indestructible, absolutely independent thing. Ideas are by no means essential to the soul; they are sparks that fly from it when it strikes other atoms. The substances remain unchanged; but beside them arise certain groups of appearances, of changing effects, which express the relations of contiguity that exist at any moment among these unchangeable things. At first we might be at a loss to understand why any set of these ideas—any human life—should be said to belong to any one of these monads in particular. But a reason can be given. The relations of contiguity of one monad *A* to the world of monads are different from those of any other monad *B*. For there is a uniform medium which is the locus of these relations, a kind of real space that Herbart calls an objective appearance. This expression is contradictory, but its sense in Herbart's system is not doubtful. Space is apparent, not real, because it is not anything in substances, nor indicates any principle of change in them; for they do not change. At the same time space is objective because it is, together with substance, the ground for the order of phenomena. Phenomena refer to two sorts of things, necessarily distinguished by reason. One is a plurality of distinct and independent things; the other is a single order or medium in which these things have changing relations. The latter is space. Instead of objective appearance we might call it the objective condition of appearances. For the monads, existing simply and out of relation, could not produce any phenomena. But because of their contiguity in space a ground is furnished for the intervention of phenomena, which are nothing but the representation of the fortunes of one of these monads in the medium where it coexists with the others. The singleness and uniformity of space, in which all monads are, make it possible to trace the movements of each in reference to all the others. This the flow of ideas does, although perhaps imperfectly. Our conscious life is the partial representation of the changing relations of one inwardly unchangeable atom to the atoms that are contiguous to it. The soul is therefore that atom in space whose changing relations our consciousness expresses. That is all Herbart means by calling ideas the acts of self-preservation of the soul. Lotze makes a needless criticism of Herbart when he says that the soul must notice the threatening changes in order to execute an appropriate act of self-preservation; and that therefore the soul must first have been affected by the changed relations in which it stands. For Herbart the changed relations of the soul need not affect it at all. The soul is only one atom among others, and it may well remain unconscious of all threats, since the threatened effect is entirely impossible. An atom cannot be destroyed, mutilated, or impressed in any way. Herbart speaks figuratively of threats and of acts of the soul. The soul acts in the same sense in which the pieces act in a game of chess. As the *King's* interests may be said to be represented in the player's imagination, and as all his ideas may be called acts of self-preservation of the *King*, reactions on the *King's* part against danger; so the ideas of a man are acts and precautions of his soul. The soul is no more really threatened, no more really acts, than the wooden or ivory *King* on the chess-board. The soul is only that atom whose vicissitudes in the constellation of atoms a series of ideas represents. And, just as the pieces, when the game is over, are thrown into the box, and remain inwardly unchanged although their relations have ceased to call for representation by an interesting series of ideas; so the atom called the soul, before it enters the brain where its game is played, and after it passes out of the brain, remains itself unchanged, but is not the occasion for any ideational process. Herbart's doctrine is thoroughly materialistic: only the spirit of his age, and the recollection and attraction of Leibnitz, gave it a somewhat spiritualistic vocabulary. For Leibnitz monads are essentially spiritual; if they ceased to be conscious they would cease to be. They are not in space, they are not in relations of any kind to one another; space is within them, and within each is the representation of all the others. We know the existence of the others simply because we find within ourselves a picture of them; we feel the impulse, which we have no reason to withstand, to believe that something like what is represented within us exists also for itself. This is a true pluralistic idealism, a solipsism multiplied. But Herbart's pluralism is materialistic; and the ideas, which of course no materialism seeks to pass over, appear in his system as superadded representations of the flux of atoms.

Only one point separates Herbart's theory from what would recommend itself to a modern materialist. He regards ideas as reactions of a single atom; it would now seem more natural to regard them as reactions of many atoms, say of all the gray matter of the brain. There would be no inconsistency introduced into Herbart's system by this change, which he would make, perhaps, did he live in our day. For what ideas represent is by no means the internal changes in the monad; for there are no such changes. Ideas represent its external relations, and these already involve a plurality of atoms. Herbart was led to this unnecessary identification of the ground of consciousness with a single atom by several considerations, some of which are not without influence on Lotze also; we may therefore briefly refer to them here, in anticipation of the longer treatment one or two must receive later on.

First among the considerations that lead to the identification of the soul, or ground of consciousness, with a single monad or atom, we must place philosophic tradition. Descartes already sought for the unit of extension that should transmit all the shocks it receives to the soul as ideas. But the analogy between Descartes and Herbart is superficial: Descartes looked on the soul as essentially conscious; for Herbart the soul is the material atom with which Descartes wished to connect but never to identify it. Leibnitz, as we have seen, continued this tradition by actually treating atoms as representations of souls; but we have also seen how little real agreement there is between Leibnitz and Herbart. The motives that made Leibnitz regard the soul as a monad were idealistic; they arose from difficulties in passing from a subjective to an objective world. Such difficulties do not exist for Herbart, nor for Lotze either; both accept as inevitable and legitimate our spontaneous belief in the objective validity and transcendence of our ideas. But in spite of this essential divergence, the example of Leibnitz doubtless predisposed both Herbart and Lotze to treat the soul as a substance, to make it one of the real elements of a pluralistic world.

Another consideration that may have led Herbart not to regard a mass of atoms as the basis of consciousness is the belief that, by making one atom the basis, the unity of consciousness is explained. But there is no conceivable reason why it should be easier to enumerate and classify the shocks received by one atom than to enumerate and classify the relations between a large number of atoms; the atom surely is not an act of enumeration and classification. We are here touching a question of moment in Lotze's philosophy, and we may seem to be neglecting his arguments. But the unity within which Lotze demands that all comparable effects should fall in order to be added together into a total effect is not a material unity; it is not an atom but a series of events. The summation of effects is only possible, Lotze tells us, when the effects are modifications of one thing, as the wind and tide do not seem to join themselves into one resultant force, but the two forces, acting on the same unit, the ship, produce in it a resultant motion. This train of thought leads Lotze, however, to alter the definition of a thing so as to make it the historical unity of its own successive modifications. The whole treatment of effects as modifications of substance is foreign to Herbart's thought, and would lead, as Lotze shows, not only to making the soul a unit like an atom, but also to making all units fictitious and progressive unities, like that of the soul. For Herbart the modifications of consciousness leave the substantial soul unaffected; the unity of this soul does not help at all to make the unity of consciousness comprehensible. Ideas do not represent affections of the atom but its external relations. Therefore it is not the function of the atom to think, but the thought refers to the motions of the atom as to an object, and refers no less to the presence, approach, and collision of other atoms contiguous to it. The presence of other atoms is not discovered by any inward modification of the atom itself, but by the "accidental aspect," as Herbart calls it, presented by an atom in reference to those about it. The point of view is therefore external to the atom; something external to it is the ground of consciousness. And besides we should remember that the unity of consciousness is nothing but the fact of consciousness. If not united a thought would be simply so many detached and mutually unattainable thoughts, each no greater than the sphere of its own content. To talk of uniting thought, as if it were naturally separate, is like talking of uniting the three dimensions of space which nothing but abstraction could ever sever. The only question is, is there any thought at all? If there is its unity is taken for granted. Philosophy may some day class the desire to account for the unity of consciousness with the desire of accounting for the existence of something rather than nothing, and with kindred expressions of a vaulting ambition that o'erleaps itself. As Lotze often repeats, our problem is to discover the nature of things, not to make it. Given the unity of consciousness our business is not to explain how nature manages to produce it, but only to note what materials she employs. And if we keep this limitation of our philosophy in mind, we shall be willing to admit that any mass of atoms may as easily be the physical basis of a single consciousness as one atom. We shall then see the futility of those attempts, begun by Descartes and not abandoned by Lotze, to discover the seat of the soul, and the particular atom of the brain with which the soul is to be identified.

The points in which Lotze follows Herbart are the incidental views in which Herbart is least consistent with his own materialistic principles, as in regarding the soul as one of the real things that are the objects of thought. And the points where Lotze rejects Herbart's authority are the most fundamental, as, for instance, the necessary plurality and immutability of reality. In spite of this opposition Lotze, at least in his method and starting point, resembles Herbart very much; but he is not a consistent and thorough realist like Herbart; he is a realist not from metaphysical conviction but only from scientific sympathy; he likes to place himself at first in the familiar and objective field of real things with external relations and changing aspects. Lotze's arguments then are brought in to compel us to abandon these provisional and natural conceptions, and to adopt others of an entirely different sort. Hence the double and almost treacherous attitude of Lotze to Herbart: in the beginning and on the surface great similarity, so that some have treated Lotze as a disciple of Herbart; but at bottom a complete disagreement which in the end becomes explicit.

The external relations of things are the first difficulty in the way of Herbart and Lotze; Herbart solves it in a manner consistent with realism and with the immutability of substance. Lotze also retains the realism for the true being, but at once sacrifices the immutability. The units of substance are to be changeable, so that relations between them may be reduced to modifications of them. This denial of external relations between things is a prominent characteristic of Lotze's system. Relations are to be regarded as projected from real things; a change of relation means a change in the internal condition of the related objects. Lotze thus takes the position of Leibnitz as against Herbart; relations are not between things because nothing exists at all but things; it is impossible that anything at all should lie between realities, for either it is nothing or it is itself a reality; and if a reality, then it is not between things but *ipso facto* one of these. Herbart, as we have observed, establishes the world of phenomena as distinct from the world of reality; this is essential to realism and is also consistent with Kant. For if by the reality we mean ideas also, and make no distinction between the actuality of phenomena and the reality of things, then we evidently give up realism and become at least partially idealists. This Lotze does; substance for him means the ground of things in a different sense from that intended by Herbart. For Lotze a substance must contain all its accidents and effects; the phenomena must follow necessarily from the nature of the thing, and therefore the ground of change in the phenomena must lie in the thing. Thus Lotze is led to the paradoxical doctrine that substances suffer change, that they are processes; he defines a "substance" as the "property" a series of events has of producing the idea of a substance. This illogical definition may be paraphrased by saying that substances do not exist; that what produces the idea of substance is a series of unsubstantial states; only as there is no deeper and firmer reality than this succession of phases, we may call this series itself a substance. Lotze is inclined to give old names to new things; he is fond of a metaphysical nomenclature, and his terms are generally more mysterious and old-fashioned than his ideas. Thus he speaks of the soul, of substance, of free will, of efficient causation, of a personal God; but these phrases stand in his system for comparatively modest and legitimate conceptions. The words may please us in themselves; but we shall be disappointed if we welcome the things for love of the names they bear. And it may be said in passing that a certain acceptance which Lotze has found in conservative circles is perhaps due to insufficient consideration of his meaning. His adoption of scholastic terms shows his benevolence toward earlier philosophy; but his own is none the less essentially modern and draws its inspiration from a very different quarter.

Thus although he retains the word substance he abandons the notion for which it commonly stands. A substance that does not lurk behind phenomena, a substance that is the series of appearances themselves, depends for its existence on its accidents, instead of being something that the accidents need for their support. A series of phases is subsequent in nature to all its components, and subsequent in time to the first of them; it cannot exist except as an idea, and in calling it a substance we misapply this tolerably expressive word. Another definition of substance that Lotze gives is that "substance" is the "faculty" of being effective and affected; again a definition that makes substance subsequent in nature to something else, namely, to the phenomena forming a series that changes in reference to another series, that thus affect or are affected by each other. This surrender of the idea of substance, this willingness to see variation and mutability in the deepest reality is a potential idealism; Lotze continues to speak of objective things, but among these real things we shall of course find him enumerating the soul. The soul is a substance, i.e. it is that faculty our successive states of consciousness have of producing the idea of a substantial soul. Herbart too calls the soul a substance; but his misuse of words is here distinct from Lotze's. Lotze misleads us in the use of the word substance, which is not applicable to an ideal unity projected from the self-existent states it looks back upon. But he does not misuse the word soul which naturally describes that unity of personal life we are aware of in surveying our experience. Herbart on the contrary abuses the word soul; for the atom to whose fortunes our mental experience is attached is not a soul, but an atom. Consciousness is by no means native to that atom, or internal to it; consciousness is only an expression of the complicated relations in which the atom stands to other atoms, presumably in the brain,—relations, however, that are entirely accidental and indifferent to that atom. Thus it might turn out that what Herbart religiously calls a soul is an atom of nitrogen. Such a thing is properly called a substance, but even if it is the kernel of our thinking, it is no soul. Herbart's soul-substance, then, is a substance but not a soul, while Lotze's is a soul but not a substance.

[III]

Lotze's atomism:

his argument for idealism

A POINT OF fundamental importance in Lotze's realistic philosophy is the atomic nature of reality. I say his realistic
philosophy, for we may properly speak of two distinct parts or
stages of his thought: one is an analysis of our conceptions of the
phenomenal world, treated as a reality, and the other is the
idealization of this reality. Lotze intends these two trains of
thought to fall together, and appear as one; indeed the argument
of his chief work, if we look for a general argument, is that analysis of the reality, treated as an object, will lead us to regard it as
a spirit; that we should see our conceptions of the external
world necessarily become of themselves conceptions of super-
sensible living beings. In other words, Lotze's system, if we regard his works as developing one philosophical thesis, is that
scrutiny of things, of a multiple material reality, will prove to us
that they are ingredients of a single spiritual process. But we are
not compelled to regard the steps of this metamorphosis as the
vital element of Lotze's thought; it is rather a somewhat fictitious and external logical unity imposed on a collection of little
treatises on a variety of metaphysical questions. To judge Lotze
by the logical concatenation of his system would be as unjust as
to judge Spinoza by the cogency of his geometrical proofs.
Lotze, like Spinoza, has a system, and no inconsistent system; but
its unity is psychological, it is a personal manner of regarding
things, a poetic intuition of the cosmic life; the various doctrines
are congruous, they appeal to the same mental constitution and

aspiration, they can be held together without contradiction. But the logical sequence of the arguments is a purely formal pretense to philosophic construction. And just as the total conception of the world that Lotze presents to us has a value in itself, apart from this attempted construction, so the various arguments and analyses that enter into that construction have each its own value, apart from the general thesis they are intended to introduce. Lotze has very interesting and cogent arguments; but they are not the links of a single chain, they are only criticism of certain traditional conceptions. Of course these criticisms are made in the spirit of the man; we find a certain congruity, and sometimes an apparent inconsistency between them; but this congruity and inconsistency are both effects of Lotze's personality, of his general temper and postulates. Thus very different points are fundamental with Lotze; if we regard his system, or total conception of the world, what is essential is his rationalism, his aestheticism, his optimism. If we regard his philosophical argumentation, however, what is essential is his atomism, his insistence on the discrete nature of the reality. To this latter principle, and the considerations connected with it, we may first turn, reserving the final philosophy of Lotze for the sequel.

Lotze regards metaphysics, as distinguished from logic, as a study of the given reality; the realm of ideas, with fixed natures and unchanging relations, exists in a certain sense; i.e. what logic discovers about it has validity, it holds and is true. The opposite can never be, and therefore the science of our meanings, as this might be called, is a science about something in one sense real and fundamental. At the same time these ideas exist only as intentions of our thought, as our meanings; metaphysics is not concerned about them, but only about actually existing and changeable things. It is of the greatest importance for us to remember that the world of reality is for Lotze necessarily a world of change; were it a world of eternal things it would belong to the province of logic. Two familiar types of metaphysics are thus excluded *in limine:* materialism, or any philosophy of an unknowable substance, and Platonic idealism, or any philosophy of eternal entities. We see that Lotze's difference with Herbart is fundamental; the two part company at once. The monads, or rather atoms, that are to be unchangeable are impossible for Lotze; such things do not belong to the real world. The only philosophy that remains for Lotze is some form of phenomenalism; the reality must inhere in the world of change. Not the ὄντως ὄν [really real] but the γιγνόμενον μὲν καὶ ἀπολλύμενον ὄντως δὲ οὐδέποτε ὄν [what is coming into being and being destroyed but not ever really real] is the subject of metaphysics. With this beginning Lotze has no need of arguments to prove the unreality of space or matter; these things are eternal and unchangeable, therefore out with them; they are ideas, they are not a part of the content of reality. But Lotze nevertheless gives arguments to disprove the reality of matter and space; these arguments are founded on the discrete or atomic nature of these objects. And on the same foundation Lotze constructs a number of other theorems about the phenomenal reality.

Connected with Lotze's definition of the object of metaphysics as the given and changing reality is another important axiom. It concerns the locus of relations. Between abstract ideas there are fixed relations; the mind, seeing always the same thing in each, places them always in the same relation. The constancy of our meanings involves the constancy of the relation between these meanings; for what could a meaning be unless it was the consciousness that the direct object and content of our thought was linked in certain ways to certain other objects? This reference, this comprehension of relations, is the essence of an abstract thought. But all is changed when we pass from absolute ideas and fixed meanings to real and changeable objects. Where can the relations between them lie? Surely not "between" them, as we say following the analogy of ideas. Relations can lie between ideas because the essence of thought is to pass from one mental image to another; and the sense, the significance, that distinguishes a thought from a mere image or sensation is precisely the feeling of direction, the drift (as we significantly call it) of what we have in mind. Thus the locus of the relations between ideas is simply the thought that understands what those ideas mean. Twice two is four; this relation lies in the thought that constructs the idea of four, and knows what four means. But this mental activity, this flash of intelligence connects only what enters the mind; the relations between external objects must have some other locus.

The difficulties of this question are always great; but Lotze has shut out the most obvious attempts at a solution by making the reality essentially changeable. For many systems, such as Herbart's, for example, the solution lies in making reality consist of substances that suffer no change, to which all relations are external and accidental. The problem of relations does not disappear, but is pushed back from ontology into psychology; the atoms are independent of all relations, each is a world to itself; only the external observer, collecting impressions from all, conceives how they stand to one another by perceiving how each stands to him. The effort of all materialistic systems is to make relations accidental and adventitious things; the substance of the world is to be discovered and described without considering relations. Thus Herbart calls relations accidental aspects; it is only the mind, he seems to say, that endows atoms with external attributes which, each in itself, and therefore all of them, are entirely without. Yet we have seen that Herbart was compelled, as a preparation for his psychology, to admit an objective locus for the relations of atoms to exist in, a medium of contiguity, *das Zusammen*. He might, perhaps, have made this field of relation wholly subjective and mental had he not made the soul itself one of the independent atoms. The *Zusammen* had, however, to be external to the mind, since it was the locus where the mind existed side by side with the realities that it knew.

This weakening of Herbart's realism, this breach made by himself in his system, is what Lotze takes advantage of to discard the entire realistic philosophy. Relations, he tells us, and this is the important axiom to which I referred just now, relations "between" real things are impossible, but must consist in internal modifications of the things themselves. The two parts of this proposition are habitually given by Lotze as inseparable; he seems to regard the internal modification of the elements of reality as the only alternative to real relations between them. But a middle term is not excluded. If we accept the realistic hypothesis, as Lotze appears to do, we admit a double object: there is the reality self-existent and objective and there is the phenomenon in us. Now relations "between" the elements of the reality are indeed impossible; for if they are real, then they are not "between" realities but integral elements of the reality; and if they do not belong to reality, they must belong to the phenomenon; i.e. they must be subjective and be relations, not in the object as it is in itself, but between the representations of that object in us. And between ideas we know that relations can perfectly well exist, since it is the nature of ideas to involve such relations among themselves. This is the position that any materialistic or realistic system must in the end assume. But this possible position Lotze ignores. Following Herbart in his inconsistency, and laying stress on the admission that monads stand in real relations to one another, Lotze proceeds to criticise this admission and to show that it involves the inward modification of the monads themselves. In this way the fixed and simple nature of substance, as conceived by realism, is exchanged for an idealistic conception that sees the reality in a series of unsubstantial states. The claim of this series to the name of substance is made to rest on the fact that it produces the illusion of substance; substance thus becomes a name for the impression produced by a certain series of phenomena. This abandonment of realism and of the validity of the concept of substance is the result of admitting relations between things; for if there are such relations the things must be changeable and ideal. They cannot be real and immutable if they stand in essential relations to one another. The position of the atom, in other words, or its proximity to others, must not be regarded as affecting the atom in itself; the atom must have nothing to do with such accidental and adventitious considerations. They appear only to the external observer. By admitting that they are elements in the internal nature or life of the atom, we are untrue to the realistic hypothesis; we abandon in principle our whole point of view.

It is not in these allied principles of the essential mutability of the reality and of the internal nature of the relations of its elements that lies the point of Lotze's realistic argumentation. This is anti-realistic argumentation. It is the leaven of idealism that is to leaven the whole realistic mass. But it is idealism from the beginning; it does not grow out of the realism. The force of Lotze's argument must be looked for in the developments he gives to various conceptions, not in the variety of conceptions he combines. The argument is one thing, the system another. And the argument rests on his principle that the elements of reality must be atomic; that extension, for instance, is a relation between two points, which alone can be real and independent. The *res extensa* of Descartes and of common sense Lotze analyses into two elements, one the substantial and self-sufficing points that make, as it were, its skeleton, and the other the unreal and objectively impossible distance that separates them. Out of this analysis flow the important consequences that Lotze insists upon. If we accept this analysis, we really discover something about the implications of our metaphysical conceptions. Such an analysis does not abandon the realistic hypothesis; to consider it is not to introduce a foreign conception into our system. If the analysis really unfolds the sense of our feeling of reality, if it really points out what lies in the conception of substance, it is an invaluable contribution to philosophy, for it clears up one of our most primitive, most inevitable and most tenacious ideas, that of an external and extended substance. And this analysis would have to be accepted by all realists; for it does not rest on any idealistic principle surreptitiously introduced. Such was the case with the principle of internal relations, or of the mutability of substance. A substance, by definition and common accord, designates an unchanging thing, something self-sufficing and unaffected by what may go on about it. To call it mutable and make it the locus of relations is to describe an entirely different thing which we abitrarily choose to call by the same name. But if our concept of reality, on being scrutinized, breaks up into an infinity of real points, each without extension, and into the complex of their external relations, then we have entered upon a line of thought that may lead us very far indeed. We must therefore consider attentively what Lotze tells us on this subject.

In the first place, we must remember that immediate perception does not discover matter in the abstract, does not discover any continuous substance, but only a plurality of various material elements. The atomic structure of these objects is evident sometimes to our unaided vision; and although the fact that apparently continuous bodies are found upon closer scrutiny to be made up of discrete parts does not prove that all bodies need be so made up, yet it does prove that the appearance of continuity is no argument against the atomic structure of a body. I am not able to make out how much Lotze intends to say by this assertion; if he means that because an apparently continuous surface can be composed of various parts, themselves still having extension, therefore any body may be composed of unextended points, the inference is evidently false. For the obvious reason why a collection of units appears to sense as a whole is that each unit contributes something toward a stimulation which, owing to the indistinctness of our perception, reaches consciousness only as a total; were the stimulus from each atom absolutely null, then it is hard to see how a collection of such atoms could constitute an object of sense. All that Lotze's argument shows, and perhaps all he meant to show by it, is that we can never be sure that the units we have are not composed of smaller units; we find the appearance of continuity produced by discrete, but extended, units; therefore these units themselves may conceivably in turn be but sensuous resultants of a variety of stimuli. Nothing could induce us, therefore, to assert that this possibility of subdivision must somewhere cease, unless it were the purely intellectual ἀνάγκη στῆναι [necessity of an end]. But Lotze's argument, so understood, is really irrelevant; that the size or number of the extended elements of matter can be respectively decreased and increased *ad libitum,* does not affect the question whether absolutely unextended atoms can compose an extended body. The smallest atom we care to imagine is as different from a point as are the heavenly bodies. By talking of the very small size of atoms we may predispose the imagination to regard them as absolute points; but for reason and logic the question of size has nothing to do with the question of nature. And it is a question of nature that we are discussing; the whole desire we betray to refine extension into unextended being, is a desire to get rid of matter altogether, and to deal with a world of intelligible entities that may prove more docile and pliable in our hands. But in truth, the fact that we have no reason for stopping anywhere in our subdivisions of matter, does not help us to get rid of that troublesome spectre; for even if we never stop we shall at every point in that infinite process have the same matter, quite as extended, quite as far from vanishing into air, as at the beginning. There is reason to wonder at the impatient imaginativeness of men who allow their thought to be so easily confused, and resign logic and neglect definitions in the heat of their enthusiasm for some new and irrelevant conception. The case before us is typical. There is on the one hand a vision of extended objects, and the knowledge that they are divisible; on the other hand is the conception of a world of mental or passionate forces, more analogous to our consciousness, and therefore more congenial to us than the unyielding and foreign world of material realities. And the ingenuity of desire at once becomes evident; the feeling arises that, since matter can be broken up into parts too small to be seen, and since this subdivision may go on indefinitely, matter may not be extended at all in reality; and if not extended, why, its nature can be none other than the nature of that imaginative world of foreign consciousness that we spontaneously construct. In this foreseen transformation of the reality lies the whole force of that impulse to contradict our conceptions, and to declare that extension is made up of unextended elements. If we forget this transformation of the reality, the logic of our conceptions themselves will be evident. A body, an extended thing, can be composed of parts; experience shows that an apparently continuous surface may in truth contain breaks, and be only the sensuous union of stimuli from various scattered units of extension. But the nature of extension, and its essential and infinite diversity from non-extension, belongs to every one of these units, at every stage of the process of subdivision. There are indeed considerations of another sort that may induce us to doubt the reality of extension altogether, whether of space or matter; these idealistic arguments do not concern us here, for they apply to the conception of matter and space as a conception in the mind; they look at it from the outside, and consider its locus, its origin, and the sort of validity it can have as a form of perception and as a category of human thought. And if we are inclined to postulate any reality but that contained in human thought, and subject to its categories, then we may justly say that extension does not belong to that reality; that reality would indeed be unknowable. But if such objects of consciousness as extended things are allowed to retain the primal reality that we spontaneously attribute to them, then any criticism of extension as a form of human perception, any denial of its applicability to objects on account of its own subjective origin and function, is idle and futile. It is this right understanding of the practically realistic and materialistic outcome of the Kantian philosophy that makes Lotze return to an analysis of our conceptions in regard to their content and intention; he gives up the question of the validity of the predication of these attributes of the reality, and discusses instead the question of the meaning and sense of the predicates themselves. The value of Lotze's arguments rests entirely on the analysis of given conceptions; the question whether these conceptions, simply because they are human conceptions, are applicable to the reality, is justly passed over by him as a question altogether idle and ill considered.

It is to the intrinsic logical difficulties of the idea of extended atoms that Lotze accordingly turns. In the first place he refers to Fechner for a proof of the scientific utility of atoms as opposed to a mysteriously extended material substance. But we are not concerned with this; for the atoms that have been useful in science are extended atoms still; they are still bodies, and what we are investigating is whether body must be composed of things that are not body. We measure atoms by weight and not by size, for they are not visible; but although this circumstance makes it possible to forget their extension and abstract from it, it cannot excuse a denial of their extension. A philosophic reason must be found for that denial; a practical reason there cannot be.

But now let us consider what we do in supposing an atom to be extended. We leave, says Lotze, the problem unsolved, for the nature of matter is no more explained by a small piece of it than by a large piece. And here we must at once stop to make clear the true question before us. Lotze seems to expect an analysis of the nature of extension, an analysis that of course cannot be accomplished until extension is reduced to elements of a different nature. If this problem be the real one, of course an attempt to solve it would exclude *in limine* the supposition of extended atoms. Our choice would be confined to the various possible metaphysical geneses of extension; the elements from which it springs, whatever we might decide that they were, must at any rate be immaterial and unextended. The sense, therefore, that there is such a problem at all is already the sense that extended things cannot be real. In other words, if what we want is a reduction of matter to the immaterial, of extension to the unextended, of elements of perceived objects to intellectual conceptions, then indeed by our very demand we set out on the road to idealistic conclusions. No wonder that we should transform matter into something entirely different, if what we propose to ourselves is to discover into what entirely different thing matter can best be transformed. But the problem that meets the unsophisticated inquirer is not this wholly metaphysical problem. If we are led to inquire about the composition of matter at all, it is not by a dislike of matter as such, and a desire to metamorphose it into some more inspiring form of being; we inquire about the composition of material objects because we observe that they are actually decomposed at one time or another. We wonder what can be the elements into which objects break up; in other words, we wish to follow the transformations of matter that actually occur, we wish to see into what shapes it changes. But we are not naturally dissatisfied with the supposition that matter itself in its various forms is an ultimate reality; in truth that belief is one that we can never practically abandon. To ask, then, what matter is composed of, is only to ask for the complete series of its transformations; the smallest element of it that is ever found alone will be its ultimate element, and we shall feel that we know what things are made of if we know what the matter of them looks like when it loses its present form. The problem, therefore, in so far as it is inevitable, is only a physical problem, one that might be solved by a completed physical science. The existence of a problem about the composition of bodies is therefore no proof of the existence of a problem about the possibility of body at all. The second problem is invented by metaphysics, while the first is suggested by common experience. A physical theory like that of Lucretius cannot be blamed, therefore, for retaining extended atoms. The only problem that exists for such a system is the physical problem, and to that it suggests such answers as the state of science at the time warrants. The metaphysical necessity of explaining matter away entirely such a system does not recognize; the metaphysicians have the burden of proof to carry, and their criticism must first show that there is some fatal impossibility in the natural supposition that there is such a thing as extended matter. After they have shown the reality of the problem, they may go on to consider what sort of being may be substituted for extended matter as the external seat of reality.

The metaphysical criticism of the idea of body is to a great extent founded on the arbitrariness of the assertion that extended things are indivisible. Why should a body be indivisible while the space that it fills is divisible *ad infinitum?* Yet this objection is founded on a metaphysical misinterpretation of a harmlessly physical expression. The indivisibility of atoms is a mere fact; an atom being the smallest mass of matter ever detached, its indivisibility is only a synonym of its definition. Of course, as the atom still occupies space it can be conceived as smaller than it is; just as if instead of an element of extension we should place an element of measurable force, we might conceive that element of force smaller than it actually is. Nevertheless, if in a dynamic system individual forces were distinguished and regarded as elements of nature, each would properly be regarded as a unit, and as indivisible, although no possible reason can be given why it should have precisely its actual intensity. So also with the atoms. They are units, because they are the counters with which nature actually plays; and the possibility of their having been larger or smaller does not prevent their actual unity.

Yet it is against the supposed unity of the extended atom that Lotze directs his attack. The supposition, he says, of indivisible atoms would require an absolutely infinite force of cohesion in them; and this supposition is repugnant to our scientific conceptions, at least if it is supposed to maintain the atom absolutely unchanged in shape under all conditions. Now this objection, which although advanced as not wholly conclusive, seems to have influenced Lotze, and which is repeated by him, consists in an appeal to the scientific temper and manner of conceiving matter and force. Yet from the scientific point of view the objection is hardly called for; what indivisibility stands for is a fact and not an indefinable possibility. If an infinite force (per impossibile) were observed, and if it could be applied against the cohesive force of an atom, then we might have occasion to see whether the atom was divisible by an infinite force; meantime all we need know, and all we mean to assert, is that the process of nature is a play of detached and individual material particles. The forces at work are nothing but descriptions *a posteriori* of the motions of these particles and their aggregates. Their indivisibility is a cause and condition of our observing force at all; for what forces would there be in a world of vanishing objects? But quite apart from this, a believer in extended atoms would not be in the least disconcerted by Lotze's objection; he might grant that a greater force than any now at work in nature might, if properly applied, split up all his atoms; that might involve a thoroughgoing change in all physical and chemical laws; the world might be greatly transformed; but it would still consist of individual particles and their aggregates. The indivisibility would in the new order attach to smaller particles than in the old order; that would be all. For, I repeat, by indivisibility is meant no unintelligible possibility, but a fact,— a hypothetical fact, to be sure, but something perfectly simple and intelligible in its nature. The difficulty does not appear until we try to read some mysterious necessity into this fact; but we have no cause to inquire what is or is not possible *a priori* in nature; necessity and possibility are internal to that system of things that our intelligence conceives. This system itself is neither necessary, nor probable, nor possible *a priori;* we simply cannot get out of it. So if we must conceive of matter, and if matter is divided into atoms, and these are not further divided, it is idle to discuss whether, although undivided, they are divisible. Their unity is just the sort of unity that ordinary material bodies have; we should never have learned to regard these as divisible were they never actually decomposed. And where, in the process of nature, decomposition ceases, there, in the system of our science, indivisibility begins.

It is not, then, in any incongruity with our physical conceptions that an objection can be found to extended atoms. The unity that they are supposed not to have is not a physical unity; they must be admitted to possess the unity of physical elements, a unity that enables us to use them as counters, as points of reference in our calculations. This is the unity possessed by planets in astronomy, by individuals in society. Such a unity extended atoms possess in an eminent degree. And it is the only unity that they need possess to be the ultimate elements of reality in an objective and materialistic system. If we demand some other kind of unity, we abandon the realistic point of view altogether. We seek a "metaphysical unity;" and Lotze, in using this phrase, gives us fair warning of his altered attitude. Only it is to be regretted that these changes of front are not more pointedly and frankly confessed by him; there is nothing unphilosophical or contradictory in them. We may legitimately consider a question from various points of view, and with various problems in mind; what is unphilosophical, and what alone introduces inconsistency in our thought, is the attempt to deduce from premisses of one sort conclusions of quite another, to extract, for example, a spiritualistic idealism out of a system of molecular physics. We cannot distinctly charge Lotze with such a piece of sophistry, for he does not distinctly undertake it; but a certain suavity and treacherous facility in his transitions and changes of attitude lend color to the idea that he believed himself to be accomplishing some magical feat of that kind. But we shall have occasion continually to show that all conceptions, treated logically and with regard to their meaning, are static and fixed, and that the only *treibende Kraft* [driving force] that can hurry us from one to another is our psychological instability, the loose hold we have of everything in the flux of impressions and emotions. And we can with greater propriety insist upon this self-sufficiency of our conceptions, in as much as Lotze himself insists upon it in his logic. It is only in the attempt to construct for himself a coercive system of metaphysics that he is in danger of falling into the mystifications that he has exposed.

The metaphysical unity that Lotze fails to find in an extended atom is that unity which would require that the state of each part should be at the same time and *ipso facto* a state of the whole unit. Thus a shock sustained by an extended atom at one point of its surface would have to be simultaneously felt at every other point of the atom. The velocity with which the shock is propagated would have to be absolutely infinite. And the attraction of another body would have to be felt equally at every point of the atom; else an affection of one point of the atom would differ from an affection of another point. This would destroy the required metaphysical unity. And finally an infinite cohesive force would be required to keep these various points within the atom, did we regard them as affected differently, in a constant relation to one another. The cohesive force would have to be infinite in order to make the difference in the other forces working on the parts of the atom absolutely disappear. All these suppositions, Lotze tells us, are incompatible with our physical conceptions. For we must regard bodies as acting with equal force at various distances, and motion as propagated with infinite velocity. It is perhaps worth while to observe that really one of these unnatural suppositions would suffice; for if, upon touching the surface of an atom, the shock were propagated with an infinite velocity, we should not then be compelled to assume that the attracting or repelling force acted with equal intensity at both surfaces; the simultaneous motion of the whole atom would be accounted for by the instantaneous propagation of the effect on any point to all the others, by virtue of the absolute cohesion of the substance of the atom. Only if we refused to suppose this infinite cohesive force should we be compelled to attribute an equal efficiency to the external force at every point in the atom. But since either of these suppositions would involve an exception to our received physical principles, we need not dwell upon this detail. Lotze's objection would still remain that the hypothesis of extended atoms is inconsistent with our accepted scientific theory.

Had Lotze's analysis been carried one step further, however, the assumptions and presuppositions of physical science might have appeared in a different light. For when he speaks of an external force acting upon the various points of the atom, does he not already suppose these points to be independent and to contain reality? But in order to regard these points as containing reality and as propagating motion to the surrounding points, they must be regarded as extended, i.e., as not really points at all. A point cannot move, much less can it by its motion drive out other points from their positions. For a point is a limit, and is therefore determined in relation to the figure of which it is a limit. The whole possibility of treating the world physically and dynamically disappears if we insist on regarding forces as acting on points primarily, and on bodies only derivatively. Force is an abstraction from motion, and motion is an affection of extension; the idea of body lies at the bottom of our whole series of physical ideas, and the notions of force and of motion become absolutely empty and senseless except as they refer to bodies. Lotze's supposition, then, of a force affecting a "point" on the surface of an atom, whence it must be propagated to other "points" is fundamentally inadmissible. The terms of it are not congruous and will not combine. Points are geometrical limits, force and motion are physical terms that derive all their content and meaning from the idea of body. And what we really think of when we read Lotze's phrase about a force affecting one point and being thence propagated, is a motion of a mass of matter whose centre of gravity is at that point. Nothing is more important for us than to remember the natural order of ideas. What is given is the concrete thing, the total obscure object; out of this we spin out our abstractions. But these, while they clarify the object, are themselves intelligible only with reference to it. So the ideas of force, of centres of gravity, of distance, and of points make body and extension clear and manageable for our thought; but they become themselves nonsensical if divorced from that idea of body and of extension from which they are derived. And it will be an easy thing indeed for any man who so divorces these terms from their subject-matter, to prove that they have no subject-matter at all, and that they dissolve in contradictions. And it will be easy to show that realism is untenable and overcomes itself, when we have substituted for the actual objects of perception purely intellectual and methodological abstractions. Thus Lotze has no difficulty in showing that an atom cannot be affected as a unit if what is first affected is an unextended point on its surface; but the unwelcome and paradoxical conclusions that he draws follow, not from the supposition of the extended atom, but from the supposition of the really affected mathematical point. In this impossible and contradictory conception lies the source of the entire difficulty. It introduces the incongruous element that, by being alone insisted upon, is destined to drive out the original realistic conception into which it has been ingrafted.

For if the external force playing on the atom affected only a mathematical point on its surface, it would leave the matter of the atom absolutely unaffected. This mathematical point could be pushed in or drawn out without even tending to affect any change in the atom; no man can be killed by a bullet of absolutely no diameter. Forces affecting mathematical points are powerless in the world of matter, because they do not pertain to an element of body, but only an immaterial and in itself non-existent limit of extension, the point. A force cannot affect matter by virtue of affecting something immaterial. If the drawing out or pushing in of a point on the surface of an atom is to have any effect on that atom, it can only be because that point is the centre of a tract which is drawn out or pushed in; some element of body, however small, must be the starting point of a shock that is to affect body. After we have observed the motion of this region as a whole, we may discover that the motion is not the same in every part. In that case we but repeat the previous process, and subdivide the moved mass into various tracts, each moved to a certain distance. This process can go on indefinitely. But it would be a notable blunder to imagine that because it can go on forever this process ever threatens to leave us with no space and matter at all. This possibility of infinite subdivision, far from being an argument against the continuity of space or matter is a corollary of their continuity. So long as we have space or matter before us at all, so long therefore as we can talk of motion and force, we have space and matter as truly and hopelessly extended and continuous as we have at the beginning. No matter how much we divide, what remains on our hands contains as much room for subdivision as what we had before; and hence it is that we must treat given elements of space and matter as permanent units; all units of extension must be given by perception and by objective experience; there are no logical and necessary units of this nature. From the *a priori* point of view all units of extension are equally satisfactory; where we shall stop in our subdivisions must depend exclusively on our practical convenience. The moral of this infinite divisibility of extension is that we must be satisfied with the units of matter that observation discovers to us; there is no possible theoretical objection to them. And since observation can never by any possibility discover to us unextended units of extension, or immaterial elements of matter, the ideal divisibility of the elements we do discover must pass, not for an unavoidable difficulty, but for a necessary qualification in them. Were they not ideally divisible they would not be component parts of space or of matter.

When it is a question, however, of measuring the motions of bodies, we are obliged to select some point upon that body from which to measure the distance traversed. Hence the habit of regarding bodies as moving in obedience to the motion of their centres; a habit perfectly harmless and proper, especially when we reflect on the crying absurdity of supposing that such a method of treatment describes the actual genesis of the motion. No one would think of attributing the motion of a planet to the attraction exercised on an immaterial point at its centre, which not only had the wonderful property of moving itself, although it had no extension or figure but existed only as the limit of a figure, but had also the still more wonderful property of dragging an extended mass after it in its flight. We have not yet heard of the cohesion of a molecule and a point, or of the friction of the earth upon its axis. Yet not different in principle from this is the confusion of thought that regards the motion of an atom as affected by a force working at a point on its surface; and on this latter supposition Lotze founds his criticism of extended atoms. Of course, he makes this supposition only to reject it in the end; it serves him as a lever with which to remove the conception of matter entirely. But the supposition is incompatible with any theory of matter whatever, and therefore the arguments resting on it prove nothing against the theory of extended atoms.

What we should strive to keep in mind in this whole discus-

sion is that extended elements cannot act or move except as
wholes, because only as wholes can they exist or be observed at
all. If a subdivision is possible for us, it is possible only by virtue
of the discoverability of smaller wholes within the larger, and
these smaller wholes can be discovered only by virtue of their
extension and cohesion. Lotze, we remember, has raised the objection that this cohesion would require an infinite force, if the
unity of the atom were to be real. What sort of unity atoms can
and should have I have just tried to show; but although Lotze's
objection is thus sufficiently met, yet it is worth dwelling upon
for another reason. It is Lotze's merit, and a sign of his real
value as a philosopher, that even where his conclusion and
arguments are least satisfactory, his treatment of the question is
full of suggestions and opens up a great variety of problems. And
so in this place the interesting point is brought up, in what
sense we must consider the cohesive force of an atom to be infinite. Force is a principle of motion, betrayed only by its effects.
Although we tend to make it the ground and explanation of
motion we should remember that it is only ideally prior to
motion; in the genesis of conceptions it is derived from motion,
and therefore has a right of citizenship in our thought only by
virtue of the existence of motions. And motion in turn is dependent on the existence of figures and occupied space. Only
therefore where there is form can we speak of motion, and
only where there is motion can we speak of force. Whether the
cohesion of an atom can be attributed to a force at all will therefore depend on the inclusion of this cohesion in the system of
motions in nature. If any change in nature is traced to this cohesion, then it is a force. If any motion seems to be arrested or
created by this cohesion, it is a force. But evidently this will be
the case only if the cohesion is actually overcome, at least in
part. The supposition of an infinite cohesive force in atoms is
therefore only a verbal necessity, for cohesion, if it is a force and
not a mere fact, presupposes possible disintegration, in reference to which that cohesion can be regarded as a cause of (pre-
vented) motion. Two atoms may cohere, or two molecules, but

the force that preserves an atom is no longer called a force of cohesion properly, but only by analogy; were the body not an atom, but dissoluble in the operations of nature, we should call the force that now held its parts together cohesion—and this force would not be infinite but would have a fixed proportion to other forces, viz. to those that would separate the body into its atoms. But if the body is an atom the force (so called) by which it subsists no longer enters at all into combination with other forces; it is not a force governing changes in nature, but that metaphysical force or fatality by which things exist, by which they are thus and not otherwise; it is not that phenomenal and calculable force that alone is to be considered. Therefore if we say that an atom is held together by an infinite force of cohesion we speak improperly. In the first place the atom does not exist by virtue of its parts, but by virtue of the larger masses of matter of which we discover it to be an element; we get at the atom by division, not by aggregation, of the given objects that alone have primary reality and that are the sole basis of our knowledge of matter at all. We have no occasion to speak of cohesion in the atom, since its function is to contribute to larger wholes, and its own consistency needs no explanation because it is a primary and given fact. And then, if in expressing this fact, we say that the atom is maintained by an infinite cohesive force, we employ an objectionable phrase. An infinite thing is not properly called by the same name as anything finite, for it can have no determinate relation to finite things, and is incomparable with them. An infinite force would no longer be a force, because it would not stand in any relation to real forces. It would be a cause of being, not a cause of motion; it would overwhelm and include all real forces, and yet leave to them alone the possibility of accounting for phenomena. Now this sort of force, if we may call it so, is what constitutes atoms; they are units not by virtue of a constellation of phenomenal forces, such as hold together composite objects, but they are units by virtue of the primary constitutional necessity of things, that compels us to see in extension a total, and in all its parts totals and units. If we subdivide these units, we thereby perceive new units, as extended and ideally divisible as the former; and this necessity, which is not a result of physical forces, but of the nature of body itself, is what guarantees the indestructibility of atoms;—an indestructibility which inheres, so to speak, not in their persons but in their office, for the particular atoms in our world might conceivably be broken up, yet their fragments, which would be the atoms of the new cosmos, would succeed to all the rights and duties of their predecessors. Unity and extension would come to them together by virtue of the application to them of the category of body; for the conception of body and of an atom are essentially identical, the atom being the type of body. Only the proof that the bodies we perceive are actually dissolved, and are temporarily held together by real finite forces, can prevent our regarding them as units already; in the case of atoms we conceive of a body in which the proof of such physical dissolubility would not be found, and then—not by any new postulate, but merely by our original conviction and knowledge that it is a body—we declare it to be at once extended and indissoluble. This indissolubility does not mean that it is not ideally divisible into parts; it means that the nature of extension is itself indissoluble by divisions, and that therefore the portions that actually figure as units must always be extended portions.

If we grant, however, the possibility of effects propagated from points, Lotze's various conclusions follow inevitably. Contact is impossible, and all forces must operate at a distance. For suppose, says Lotze, two spheres of matter; for them to be in contact one point must be common to both. But if the substance of an atom is present at the same point as the substance of another, evidently no reason appears why the commotion that we may suppose to result should cause a motion of the atoms in one direction rather than in another. The tendency to push or pull must appear by virtue of the previous position of these substantial points; when they are coincident their action and reaction cannot be expressed by a motion. And beside this argument Lotze might have pointed out that if the substance of matter is concentrated at points, even if one of these, on the surface of the sphere, for instance, were pushed or pulled in some way, it could communicate this motion to the neighboring points only by virtue of action at a distance; for the nearest point is still at a distance, else it would be the same point. Indeed, on the supposition of real points and of unreal distances between them, the determination of points and therefore their very existence becomes impossible; it is on this that Lotze builds his intricate arguments against the reality of space. These arguments Lotze advances as not convincing; he seems to suspect that they have no value from the realistic and objective point of view; for anyone who believes in the reality of space and matter does not place that reality in unspatial and immaterial points. Yet Lotze does not tell us that this is the reason why his arguments are inconclusive; he seems to attribute their doubtful validity rather to their subtlety and complication. He strives to show that the various points of space must have an internal note that distinguishes each from the others; each must "feel" differently, must have a consciousness, as it were, and a personality of its own. For since they are to contain the reality of space, and not merely to limit it, we cannot rely on an external relation between them, such as distance or position, to distinguish them; it must be a qualitative difference in their content that makes them separate and distinct. And hence it follows naturally that extension is a scheme for the expression of intensive relations; it is the comparative feeling and inward state of realities that we express by attributing to them a position in space. And in this way we have successfully done away with the reality of space, and reduced it to a subjective interpretation of non-spatial external facts. I need not stop to repeat what I have said in relation to the composition of matter; the absurdity of a point with an internal constitution, and almost with a personal consciousness is crying enough. It is not from a consideration of space that such notions are derived, but by pure analogy of conscious being. The reality of space is thus disproved only by first eliminating all that in space that can possibly be real, and substituting for it a helpless abstraction. A space composed of points, that must keep themselves apart without admitting any distance between them, is of course impossible; it simply ceases to be space at all. And this consequence is obvious enough. The doubtfulness of Lotze's analysis does not lie in the idealization of such a space as this; what invalidates the whole argument is that the premisses are inadmissible, and that therefore all the consequences drawn from them are irrelevant.

After all we have said, it remains perfectly possible to deny the reality of matter and space, and interpret them as phenomena representing some reality unlike themselves. We may perfectly well agree with Lotze's conclusions; but he has sought to establish these on a basis on which they do not rest. What Lotze says of Kant's arguments must be applied to Lotze's own; they advocate a congenial and probable opinion but as arguments they are inconclusive. Lotze rejects Kant's arguments, psychological and metaphysical, for the ideality of space; for Lotze rightly insists that we have not to pass judgment on the possibility of the existence of things. We are not called upon to make the world, but to see it as it is given. Herein lies Lotze's objective and positivistic method. We have no standards of possible and impossible existence by virtue of which we can declare a finite space possible or an infinite space impossible. We have only to ask, what sort of space is this that is given. And the fact that it is given as one, or infinite, or a total, cannot be an indication of its subjectivity, for we lack a faculty by which to judge what sort of things can be subjective only, and what sort are capable of existing also in a world beyond our thought. An absolute idealist, who regards the world as a product of mental operations, has a right to assume a different attitude; but Lotze's peculiarity is that he strives to attain idealistic conclusions on a realistic basis. On the same principle he rejects all *a priori* and shorthand arguments for idealism of the common type; he would not say with Berkeley that we know nothing but our ideas, therefore our ideas are all that exist. We have no authority to judge whether these ideas are not in truth what they give themselves out for, viz. pictures and doubles of independent and objective realities. Over the whole attempt to criticise our faculty of knowledge Lotze throws the obvious but too often suppressed suspicion, that this faculty judges itself by its own authority and that therefore its judgment neither confirms nor invalidates that authority. The fact that all our knowledge is contained in our ideas is not a proof that nothing can be known, that there is nothing more to which these ideas correspond. Of course we cannot know what we have no idea of; but the question is whether we know that of which we do have ideas. It will not do to beg the whole question and say that because knowledge is contained in ideas, knowledge is impossible. That is a denial of knowledge not founded on any grounds whatever; it is simply a perception that, as Lotze says, knowledge knows its objects and does not create or constitute them. In other words, knowledge pretends to have a transcendent significance; it pretends to represent something that it is not. To tell us what knowledge is formally, viz. that it is a mass of ideas, does not determine the question whether it represents anything else or not. Idealism therefore must be based upon the contradictions of our ideas, not on their nature as ideas. To be convinced that our knowledge is simply thought and not information we must find that our knowledge is self-contradictory. In that case we shall be forced to believe that it is mere thought, mere ideas, and that nothing corresponds to it in reality. But if the message that our ideas bring is not contradictory then we shall certainly continue to believe in our ideas, and to conceive that they inform us about the nature of things. Why should we doubt it? Indeed, no proof of the transcendent validity of knowledge can ever reach us, since all proof is but added ideation; but the nature of ideas is such that every image in the mind *claims* to represent a reality; our minds have the form of objectivity, and an idea is always the idea of something. Not until we discover conflict in these ideas do we begin to doubt that they correspond to the truth; and such doubt can be maintained only in so far as these ideas are really contradictory. The most idealistic of systems believes in a reality of some sort; it believes in the representative value of its own conceptions. Therefore we must distinguish carefully between a sudden, dogmatic, and in the end self-contradictory idealism, which is based on the denial of the representative character of knowledge, and a partial, critical, and progressive idealism that by study of our ideas seeks to clear them of contradictions, in order to attribute objective validity to those that are really unassailable.

On these principles idealism cannot be carried further than to the Lockian stage; the primary qualities of matter must remain objective, because any further reduction would involve, not a comparison and coordination of the objects of sense, but their total annihilation. The idealism of Locke is simply a translation of sensuous experience of all sorts, into terms of one kind of sensuous experience. The object is thus simplified, and a mechanical treatment of it is made possible. Science has therefore adopted this form of critical idealism; it enables us to treat mechanically the object that remains real, while its secondary qualities, which are without influence in mechanical motions, remain objects for other sciences, such as psychology and aesthetics. This is as far as the idealization of nature can go by virtue of mere analysis of the object as a thing; that mere analysis can never do away with the object is a matter of logic and first principles. A further idealization of nature must proceed from very different motives; it must in some form or other repeat that ancient and ever new reflection that the world is my vision, that all I pretend to know is projected from the unity of my present consciousness. Lotze has not considered this point of view as the right one in philosophy; it belongs according to him exclusively to mysticism. Philosophy is a discussion of the given reality as an objective reality; yet on this positivistic basis Lotze has tried to build that absolutely idealistic system that properly rests on that insight into the subjectivity of all things which he has intentionally ignored. I have tried to show in a typical case—that of extension— that this attempt of Lotze's has failed. But it has not failed for any lack of ingenuity or insight on his part; it was condemned to failure by its very nature and pretensions. By no inward logic of the idea of extension can we be driven to renounce the idea of extension; that sort of self-annihilation of definitions is necessarily sophistical. If I say: here is a body, and mean something by what I say, I can never, by seeing what I do mean, see that I mean something quite different. I can never by analysis of a concept find in it a different meaning from that which the concept stands for. I may abandon my concepts in favor of others recommended by new experience, or more congruous with my temper and interests; but I can never abandon a concept by retaining it. There is, to be sure, a suggestiveness in such paradoxes that gives them a certain rhetorical force; for we do undoubtedly in life and meditation pass from one phase to another, carried along by the stream of our ideas. We find that one thought, if we attend to it long enough, will of itself lead us to another; but only as youth, if we are young long enough, will lead us to old age. The fact that we thus describe is not that one thing transforms itself into its opposite, but that we are driven by new experience, by altered circumstances, by modifications of our organism, to exchange our attributes and to abandon our old selves for new. It is the psychological, the biological, process that controls this development, not the logical concatenation of concepts. An idea of itself has if anything a certain inertia; far from being the inevitable step to another idea it is, in so far as it is vigorous, an absolute impediment to the production of different thoughts. Thus the idea of body, the idea of extended objects moving as units and remaining internally unchanged in that motion, far from leading in itself and by virtue of attentive analysis to any other conception of reality, inhibits and prevents any other conception. Yet perhaps any other conception would be as good did it actually establish itself in our minds and become natural and familiar to us. These various conceptions have their own seeds in the mind, and they will spring up there if the soil be congenial. But the grapes of idealism do not grow on materialistic thistles. Lotze might have developed these other thoughts, without seeking to engraft them on heterogeneous matter; he might have plunged like so many others at once into the rapid current of idealism. He preferred to reach the same goal by a circuitous journey on terra firma. But unhappily he is not satisfied with advancing himself; he does not say to himself, "If you change your point of view, if you travel from your present position, you may gain the position held by yonder enthusiasts; move, be changed, cultivate different thoughts and different interests, and the entire sense of reality will change for you; what was real to you will become figurative, what was figurative will become real; rocks and trees will become symbols, theodicies and mystical unities will become realities." To speak so would have been, perhaps, to draw a moral from the history of human conviction; it would not have been to construct a *System der Philosophie*. Lotze wishes to coerce the mind with arguments, he wishes to make idealists of us by an artificial process. He tries to compel us to admit conclusions suggested by metaphysical and poetic insight as the results of an *argumentum ad hominem* addressed to the positivist. And the artifice employed to this end is the familiar one of constructing a series of stages, so that by imperceptible variations the unsuspecting student may be led from his native conviction to a diametrically opposite assertion. The Platonic Socrates has with admirable irony shown us how a man thus led to contradict himself may by the same arts be recalled from his perplexities and happily be restored to his familiar thoughts. Lotze might undoubtedly have cancelled and retraced his entire argumentation, had he desired to bring us back to positivism; but a different side of his nature attached him to idealistic beliefs; he therefore insists upon these, and develops them into his system of philosophy. We must now turn to a consideration of that; and this constructive and imaginative side of Lotze's thought will offer a more grateful subject than the critical arguments on which it is supposed to rest. That its true foundations are the demands of our ethical and religious imagination will sufficiently appear from the nature of the construction itself.

[IV]

Monism—Causality—Indeterminism

THE PROOF OF the unity of nature, the basis of monism, is really very clear in Lotze, although the thing proved is perhaps less momentous and novel than we might be led to think it. The words monism, pantheism, the One, have such a profound and mystical sound, they seem to contain a doctrine so much more difficult to understand than the conceptions of common sense and natural science, and in fact such far-reaching theories are often designated by these names, that we may be a little disappointed, and possibly a little relieved, to find that for Lotze they designate almost a truism. For we must remember what Lotze means by a thing, and what in his system constitutes substantial unity. A thing, a being, a substance, is for him the "actualized law of its behavior" (Verhalten), its unity is its history, the melody or movement of its variations. Now all the objects that enter our world enter it by virtue of their relations in that world; they must occupy some place in it, figure in its history, and be parts of its process. This is nothing more than saying that the thing exists, that it has come into the world. It follows therefore by definition, and without any further argument that the world is one thing; for only by being events within it, only by having relations to one another can things enter the world at all. Things utterly separated and out of relation are simple possibilities, not parts of the given reality; they are other independent worlds, that may possibly exist for all we know, but that by definition are not elements of the knowable reality. Their existence or their destruction makes no difference in our world. But the existence of these relations between the elements of a world is enough to make them a series, an actualized law of behavior. We are using the word law here in a slightly modified sense; in natural science a law is an abstract type of event that can be recognized in many given examples; but for Lotze repetition of similar events does not follow necessarily from the presence of a law, for the law that in being actualized constitutes a thing is exemplified only once. Until the last moment or state of the thing has been realized the law has not been fully exemplified; unlike an abstract law that is fully exemplified in every part of the series that it describes. The law that makes the substantial unity of a thing is an individual law; it is conceived on the analogy of human character, or of aesthetic unities like melodies, that are principles that are exemplified throughout the object, but not fully exemplified in any part of it, and that therefore require the union of all the parts without involving necessarily the repetition of anything. We may note in passing the profoundly and well-nigh exclusively aesthetic nature of this conception of unity and of law; Lotze betrays in it the sort of thing he looked for in the world, and the sort of thing he saw. And consideration of the aesthetic nature of Lotze's conceptions will lead us, I think, to see how consistently and naturally his various doctrines hold together, although the arguments by which they are supported may be drawn from the four quarters of the heavens. For such aesthetic unity, while it allows Lotze to speak of universal law, of universal purpose, and universal value, requires no inward and mutual determination of the parts united; and hence a truce is declared between the naturally hostile ideas of perpetual variation and total unity—a truce that would be impossible if we regarded these ideas logically or in the manner of natural science, but that becomes possible on aesthetic ground. For a total aesthetic impression, such as is produced by a melody or by a story, does not involve any repetitions of sequences within the given whole. What is common to all the parts being only their contributing, each in its way, to an emotion, which is itself very vague although possibly very intense and real, this common element in all the parts cannot determine *a priori* what each must be. The unity is not capable of formulation in the same terms as the objects that it unites; the unity is a function while the objects united are individual things. Yet we must remember that this functional unity is what Lotze declares, in a paradoxical definition, to be the "substance" of a thing.

Since the unity of being is nothing but the concatenation of elements, and as no element out of all connection with others can appear as part of the same world with them, the realities that exist are all inevitably notes in one melody, events in one history. Thus we have all the required unity in the world; we can with the same right call it one being, as we can call any single object one, whose states are connected together and recognizable. For if any series of events stopped short, if the aesthetic law by which it was a series ceased to be exemplified, we should say that the thing had ceased to exist. Thus we notice when one tune ends and another begins, when one nation dissolves and another is formed; yet the latter example may serve to point out how vague and arbitrary such aesthetic unities may be. Yet we know the world from moment to moment to be the same world by a similar test, because the laws of the same nature continue to be exemplified in it. And Lotze's system proves no other unity to exist than this unity given by continued exemplification of aesthetic laws; with accurate mechanical laws he is not unwilling to dispense, although he is willing also to admit them in a subordinate place. Since the unity of things is for him essentially a historical unity, the fact that what arises in nature necessarily bears some relation to what existed before is enough to prove that the world is one thing, or one being. And the unity thus ascribed to the world implies nothing more than this identity of the world with itself. It does not imply any mysterious identity of one thing with another. It only dwells on the familiar and undenied fact that these different and independent things are forms of the same space and events in the same history. No wonder, then, that Lotze finds no difficulties in his monism; he says that of course the unity and multiplicity of things are not identical but opposite; they are both applicable to the world, as what is one in one respect may be many in another. The aesthetic law that is realized in the successive states of the world is one; yet there are many cases and progressive exhibitions of this law, each having a certain history and make-up of its own; and the parts have for that reason the same right to be wholes as the total has. So a multiplicity of notes makes a single melody, and the unity of it does not exclude but in fact involves the multiplicity of its members. The danger that threatens Lotze here is that this simultaneous attribution of unity and multiplicity has become so necessary that he cannot attribute unity to anything without attributing multiplicity to it, and his atomism runs great danger of contradicting the theory that it was destined to introduce. The soul itself becomes an aesthetic total; and its momentary states, the law of which is the "substantial soul," seem in turn to require dissolution into their elements. But since Lotze has not discussed this difficulty, we must be satisfied with pointing out its existence.

Yet Lotze goes, perhaps, a little too far when he says (*Metaphysik,* p. 146.) that being may be one and many, just as a body may be extended and heavy at the same time; for extended and heavy are not contradictories as are one and many. Nor can he make his position clearer by quoting from Plato the passage where the possibility of being at once like and unlike is maintained; for here the possibility rests on the relative and transcendent nature of the predicates; a thing cannot be simply like, but must be like something else; and all that is necessary to clear up this verbal question is to point out that for A to be both like and unlike there must exist two other things B and C, themselves unlike each other. There would be contradiction only if A were said to be both like and unlike the same thing B. And in this latter form only does the example at all resemble the case of unity and plurality. For here too the explanation of the phrase consists in saying that the predicates apply to the subject in different respects; that while one element or phase of A is like B

another element or phase is unlike it. That is, the subject, instead of being A as a whole, must be transformed into unlike elements of A, which now, being unlike each other, may be one like and the other unlike B. So that to call A both like and unlike B is really an impropriety of speech, since the meaning is that m, an element of the complex thing A, is like B, while n, a different element of A, is unlike B. And the justification for Lotze's saying that being is both one and many is just of this sort; for the reality, as he elaborately shows us, is not simple, but essentially complex; the reality cannot be in a simple quality, it must lie in the relations of states, in the behavior of things. And in this, without going any further, we have the solution of the puzzle. For we see that, in order to be one, a being must be composed of elements; its unity is the unity of a series, which to be realized, calls for a series of examples or applications. So that in saying that the world is at once one and many we express in an obscure and misleading way a very homely and indubitable truth. We only mean that the world, in order to be real, has to be a series of separate events, a galaxy of distinct realities; that its unity is that order, that scheme, which makes each of these events and realities a member in that series; for evidently a star that was not in space or an event that was not in history would be a non-existent star and an imaginary event. This procession, therefore this order, apart from which nothing can be actual, is the unity of the world; and its plurality is the distinction and separation that must exist between the elements of any plan, between the members of any procession.

This is all that Lotze's arguments show, all that his premises involve. Perhaps it is not all that he believed or wished to have us understand. There is in his conception of the argument a dynamical element; the emphasis is laid everywhere on the necessity of unity to explain action and reaction; the ability of things to affect one another involves their unity, and we are told that interaction is conceivable between the various states of the same being, but not between different beings. And all this naturally suggests a deeper and more mysterious unity in things than that of which we have been talking. If we turn to Lotze's own exposition of the argument we may find that our statement of it has not been fair; we have missed the significance and real momentum of it. The unity he has in mind is a unity of force; the One is an all-sustaining power, an efficient cause of all existence; and the many are not so much elements and indispensable parts of the One, as its creatures and products. But this sense of the dependence of the many on the One does not have its source in the argument itself; it is the anticipation of an identification of the world, regarded as one, with a personal God or Creator, the motives for which we shall consider in the sequel. As yet such an identification is wholly unwarranted. For the sense in which the existence of the many depends on the One is not dynamical. If anything, the parts are the creators of the whole; for there is more reason in saying that history is a product of events, and a melody of its notes, than to conceive history as a power producing its events or a melody as a force bringing forth its elements. Such a view could only be aesthetic and teleological; the beauty of the result, its value in emotion, might be regarded as the final cause or moral justification of the existence of the objects that possessed that beauty and value. But from the logical and ontological point of view of our argument hitherto, we can only say that the unity is as essential to the presence of the parts as the presence of the parts is to the existence of their unity; if not an element in some whole a thing would be a universe in itself and could never enter our world. The cosmic laws to which things conform are their title to existence. And therefore in one sense, although not in a dynamical sense, the unity of things is prior to them individually. The law is in one sense prior to the cases in which it is exemplified; for their conformity to the law, the fact that they exemplify it, is their passport to existence. But in another sense the cases are prior to the rule; for the rule is the description of the cases. Thus we may say that the One determines the form of the many and their places within itself; but the many give existence and actuality to the whole. A causal dependence of the many on the One is therefore not justified by what Lotze has hitherto shown us. Nor is it justified by the principle of causation as he explains it. To this we must now turn our attention.

How one event follows another, says Lotze, must ever remain inexplicable. "For whatever process (*Microcosmus:* Vol. III, p. 486.) should be devised to fill the apparent gap between cause and effect, it would still be composed of a chain of events; and every two of these events would be bound together by the same unthinkable causation, the possibility of which was to have been explained by introducing this series." The process of causation approaches a solution no more by being traced inward into the minute constituents of the process, than by being traced backward to a first event. In neither direction should we be helped by discovering a limit. The question must be confined, then, to asking what happens, not how it happens. And we see that Lotze, whatever arguments he is about to present to us, can never put a dynamical and efficient element into causation; he must always be satisfied with a description of actual sequences. Or if he finds another aspect, the teleological aspect, in which to view the question, he cannot institute an enquiry how causation is possible; this question he has explicitly and even impatiently rejected as unanswerable and ill-considered. "Would I might have succeeded" he exclaims (*Microcosmus:* Vol. III, p. 486. Cf. also, *Metaphysik,* p. 91.) "in making evident the senseless circle that lurks in this curiosity" regarding the causal operation itself. If any light is to be thrown on the subject, it can only be from the point of view of final causes. We may see a reason why such and such a sequence is desirable, why things do well so to succeed one another. But by what process this comes about we must not inquire; the process is here already; it is nothing but this sequence of one event after another, this fact that upon one state another state regularly follows.

To note and describe actual sequences seems to Lotze enough when these sequences are among states of the same thing; but he wishes to find some further explanation for the succession of the states of one thing upon those of another thing, i.e. some explanation of action and reaction. In discussing, however, the possibility of interaction Lotze seems to discuss something that his definition of a thing has already made inadmissible. For if the law that the successive states of a thing illustrate does not cover all the states of that thing, then evidently the definition of a thing by its law is impossible. Some states belong to that thing which are not elements in that series which is the thing. Either, then, Lotze here gives up his definition of a thing as a series, as a melody, as a history, and reverts to the uncriticised notion of a substance, of an unchangeable kernel of reality with variable husk, or he is guilty of an evident contradiction in even considering the possibility of action and reaction between things. For interaction means that the law which the changes in a thing obey is not the private law of that thing, but a law covering the changes in various things and connecting them. If in the law, then, is to lie the essence of the thing, the thing must be coextensive with the law, and any states connected by a law are *ipso facto* states of a single thing. Lotze, I conceive, would have admitted the justice of this inference, and declared that it constituted the proof of the unity of nature; no law can adequately describe the nature of a thing subject to influences not included in that law; hence we shall never be able to discover a real law until we include all things under it. Then we shall have a law that adequately describes the series of states or phases before us. But there can be no law for a particular thing if the phases of that thing are effects of other things; evidently the law of that thing must include all the states of the given series, all the causes of effects in the given thing. Thus appears the impossibility of having anything less than an entire universe; either things have no relations, and then there is no passing from one to another, no interaction, or else they form a single series of states, a single process, and, by our definition, a single thing.

But if we hasten in this manner to the implications of Lotze's doctrine we pass over a great part of his discussions; the problem that most seems to occupy him disappears. For if we begin at once to treat the universe as one thing, and to insist on the imperfect nature of all other unities, we cannot go on asking how different things manage to affect each other; all things are one; and we know how idle it is to look for the reason of that causality which connects the various states of the same thing. To note and describe sequences is all we can do in such a case; the ground for these sequences is simply the nature of the given thing, which is nothing but the law which those sequences exemplify and actualize. We have no business to ask for any further ground for these sequences; they are the nature of things. All we can do is to reconcile our will and imagination to this given and unexplained order, by showing that it gives rise to aesthetic and moral values; we can justify the given dispensation emotionally and see that it is very good, but we can not further give an explanation of how and why it came to be what it is. And to this conclusion Lotze finally comes; his ultimate attitude is consistent with his first principles, and makes explicit what is implied in them. But it is characteristic of Lotze that he does not at once draw the conclusions involved in his own premisses, although, as we see, they are evidently involved; he prefers to delay, and discuss intermediate problems which in truth arise only for those who take points of view different from his own. So in this question of causation he avoids any appeal to that monism which he has already established; he takes for granted the plurality of things and his discussion only serves to point out the impossibility of explaining changes in one thing which follow upon changes in another, without supposing a real influence to be exercised by the latter on the former. Since this influence can never be discovered except by virtue of the fact that upon the appearance of the state β in the thing B, the state α appears in another thing A, and since this is defined to be transeunt causation, we are left with the fact of causation between things but with the impossibility of accounting for it. Lotze here exerts himself to show that there is interaction between things, and not mere correspondence; we may best understand his meaning by considering his objection to the three theories of correspondence that he discusses: the theory of regular sequences, or of correspondence of one phenomenon with another; the theory of occasional causes; and the theory of preestablished harmony.

The theory that reduces causation to regular sequence Lotze puts aside by saying that the succession depends on the nature of the events; that for a definite thing to succeed to a definite thing, and not anything to anything, the contents or natures of these things must determine what is to come after them. And this is undeniable. However much we may incline to regard causation as the *a posteriori* association of the members of a sequence we must admit that the causation involves the regularity, the fixed character of that sequence. The fact of regularity and the fact of efficiency are indistinguishable. The only quarrel is about the possibility of discovering *why* this sequence is such as it is; a certain type of philosophy treats the matter as if causes must inevitably have had such effects as they do have, as if the *rationale* of causation were clear. That is what Hume and his school wish to protest against; and they emphasize their protest by saying that only the fact of sequence leads us to perceive a causal relation, and not any insight into the necessity of that sequence. And on this point Lotze agrees with Hume; he protests also against a desire to discover the process of causation. And with his usual avoidance of Kantian attitudes, Lotze does not put the necessity of causation on a subjective and *a priori* basis; for such a basis makes the law abstract, and Lotze takes little interest in merely abstract and formal principles. He does not care to tell us that although only observation can show what effect follows what cause yet the nature of our minds makes it necessary for us to seek some causes for every event; indeed he denies the latter proposition altogether. Therefore he is on this point in full agreement with Hume. And considering this agreement we may be a little surprised at the summary way in which the phenomenalistic theory of causation is discussed. But it is dismissed so summarily because what removes Lotze from it is not an argument but a definition. In general we have seen that Lotze's nomenclature is much more metaphysical than his doctrines. In this place he likes to speak of efficient causation, and is impatient of a phenomenalistic statement of the matter; but in what does his objection consist? In the fact that the content of the various states, the nature of the successive events, must be taken into account in tracing causes; the process of the world does not let any event follow any other, but only a given event follow a given event; therefore, says Lotze, it is absurd to say that we have only succession for we have evidently causation and efficiency. The second event does not follow after the first but comes out of it. That is to say, events follow one another, and we have only sequence, when there is no law that unites them, no regularity in that sequence; but events follow out of one another, and we have efficient causality, when they are connected by a law, and the sequence is regular. Thus Lotze only apparently rejects Hume's doctrine; the difference is not one of meaning, but one of emphasis and method of approach. The regularity of sequence that Hume regarded as the objective condition of our idea of cause, Lotze regards as the meaning and real content of that idea; so that for Lotze the category of causality actually predicates of the world that uniformity which Hume assumed as an explanation of the presence of the category in our minds.

Lotze's rejection of Hume's theory depends on a failure to distinguish the two very different senses in which the nature or content of the antecedent may be said to involve and determine that of the consequent. In one sense the antecedent upon inspection, and prior to any association of it with the consequent, betrays what that consequent is fated to be. In this sense Lotze denies any determination of the effect quite as much as Hume does; only from the teleological point of view does he admit *a priori* insight into the direction of causation. But *a posteriori*, and by virtue of observed regularity in nature, the antecedent involves and determines the consequent even more surely for Hume than for Lotze. For of course it is the content, the nature, of the antecedent that is associated with the content or nature of the consequent; a law that said that anything whatever is regularly followed by anything else, would evidently apply to nothing. The laws that are observed among phenomena are observed to hold of *given* phenomena, of things of a given description and content. Abstracting from that content, no law could have any terms to associate. Yet only this necessity that the connection should be between the natures or contents of phenomena Lotze declares to be proof of efficient causation; and he seems to imply that something else is the meaning of phenomenal laws. Herein lies the confusion. It would be absurd to say that any event is the cause of any event, picked at random from all that occur in the following moment; but not because this event, once picked out, might not as well as any other be the *regular* consequent and therefore the effect of our given antecedent; but only because, before that regular sequence had been noted, there would be nothing to associate the antecedents with this particular consequent, rather than with any of the other events simultaneous with this consequent. When, attending to the character of events, we select those that habitually succeed one another, and name this habitual succession causality, we have in mind not abstract succession, but the actual and given succession of this antecedent and this consequent. Had the nature of these not been considered, their recurrence could not be known, since they could not be recognized. And the psychological basis of the idea of cause is not succession as such, but observed succession of the same experiences, whereby they form a whole in the mind, one element of which requires and calls up the other. This sense of the necessity with which one thing produces another is very easily awakened; a single striking coincidence is enough to give rise to the idea of necessary connection, as in superstitions. The events themselves are primarily the objects of attention; their connection is only dwelt upon for their sake and as a guide to our expectation. And therefore causation, even from the phenomenalistic point of view, is not independent of the characteristics of the antecedent and consequent, but consists in the association of these characteristics. This phenomenalistic theory is therefore not open to the objection Lotze brings against it, of neglecting the content or nature of the terms of the causal relation; and the difference between it and Lotze's own, apart from the question of final causes, is more apparent than real.

The doctrine of occasional causes is also discarded by Lotze, and he even tells us that it cannot rank as a metaphysical theory at all. For an occasion—and by occasion Lotze seems to understand opportunity—that cannot be turned to account is evidently no opportunity; but whenever the occasion is made use of, we have a case of efficient causation. The occasion must be "noticed" by the thing that is expected to improve it; and this susceptibility of the thing, this fact that it is aware of its opportunities, already implies that the thing is affected by that constellation of forces that was to be only the occasion, but not the cause, of change within it. But Lotze here seems to be arguing against figures of speech by means of figures of speech even more misleading. An occasion means of course a time, a juncture, not an opportunity. And the theory of occasional causes teaches that a certain change in one thing A is regularly the occasion (i.e. the point of time, the juncture of events) for a change to occur in another thing B. B is not supposed to "notice" anything in A; it is we who notice a coincidence of the changes in both. To say that such a coincidence is impossible cannot be Lotze's purpose; for he acknowledges that no reason can be assigned for the order of events in each being; nothing, therefore, prevents a appearing in A at the same time that β appears in B; and nothing prevents the repetition of this coincidence. If we are filled with wonder at such regularity in nature we may consider that things are wonderful or commonplace only by analogy, and that to wonder at the commonplace is inevitable when we scrutinize it so closely that it loses its familiar shape. Or if we desire to cultivate our admiration rather than to live it down, we may appeal, as Lotze himself does, and as Malebranche did even more emphatically, to the wisdom of the purpose that regulates and maintains the correspondences of things. In this appeal Lotze's insistence on something more than phenomenal causation finally loses itself; we may therefore wonder the more that he does not recognize the practical identity of his theory and that of occasional causes; in this case he cannot be repelled by the denial of final causes which gives a disheartening tone to Hume's doctrine. For after all, the difference between phenomenal and occasional causes lies not in the conceptions themselves, but in their authors and in the systems with which they are associated. What makes Lotze treat both theories as essentially contrary to his own is perhaps his determination to keep his monism for the end of his system, and to approach every question from the pluralistic point of view. And occasional causes involve a thoroughgoing monism, just as phenomenal causes also in their way involve the dissolution of particular things. Both theories make all facts equally primary, and deducible from nothing but the general and total nature of the world. And Lotze seeks a more discriminating principle; he wishes to maintain the distinction between antecedent and consequent within the same being— which he does not seek to connect by any mysterious causality— and antecedent and consequent in different beings, between which some strange principle must still mediate.

For this reason, we may assume, Lotze looks upon the doctrine of preestablished harmony with comparative favor, and recognizes its virtual identity with his own view. Leibnitz himself, we may remember, recognized the agreement between his theory and that of Malebranche; but Lotze treats the two very differently. The only serious fault he finds in preestablished harmony is the determinism it involves. He wishes the plan according to which the correspondences in things appear to be no fixed plan adopted in the beginning and controlling the entire development; he wishes the plan to grow with the work. But the efficiency for which Lotze has been contending is at this point finally explained as the efficiency of a final cause; the power that at each moment arranges the correspondences in things and is the instrument of interaction, is the sense, the meaning, of the world. But essential changes can take place in the world by virtue of a double possibility: first the plan that controls reactions and determines what changes in the various elements of the world shall respond to a given change in any one element, is itself not a fixed plan, but may be a law of development; this however would not make the theory different from that of Leibnitz. For Leibnitz too what was fixed in the beginning was not a construction, not a static correspondence of parts, but a law of development; each monad obeyed such a law, and the harmony of the changes in all was itself a changing harmony. Yet all was predetermined, since the law by which changes alone occurred was given in the beginning in each case. Lotze therefore introduces a second element of change, which involves a really new beginning, something not a development, not a mere unfolding of a given law, but an absolutely unexpected and unaccountable irruption into the order of nature. For that change in a given element the response to which in all other elements the law of the world determines, need not itself be such a response to that law. It may be a spontaneous change. And thus the sense of the world, the cosmic Providence, is properly a governing power; it directs the response to actions that it does not invariably call forth. All things are subject to it, but not in all their modifications. Some modifications may arise of themselves, without being called for by the cosmic plan; and it is in reply to these spontaneous changes that the readjustment of all other things takes place, so that in spite of the extraneous interference the harmony of the world may be preserved, and it may continue to work out its destiny. Instead of preestablished harmony Lotze therefore suggests an ever-reestablished harmony. We have not merely the progressive movement of Leibnitz' world, developing according to a plan which itself provides for ever-new combinations; we have also a recuperative movement, by which the ship is headed anew in the right direction after every gust and wave. The objective point, the sense of the world, remains the same throughout; but the course actually followed is not determined by it alone, since it does not wholly account for the state of things at any moment. The response to any given occurrence is indeed determined; the nature of the universal purpose dictates at every moment what direction the world shall take; but

at the next moment it may be necessary for that universal purpose to speak again, since the world may find itself aside from
the intended course. Providence thus has a constant and real
function: it has to react on the decrees of fate.

Lotze's conception, stated in the terms used by Leibnitz would
run somewhat as follows: In establishing harmony between
things, Providence did not consider a fixed number of them, and
arrange the correspondences of their developments *in infinitum*.
But it preestablished the harmony of these developments, to
the number of x, up to a certain point of time; then, however,
a new monad appeared, to whose development the x monads
must bear relation, so that the harmony now has to be reestab-
lished on the basis of x + 1 developments, instead of on the
former basis of x. In this way a number of readjustments would
take place in the course of the process, on the occasion of the introduction or annihilation of a monad. That this involves a serious change in Leibnitz' theory is evident; for the beauty of his
system lay precisely in the independence and indestructibility
of every monad. Leibnitz can escape monism, for every soul or
monad is just what it would be if it were a universe to itself;
God is just what he would be were there no creation, for he is
the central monad by virtue of the content of his life not by
virtue of his efficiency. And each imperfect monad is just what it
would be had it no creator and no fellow-beings. Leibnitz' system
is a solipsism of the individual soul, with a dogmatic faith in the
existence of other souls. This faith rests not on evidence, not on
any possible influence these other souls exercise, but solely on
the impulse, felt by that soul, to believe in the existence of others.
And in the case of the divine life, belief in it rests on the sense
of the value it would have did it exist, and on the deep-rooted
belief we have in the reality of our ideals. What esoteric and
mystical developments this doctrine might lead to we cannot
here discuss; but it is evidently different from Lotze's in this important point, that it starts where Lotze leaves off and studies
that problem that all monistic systems create, viz. how to get
multiplicity out of the unity. The entire world is packed by Leib-

nitz into each monad; he accepts that solipsism to which idealism condemns us. And he admits the real self we know, the personal self, to be the reality beyond which we cannot pass; while
post-Kantian idealists, with all their insistence on subjectivity
and projection from the given consciousness, swamp the given
consciousness in that merely projected. Lotze falls into the same
difficulties whenever he makes his monism prominent; but among
Lotze's difficulties I cannot see that a conflict between monism
and indeterminism is to be numbered, although such is the opinion of some critics. If we compare his system with that of Leibnitz
we shall rather see that monism is the price Lotze pays for his
indeterminism. For had he allowed the immanent law of each
monad to direct all its changes, as Leibnitz did, monism would
have been avoided, but by requiring the general plan to direct
anew at every point the motion of monads, this general plan
could no longer be treated as a *de facto* correspondence among
the necessary developments of the various things. The plan became efficient; it was not only a principle of being, a description
of the fundamental nature of the facts, but a principle of change,
a power. Accidental changes can occur in the monads; therefore
the harmony among them must be maintained by an external
agency. Had the changes been all predetermined in each monad,
the harmony might have remained a mere fact, a beauty that
things possessed, and that from the teleological point of view
might be regarded as their cause or justification, as their worth,
but need not have become a force constantly guiding and check-
ing them. Thus indeterminism, far from contradicting Lotze's
monism, makes the dynamical form of that monism necessary.
The plan of the world is simply declared not to involve or call
for all the changes that appear in the world; the plan or purpose only directs what changes shall ensue in order to maintain
order in the world after the unaccountable changes have occurred. There is no contradiction in this idea. And it is moreover
a very natural and attractive idea, one that has many analogies
and habits of thought in its favor. If we try to conceive a wise
and beneficent Providence governing the world, it is in these

terms that we shall naturally conceive it. The more current statements that make the principle that directs things the principle that produces them in their entirety, really denies the idea of government, of providence, of beneficent activity altogether. The plan and purpose of things then becomes identical with their nature; no efficiency, no progressive application can be thought of in regard to that plan; it is merely the description of the facts, the constitution of nature. Lotze's instinct and aesthetic susceptibility have led him here to avoid the rash enthusiasm of those theologians who so magnify their conceptions as to make them formless. A God that accomplishes literally everything no longer has a definite function in nature, he is no longer a power that makes for righteousness, and although we may continue to use his name, we shall use it in vain, and the world will with perfect justice call us atheists. This is notoriously the case with Spinoza; and all pantheism has the same tendency. Lotze may almost be said to have reintroduced the idea of God into philosophy, where the notion of a divine being had been replaced by an aspect of nature.

Lotze's indeterminism is not only a great support to religious feeling, but it is also perfectly consistent with that mechanical view of nature which he adopts. We have seen how the three principles of explanation are related to each other; the general laws determine the interactions of real things; these real things have no explanation but are themselves ultimate facts, and their appearance or disappearance, as well as their original distribution, is controlled by no law. It is a single and irreducible fact having no cause, and comparable to nothing else. But although the appearance of realities can be traced to no prior fact, to no law, yet if they appear, these realities are necessarily subject to a law that directs their further development, and directs it in such a way that it has a meaning; it resembles a melody, it has a significant and consistent history. This significance is not the cause of those laws and original data, but is their justification. Had there been no such meaning and worth in things we should have been at a loss to understand why the world exists at all. The existence of the world is therefore made conceivable and natural by the fact that it is so constructed as to produce happiness and have value—this is its meaning, its justification. This too is its unity; for the original data are independent and are contributed, so to speak, by the four winds of heaven, which blow where they list; but these data, on entering the cosmos, fall into that vortex of interaction which the cosmic purpose presides over. The contents of the world, wherever they may come from, are from moment to moment dissolved into one fluid mass, and reformed into such figures as the ever present ideal suggests. And the ideal employs a mechanical law as its instrument; so that a mechanical law directs at every moment the transformations of nature, although the matter to be transformed may be in part a new contribution from the void. Here and there Lotze seems to say that the cosmic purpose suggests and requires not only the effects of new elements and the figure they shall make in the world, but also involves their appearance when and where they so appear. This, however, would involve a teleological determinism inconsistent with Lotze's general principles. Such passages must be understood to mean that for the cosmic purpose to produce just the results it has produced up to a certain time, the contributions of fate must have been just what they were. So that in order that the world should conform to the ideal in just the way it does, rather than in some other way, the original data have to be what they were. Had they been different, the world, in order to produce the same values, would have had to move on different lines. The ideal, the purpose of the world, is for Lotze a real end, which does not determine its means necessarily, but only determines them in view of given conditions. Here again we see how moderation saves the ideal that an enthusiastic exaggeration destroys. If the purpose of the world required, not only that certain values should arise, but that they should arise in given ways; in other words, if what is valuable is the whole world indiscriminately, no distinction is possible any more between ends and means, between good and useful, between purpose and fact. Teleology becomes a merely subjective and

arbitrary method; everything is at once end and means for everything else. The attempt to make the world perfect has led to the
denial of the validity of the idea of good; all attribution of
value depends on the subjective interest that makes it arise.
All this Lotze avoids by regarding the valuable as limited not
necessarily in quantity, but in nature and quality; the valuable
is happiness; and as evidently happiness and reality are not
synonymous, as their distribution is not even and everywhere
alike, the actual reality is really separable from the value of the
world; nature can be treated as an instrument of good, and the
ideal retains its dignity and independence over against the fact.

In this way Lotze succeeds in giving that universal application but subordinate significance to mechanism which it was his
intention to give it. Everybody will admit in one form or another
that the primary facts of being, whether they be axioms of
thought, atoms of matter, or the nature of God, are inexplicable
and irreducible facts. The only sort of explanation we can find
for them is their value, now they are here. We cannot say: this
is the cause that brought the axioms, the atoms, or God into existence; we cannot see a reason why they were necessarily thus
and not otherwise. All we can do is to discover a value in their actual constitution and result, and say, they are very good. This
moral justification, this value of what we find to exist, is the
only source of rationality in things. The mere regularity of
events, the mere fact that things instead of happening only once
happen again and again in the same ways, does not explain the
world or make it rational. Only the fact that these repetitions,
these laws and given conditions, serve to bring about a worthy
and happy consummation, that they enable us to live, to enjoy,
and to produce and discover things of value in our eyes,—
this alone is an explanation and justification of being. This
alone satisfies our reason and makes us content to accept a given
and causeless dispensation. This is the sort of explanation that
only the belief in God, the discovery of the divine, can give to
the world; a merely causal explanation does not require anything but a series of causes, and even requires this series to be in-

finite; the causal explanation therefore really fails to explain anything. This is perhaps the thought that lies at the root of the cosmological proof. For it is not the principle of phenomenal causation that requires a first cause; on the contrary it excludes that idea, for it demands a cause for everything and therefore an infinite regress. But the consciousness that such a principle, because it never completes the explanation, leaves us at the end, where we were at the beginning, and is worthless as an organon of rational explanation—this consciousness is expressed by saying that the series of causes must owe its existence to a will. This will is a first cause not by being the last link of an infinite series, which is a contradiction in terms, but by being that fact or idea to which the infinity of the series itself compels us to pass, if we wish to explain the origin of the series and find a reason for its existence. It can only be explicable by satisfying a demand, an aspiration, an ideal. The purpose of the world, its value and function, alone explain its existence; a regress along an infinite series of causes, or arbitrary stopping at any member of that series, is no progress toward an explanation of things. Only the belief that what exists is valuable and ought to exist, that it comes because it is needed and called for by an ideal of which our own aspirations are elements, only such a belief reconciles us to the fact and justifies its existence. If this belief be false, the world is irrational, no matter how inevitably each of its parts may involve all the others. The principle of causality makes not its effects rational until the value of the effects makes rational the presence of the principle. The work of causal explanation is to reduce all successions of phenomena to fixed and familiar types; when this work has been accomplished our minds can survey nature, and we have that sense of mastery that comes with familiarity and ability to predict things even if their production is wholly independent of our wills. This constitutes a comprehension of what we find, of the content of the phenomenal world; it constitutes no explanation of its presence, of the reason why it is here and is what it is. This reason can be looked for only in will. If we find what we desire, what we are half consciously looking for, what our wills fain would produce, we cannot challenge its existence; it is justified in our eyes and before the deepest part of our nature; its absence, not its presence, would require explanation. For this reason, in spite of evidence and experience, optimism must always remain the spontaneous and orthodox faith of humanity; the suspicion of disloyalty and superficiality must always attach to pessimism. For no mysteries and contradictions can appear so fundamentally irrational as the contradiction between our deeper needs and the government of nature.

Lotze's indeterminism, then, is consistent with his monism and with his belief in universal mechanism, and it helps to save that reality of the good and of a purpose in nature which his monism would otherwise have destroyed. But in all this Lotze has only met the objections that indeterminism might suggest. The motive and grounds for belief in indeterminism remain to be considered. As contrasted with Leibnitz' system, Lotze's asserts monism and denies determinism, and I have said that this denial of determinism is what made that assertion of monism, in its dangerous dynamical form, necessary to Lotze's system. For it is indeterminism, the appearance of unaccountable changes in things, that turns the harmony between them into a principle of government and efficient control, instead of a mere principle of passive beauty, and a result of the original disposition of things. Now what Lotze wishes to gain by indeterminism is vitality. He does not wish to think that the process of things (and existence for him is essentially a process) is the mere consequence of a single act, of an original state of things. It is the danger, the doubt of what sort of a reality will appear, that gives it a moral value when it does appear; this moral value Lotze does not wish to confine to the original choice of things to appear as they did appear; he wishes to distribute this moral action throughout the cosmic process, to make it possible at every point that a new choice, a new and unaccountable fact, should repeat the original and miraculous choice of things to be as they are. He would say, for instance, that the whole number of atoms did not exist from all eternity, so that the entire virtue and yield of things was the inevitable result of their primeval condition. The goodness or badness of the world would in that case depend solely on the original disposition of parts; from the number and distribution of the atoms the entire series of bodies could be constructed *a priori* by virtue of universal laws. Such a supposition takes away from all parts of the development a share in the privilege of choosing rightly, a sense that in them too is realized the act that makes the reality ideal. If from the beginning all were determined, the development is inferior in rank to the original creation of things; the creation alone is a real choice, on it alone depends the form of all reality. The development is merely the fulfilling of that primeval choice. But for Lotze the material cause of the world is not given once and for all, but gradually. For a time the laws of nature rule over a mass of matter that remains unchanged; but now and then this mass varies, new citizens, so to speak, are born into the state, new atoms drop into the sphere of cosmic attractions; the laws remain the same, but the matter changes which the laws order and control. The virtue, therefore, which the reality shows in satisfying the ideal, the miracle of seeing that independent and inexplicable facts conspire to a happy consummation, is not a virtue or miracle found once for all and seen only in the whole of nature. It is a merit distributed among the parts of the whole, each of which by an independent and timely entrance upon the scene, contributes its share to the fulfilment of the general purpose. The creation did not take place wholly at the beginning, but occurs partly also in us. Our lives are in part new creations, not mere consequences of what went before, and that momentous responsibility that falls on the determining forces of the universe, is not confined to the eternal matter and laws of the world, but falls also on the events in its historical development.

No one, I think, will fail to admire the beauty of this conception of the life of nature, and the ingenuity with which it combines various convictions which we all retain, although philosophy has often found them to be contradictory. The reality of events, the truth of our natural belief that something happens in the world, that thought, the demiurgus, has not yet finished his work, but continues to hammer at matter and transform it into new and unexpected shapes, — this conviction is reconciled with the belief in universal mechanical laws. And the responsible and original decision by which things are what they are is distributed throughout nature and not confined to the adoption in the beginning of a tyrannical constitution, which allows no activity in the world besides that which it itself directs. If the formulation of doctrines that appeal to mankind, if the explaining to men what they really believe and are trying to say of the world, be the task of philosophy, Lotze in this instance would seem to have admirably fulfilled it. If his doctrine were not so subtle, if it did not require such care and moderation in the combination of its elements, one would be tempted to predict that it would some day become the received and orthodox doctrine of the world. But whatever may be its fate, its merit is unquestionable. As a formulation of the life of nature monism, tempered by indeterminism and moralized by an efficient teleology, leaves little to be desired. The purpose in the world is the production of happiness; by this doctrine we escape a formalism that sees purpose and excellence in mere order, without reference to the realities that this order produces or their intrinsic worth. And this purpose in the world is not accomplished by magic and irresistibly, as if by the *fiat* of the Creator; it is accomplished laboriously on a foreign material, furnished at incalculable times and places. Thus the work of teleology is real work; it impresses an order on things which are not themselves produced *ad hoc*. This is one of the most subtle and beautiful parts of Lotze's conception; we must distinguish the sense in which the elements of being come of themselves, without reference to the purpose of the world, from the sense in which, at the moment of being taken up into the world and by virtue of belonging to the cosmos, they become subject to that purpose. It is the purpose that makes the unity of the world, the heat that keeps it fluid and reforms it at every moment; the contributions that the world receives from without are at once merged with it, and become a portion of its living mass. The life of nature thus is a real life, because it has something on which to feed, something corresponding to an environment. This quasi-environment is not of course an external agent; but the unaccountable incidents in the life of nature, being inexplicable by its own laws and condition, are practically equivalent to the interference of an external agent. Nature thus has a life; an internal principle and aspiration, which is its purpose, playing with phenomena which enter its life but are not products of its principle nor necessarily favorable to its aspiration. It is exactly in this way that our own life moves; the person has a certain will, a certain store of accumulated experience and digested knowledge, with certain habits and maxims which constitute the personal character; but these do not run out of themselves into a self-determined development; they are subjected to varying conditions, and the life of the man consists in his reactions, the reactions of his character, on what is external to him and not a product of his activity. And yet, in one sense, these foreign elements cannot affect the man until they enter his consciousness, until they are effects *in him;* were they not parts of his life they might as well not have existed as far as he is concerned. So also in Lotze's conception of the cosmic life. There are events that the principles of the world do not account for, and reaction on them constitutes the activity of nature and the task of Providence; yet these events exist only as events in nature, only as modifications of the one cosmic organism. Monism is therefore by no means sacrificed or forgotten in order to establish the vitality of nature; a vitality which, as I have said, indeterminism is introduced to secure.

In admiring this system, however, we must not exaggerate the value of the solution it offers and imagine that it is the only solution that combines desirable qualities. It stands alone, or nearly alone, as a satisfactory formulation of the cosmic life; but neither the indeterminism nor the monism which it reconciles are without difficulties of their own. And if the indeter-

minism seems to do so much for us in this system it is only because the dynamical monism has threatened us with all sorts of
dangers. It has in fact introduced an efficient law, a metaphysical
force that dissolves the universe at every instant, annihilating
everything, and creating it anew. Thus Lotze conceives the soul,
that "substance," as we have been persuaded to call it, as annihilated during unconsciousness, deep sleep, or even between
ordinary pulses of feeling, while the "sense of the world" produces anew detached states of consciousness when they are required by its own interests; and any set of these detached states
is known to belong to one "soul" only because of certain internal harmonies and similarities between them. The unreality
of all individual things is thus established in its most extreme
and objectionable form; what individuality, what distinction
of persons and principles can there be in a world where everything is created afresh at every moment according to the requirements of a single metaphysical principle? It is a monism of this
kind that destroys all moral independence in things, and makes
indeterminism necessary if we are to rescue anything from absolute slavery to the cosmic power. But if we had avoided monism,
or admitted only a monism of description, a *de facto* harmony
in things and a conformity on their part to phenomenal, not to
efficient, law,—then we might have secured an entire independence in things and not needed the partial and exceptional independence obtained by determinism. For individual things
would not have become mere modes of a real metaphysical being,
that supported them a moment and thus destroyed them, for
reasons all its own; but they would remain the true and primary
reality, and by being what they individually are they would
make the whole and its laws what it is. If we are not momentary
creations of a metaphysical power, but component parts of a
fraternal nature that exists as we exist, and can give no better
account of its being than we can of ours, then we share with all
nature that primary, that absolute existence that makes us responsible for being or not being conformable to the ideal. That

imagined primitive choice or fatality whence all things flow by an efficient law is now seen to be wholly unreal; there is no first fact; every part of nature is equally primitive and shares equally in that metaphysical choice by which things are as they are. No fact is prior to any other fact, and all facts are prior to the laws that express the order of their appearance. And so the analogy that may exist between my conduct and that of other men in no way takes anything from my responsibility, or from the direct and absolute relation I bear to the ideal. For it would be a curious thing indeed if I were guilty of doing wrong only if no one else ever did wrong in the same manner. Another man in my place would do as I do, but only because he would be me. If I, a constituent part of nature, fail to be as I should be, am I excused if nature has many such parts? Surely, I am not better because nature is so much worse. A man whose standard of right is not convention will not think a fault innocent because it is repeated, or a good thing worthless because it is universal. If evil consequences make evil conduct, the more such conduct the more evidence of its guilt. It is not then, the moral significance of things that requires indeterminism; such a notion can arise only if we regard laws and relations as powers that create the realities that in truth they only describe. The discovery of the uniformity of nature may affect our moral judgments in some respects, but it can never invalidate them. Good and evil do not perish because we discover their distribution, nor do moral acts lose their nature because we observe their occasions. The apprehension that they may do so betrays the extraordinary willingness we have to believe that our theory about things changes the things themselves. It can evidently change only our manner of approaching those things, or way of regarding them. And if the moral values of the world were created by a theory of how things arise, things in themselves morally indifferent, then a new theory of things might destroy values. But moral values are feelings and emotions, prior to all theories and unchangeable by them. In so far as these primary feelings are associated with their causes or concomitants, the latter become capable also of arousing those feelings; it is in this direction only that a belief in the uniformity of nature can modify our moral consciousness. In so far as the experience on which such a belief rests multiplies the associations of things it will tend to diffuse the emotion produced by each over all the others. And if the good and evil in nature appear to be woven together inextricably, we shall tend to check ourselves both in praise and blame by recollection of the opposite quality. But this amounts only to saying that the reflective habit of mind (and consideration of the uniformities of nature is an exercise of that habit) is opposed to an impulsive temperament. Much theorizing may dull the vivacity of our moral judgments. But this effect is psychological and personal; the source of moral inspiration and the reality of moral values is deep in nature, and far beyond the attack of both science and philosophy. Even a dynamical monism does not destroy at all the moral value of the world; only it alters our moral tone by bringing us face to face with a single being instead of a multiplicity of things. Our moral emotion therefore takes the form of mystical exaltation; the good, the evil, the lovable, the terrible are all attributes of a single overwhelming and incomprehensible being. Moral values are indeed withdrawn from individual things, but only in the measure in which these are themselves withdrawn from consciousness. And a change in the same direction is affected even by the doctrine of uniformity; laws and abstractions tend to replace in consciousness individual facts and examples; and the moral sense naturally follows these changed objects. It is noticeable that with meditation upon the laws of nature comes the tendency to judge nature as a moral being; optimism and pessimism are expressions of the moral sense when the object clearly before it is not an individual act but the type and law of action in the world. And therefore Lotze's indeterminism, by admitting facts and events not subject to law at all, tends to individualize our moral judgments; each of these new beginnings has an independent value of its own. But this slight advantage is greatly overweighed by the amalgamating and confusing effect which his dynamical monism produces in the same field; for evidently the moral independence of the adventitious acts is swallowed up in the moral tyranny and monotony of the single purpose that at every moment dissolves and recasts the world.

[V]

Personality of God—Aesthetics—Optimism

W E HAVE SEEN that Lotze conceives the life of nature on the analogy of a personal life; it will be easy for him therefore to regard this cosmic life as that of a divine person, that of God. At the same time, if the cosmic process is a personal divine life, our lives and the events in them would seem to belong to two personalities, and the status of the soul, of the human individuality becomes very uncertain. To avoid confusion on this subject it may be well to consider what various meanings the word "unity" may have, and in what sense smaller wholes may exist within a larger whole, without becoming independent and self-existent realities.

The first and most absolute kind of unity is the unity of consciousness, the unity of the present moment. This is a real unity, because there is nothing given that is not given within it, involved and enclosed in it. We never can have the world present to us in any shape except in an actual thought and feeling; whatever sense of past and future, of unknown, imminent realities brooding about us, we may have,—this sense is also an element of the momentary feeling; and the whole complexity of nature can never be revealed to us and impress us unless it is revealed to us at some one time, in one moment of consciousness which contains the image and impression of that complexity. The unity of objects presented in consciousness is relative to the total content of that consciousness; a single object is single because it stands out as a striking and homogeneous part of the total vision before us. The unity of objects is therefore relative, and for that reason so evident and intelligible; a star has such clear unity and individuality because it occupies but one point in space, and has such fixed and measurable relations to the other occupied points in the heavens. But the unity of consciousness is so obscure and so easily overlooked because it is absolute. Only out of its own funds can we draw any object with which to contrast it. The other moments of consciousness can never appear except as representations in the given moment. The actual, then, is always a perfect unity; the represented, as such, is necessarily a part of an actual consciousness, while as an independent thing it is an entirely separate being, and does not enter consciousness at all. This is really evident and tautological; whatever comes together in an impression and exists at once *is* one impression and a perfect whole. Here, be it said by the way, lies the objection to Hume's impressions as the original factors of consciousness: that consciousness is never anything but an "impression" and that the world is never given except as the content of a single "impression." So that although Hume's theory may be right as an account of the origin and antecedents of our moments of consciousness, it by no means meets the problem how we, who are always at one of these moments, can get out of them our knowledge of the world.—In the unity of consciousness, in the unity of the impression, we have then the first and absolute sort of unity.

A second kind appears in life, or personal history, which is projected from the single moments of consciousness. There is no actual unity between the successive states of the soul; but in the bosom of each state is a complex of memories, perceptions, feelings, intentions, and conscious directions of development, all given as a cross-section or fragment of life. But between one of these cross-sections and the next there is no *given* unity; there is only a speculative represented unity. But since this unity of form is represented within one of the states that it connects theoretically, it differs from a merely objective and speculative unity. Our life is not a mere ideal object contained in a moment of consciousness; it is a projection from that moment, which regards itself as a member of the series it considers. A third person would regard the unity of my life as theoretical merely; it would consist in the law that described the resemblances and sequences of its various states. Such is the unity of mere objects— the third kind of unity we shall consider. But my life, looked at from the inside, is a projected, a self-conscious unity, and not a mere law describing separate things. The difference lies in the fact that one of the things connected by the law is in my case not a mere object, not a presentation, but a living act, viz. my whole present consciousness itself. The other members of the series are indeed only represented things; but in putting them on a par with the living reality, I postulate more than the unity of mere objects. In the unity among phenomena the relation does not obtain between what is actual and what is represented, as in projected unity; it obtains wholly within the representation. This third sort is the unity of an ideal—the unity of treatment or conception.

Now which is the kind of unity that Lotze attributes to the world? What is the sense of his monism? He is not perfectly clear and unequivocal in this respect, and we run some risk of misrepresenting his doctrine if we insist on making it definite. We are accustomed to two types of monism, the materialistic and the mystical, and Lotze's is not identical with either. The materialists conceive the unity of the world to be a theory; the contemplation of the world shows it to be one in the sense that it obeys one law. The Idea of Hegel, in so far as it is a mere form, admits of this materialistic interpretation. The unity of the world then becomes a theoretical one, one of treatment, and in such a monism there is of course no contradiction to the fact of individual conscious unities. Our successive states are admitted to hold all our knowledge, and to be connected only as ordinary phenomena are connected by an external observer. The other type of monism is mystical; it feels that the unity of things is by no means a mere theory, which can indeed connect ideas and representations in the mind, but leaves the external realities wholly unconnected. The world must have the absolute and real unity of a moment of consciousness, of a single act of thought. And this absolute monism is not inconsistent with the existence of ideal unities under it; just as our single moments of thought include a great variety of feelings and ideas, so a universal thought, being actually and absolutely one act, might yet include everything we conceive of. All objects can without difficulty be supposed to be objects for a single moment of thought, since after all the richest conception we can possibly have of things is in our case the content of such a moment. But by no possibility can a real unity, the unity of a moment of consciousness, be taken up into another unity of the same kind. The content of our lives may reappear; but the fact that it will reappear in different relations, as an element in a wider consciousness, shows that the moment of consciousness in which it may reappear is not our moment of consciousness. Each impression, each living act, stands on its own feet and is essentially self-existent and self-contained, simply because it is self-conscious. If therefore we are to save this absolute monism from absurdity, and from denial of the reality of the only thing we know to be real, namely our actual consciousness in its actual form,—we must do what the mystics have done in practice, if not in theory. They have regarded the universal thought as eternal, and of infinite content, and therefore as divine and perfect. And our thoughts they have regarded as feeble attempts to reproduce that divine perfection. This momentum of our thoughts toward the infinite furnishes the real bond between the two; on it hang all the religious and aesthetic applications of pantheism. There can be no sense in saying that our thoughts *are* at the same time the thoughts of the infinite; but there is much meaning in saying that they tend to become thoughts of the infinite, that they are unhappy in their limitation. This infinite is thus in a manner represented within our thoughts, and appears as a goal, as an ideal for our thinking. And so a unity of projection is established between our thought and the cosmic thought; we regard our lives as stages of an expansion of which the universal life is the limit. Hence the mysticism of this view. It regards the unity of the world as actual and living, thereby excluding from it our own states of consciousness; but these are again linked to the objective reality by aspiration. The infinite appears in the finite as an immanent ideal. As the infinite includes a representation of all things and therefore of our lives, so our lives include a vague and symbolic representation of the infinite as a goal of aspiration. But only by a sharp distinction between these representations and the realities they represent can this whole mystical form of monism be rescued from the fate that sometimes overtakes it of degenerating into a riot of contradictions.

By contrast with these two types of monism, Lotze's can more easily be defined. His own method is often to put together his theories by successive modifications of those of other philosophers; and this is the method best adapted to so many-sided a system as Lotze's.—The unity of Lotze's world as a process in time resembles the unity found in materialistic monism. He insists that motion, change, is essential to the cosmos no less than to individual things; the unity of a thing we learned long ago lies in the law of its variations. And this is precisely the descriptive and theoretic unity that materialistic monism discovers. The world remains one world then by virtue of the one law that describes its successive states. But at the same time Lotze modifies this view in two respects: first he protests against the habit of seeing the value of things in their law instead of in the realities this law connects; and secondly he admits another and more intimate unity of things from moment to moment. Much as a man's life is one because of the law that runs through it, because of his character, and at the same time his consciousness at each moment is one for another reason and in a much more real sense; so the cosmic life for Lotze is a historical unity in its total extension, but is a real and absolute unity at each moment or pulse of its existence. The only difference between this view of the historical unity of the world and materialistic monism, lies in the greater prominence given by Lotze to the consciousness of unity in some of the stages of that history. The existence and personality of God seem to signify that throughout the cosmic life the representation of its total law is consciously present. A man has self-consciousness and personality in proportion as he is aware of his own character and principles, and in his thought and conduct consciously exemplifies them. So in the cosmic life Lotze supposes a continuous consciousness of its own law and a continual direction of action in conformity with it; and this self-consciousness and personality in the world give its theoretic unity the added note of a projected and personal unity. Yet in materialistic monism too there is some projection of the law, and some action in conscious conformity to it. The philosopher, namely, is aware of the character of the law of nature, and seeks to live and guide things in conformity to it. To be sure this is a very small amount of self-consciousness for the world to attain; Lotze in his personal God suggests an immortal philosopher to whom the law of things is fully and uninterruptedly present. But the difference, although great, is one of degree only. Not every part of nature is self-conscious; not every part is aware of its guiding principle and of the guiding principle of the whole. There is a great deal more life in the world than the life of God, if by his life is meant that which is aware of its own divinity. This I fancy no one will venture to deny. But it is possible to say that experience is naturally ascribed to a person, even if at the time he is not conscious of himself as a person. This self-consciousness and personality are matters of degree; they may drop out entirely and yet the feelings that they do not accompany are attributed afterwards to the person. For the cosmic life to be personal, then, it is not requisite that consciousness of its personality and nature should be present throughout that life. The cosmic soul may have its dreams, its incoherent impressions, its moments of absorption in particular objects. For it to be a person it is sufficient that at some points of its existence it should attain self-consciousness and knowledge of itself, and that from these points it should survey and appropriate the surrounding experience as its own, by recognizing it as subject to the same law as itself. Just in this way do we appropriate our dreams and scattered impressions, and call them our own. In saying that all experience is

God's experience and that God is a person we do not contradict ourselves; for all experience need not be consciously his. Lotze, by admitting change and progression in the divine life, and in making it, as it were, animal life, avoids the contradiction that so constantly threatens a religious monism. He leaves room for our experience, and makes it possible to say that it belongs to the divine life, because the divine consciousness is diffuse and changeful, admitting ignorance, illusion, and limitations of all sorts within itself. And at the same time, with an ingenuity that cannot be too much admired, Lotze knows how to endow this animal divinity with all those attributes that most engage veneration and worship. We have seen how real providence is in Lotze's world; and this providence is exercised of course by the self-conscious moments of the cosmic life. The character of a man is not lowered at all because he has seasons of sleep and relaxation when his thoughts are dissipated and he is not conscious of himself; for the perfection of character we only require that the conduct should be guided by it, and that it should consciously assert itself at the proper times. So at every pulsation of being the cosmos, as it were, recollects itself and takes a step in obedience to its knowledge of its nature; but between these moments of recollection it breaks into innumerable atoms of greater or lesser inward complexity, each a moment of finite consciousness. And when we remember that spontaneous variations may also appear in any of these finite things, variations which in the next act of the cosmos will be taken into account and reacted upon— when we consider all these elements so skilfully combined we cannot too much admire the artistic power of this philosopher. In speculations of this sort we are too far away from concrete facts to think of positive proof or disproof; the only standards by which a system can be judged are its internal consistency and its harmony with our natural and ideal conception of things. And on both these grounds Lotze's system deserves the highest praise.

We see, then, what the objects so often spoken of by Lotze— the individual thing, the soul, the unity of the world—turn out to be in his system. They are laws, schemes of relations, realized by the successive realization (in conscious states) of the elements described by the laws. Their unity but for one circumstance would be only a unity of description, a unity existing only in the mind of an observer. The successive states would possess no unity of themselves; but images of these states existing together in the thought of a third person, would by this person be seen to belong together and to fulfil a law of succession and development. The one circumstance, however, that rescues Lotze's conceptions from reducing to this rather disappointing form, is the circumstance that these related states are themselves conscious; and since they are conscious they may contain within themselves the representation of the law that connects them with the antecedent and consequent states. So that the third person, in whose thought alone the law could exist, can now be dispensed with; the law may exist in the thoughts which it itself relates. The unity of a thing, of the soul, and of the universe, thus becomes a projected unity, the unity of the life that at each moment is or may be aware of its own law and direction. Personality, or that unity which consists in consciousness of one's own character and powers, is therefore for Lotze the type of real unity; this is what makes the units out of which the universe is composed, and makes also the unity of the universe as a self-existent being.

As a further illustration of the sense and working of Lotze's system we may briefly consider his aesthetic theories. These early occupied his mind, and probably had a very great influence on his whole development. They show the point of view from which Lotze regarded the more speculative part of philosophy; they show what he looked for and what he saw in nature.

Beauty is for Lotze the consciousness of the reconciliation and harmony between the three powers of the world—the primitive facts, the law of interaction, and the purpose this law subserves. In abstract and speculative thinking these stand as essentially independent. The facts are there for no cause; they might have been otherwise. So it is also with the laws that as a matter of fact prescribe the effects which the presence of any fact must have in the world. And the purpose is again an independent item. For there might conceivably be a world of facts and laws which had no value in it; the laws might be there as it were for their own sake, as actual ways in which things drifted, not as methods by which out of the given facts an ideal and desirable state should be evolved. Lotze severely censures Hegel, as we have seen, for the reverence he showed to law as such, without reference to the intrinsic value of the states related by that law; the law and the purpose would in such a system become indistinguishable, but only because the good purposed is no longer really a good. Lotze's method of showing the essential unity of the law and the purpose—for he believes in that unity, being an optimist,— is to appeal to aesthetic emotion. There we become aware by an intimate and powerful conviction that the laws of nature do produce values; and not accidentally, for the value here lies evidently in a certain harmony, in a certain symmetry and naturalness of parts. The working of the law thus in itself seems to involve the creation of value; this is the union that we wished to find between the two. And Lotze is careful to observe (See *Ueber den Begriff der Schönheit, in initio.*) that this value resides in consciousness. At first men's sense for beauty in nature carried with it a belief in her own satisfaction in her works. They acquired this sense in exercising their plastic instinct. We do not discover beauty until we ourselves recognise in our works the fulfilment of our intention. This artistic satisfaction, this joy at the really inexplicable correspondence between our work and our ideal, we transfer to nature; we read into natural objects the same quality of embodying a thought and ideal that some of our productions possess. Lotze regards the sense of beauty as at once an emotion of pleasure in us and a belief in the objective value of what gives us this pleasure; what distinguishes aesthetic emotion is its interpretative nature. It is as it were a mythological instinct that discovers to us the life and passion of natural things. To find beauty is *pro tanto* to believe in the ideality of nature; beauty is the sense that nature has succeeded in her task, has subdued her materials and that her purpose has been accomplished. And this sense, if we trust it, becomes the pledge of the real harmony of law and purpose in the world, and of the subjection of the original facts to both.

But in the subservience of the original facts we have a great difficulty. I have not been able to satisfy myself on the point whether Lotze intended to say that in the mysterious unity that beauty discovers to us the original fact and new beginnings were also included as integral elements. If the value of the world—a value of which beauty is for us the clearest expression—demands all the facts and new beginnings just where they actually appear, we have a teleological determinism that breaks up Lotze's system altogether. We should then be plunged into a pantheism toward which all the vague mistrust that word suggests would in reality be justly felt. We should have a positive belief that the world realized an ideal, and that this ideal determined every detail in the universe, so that the omission or correction of the least apparent imperfection in it would in reality destroy its value and run counter to its principle. All our ideals, in so far as they actually condemned accomplished facts, would therefore not be merely partial and human, but they would be impious. The true value and perfection of the world would require that nothing should be realized but what is realized. The impiety of willing against God would indeed remain necessary to God's own plan, and therefore in one sense innocent and proper, wherever it was actual. But this circumstance only shows how completely such a doctrine dissolves all our standards; even the excellence of being on the right side, of serving the general good, is lost by being necessarily and evenly shared by every existent thing. And this justification of everything, were it actually intended by Lotze, would in his system be much more objectionable than in Spinoza's, where it undoubtedly occurs. For Spinoza has no God, properly so called; the world is not moral, and prescribes no particular form of being rather than another to itself; it is on the contrary absolutely infinite, and requires that every possible thing, an infinity of absolutely infinite spheres of being, should coexist. This monstrous universe rejects nothing; but it condemns nothing, and therefore, being non-moral, does not give the lie to our own moral standards, although it is indifferent to them. Nature for Spinoza produces without criticism what she must produce, and actually produces all imaginable things. Our standards of what ought to be are indeed relative to our nature and needs, but we have a perfect right to treat them as absolute, since there is no other nature or needs with higher authority or prior claims. In the moral world our standards hold universally, and any crime against them cannot appeal for justification to a standard and purpose above our own. There is no such purpose. Nature has no plan, it attributes no worth to anything; as Spinoza puts it, God cannot love any man. Spinoza's system is grim, oppressive, overwhelming; but it is not positively immoral. Its severity has elemental grandeur; it abstracts from human desire. But if we believe with Lotze in the personality of the cosmic life, in the conscious intention and providence that guides the course of things in particular channels, and at the same time if we declare that everything is justified by the cosmic plan, we establish a moral being hostile to our morality, a God indifferent to human suffering, nay, delighting in it. For we have abolished the distinction between ends and means; the sanction of providence has been extended equally and primarily over everything in nature. No moral relations are possible between God and man; the only reconciliation lies in the annihilation of man's volition, wherever it does more than rejoice in the accomplished facts simply because they are accomplished.

Such a system cannot, however, be really attributed to Lotze; I have only mentioned it to show how dangerous it would be so to interpret any of his sayings as to lead us in that direction. Lotze does not and cannot believe that the three principles of explanation are identical; he only means that they all contribute to the same result. Thus the facts of nature being what they are, the purpose of nature can also be satisfied. Not, however, as if the facts had been devised and created by the purpose; in that case no purpose, no process of gradual adaptation and idealization would be possible. What beauty discovers to us is that the idea works with the matter and through the laws; the latter conspire to realize the ideal. But this is once for all the fact: it is an accident, as Lotze himself tells us (*Ueber den Begriff der Schönheit.* § III. Cf. *Grundzüge der Aesthetik.* Chapter I) ; although, to be sure, only in the sense in which the world itself is an accident, owing to the absence of any law to determine what it must be. But the ideal does not demand this particular method of realization; it might have been realized more quickly and better had the given facts been more favorable. The unity of the three powers is in their work, not in their nature and origin. They may reduce to one process, but not to one principle. And the source and object of aesthetic emotion, like that of all value in things, is not the indiscriminate presence of them all; it is a certain process in them, a certain harmony and rhythm of their life. And in relation to this we need only to recall the sense in which life itself and personality are attributed by Lotze to the cosmos; the world is one person, but by virtue of the projection of a law or character from some only of its parts. The personality does not reside equally in every part; the consciousness of self is not coupled with every act of consciousness. So also the value. Beauty belongs to the whole world, as a process having a meaning and embodying an idea; but only at times is this beauty apparent, and it becomes perfect only from the vantage ground of the cosmic consciousness itself. Thus is admitted the fact that beauty is for us a rare exception in nature; of all the objects about us few are aesthetically interesting, few awaken the feeling that they express and embody an idea spontaneously. But another thing is admitted, that it is easier not to admit. The whole of nature, although it does spontaneously embody an idea and is by the cosmic consciousness felt to be beautiful, does not require all its actual parts in order to be beautiful; the parts, once there, have to be incorporated in the work, and the total beauty in this sense adopts and uses all the materials of the world. But it does not require them. It might have appeared differently and better had the materials been more fit. Thus the excellence of this world, in order to be just this sort of excellence, does require precisely this set of forces and events; that is obvious enough. But different forces might have yielded better excellence. Lotze is an optimist by temper; he feels that all things conspire to a common end, and that we should willingly cooperate and be thankful. But he does not attempt to defend that theoretical optimism that calls this the best of possible worlds. It is justified now it is real by the values it contains; but these values are not unalloyed, and Providence might have had an easier task had Fate been more propitious.

The seat of the value of the world is consciousness, but of course not exclusively human consciousness. Those moments that contain the sense of things, the consciousness of the cosmic law,—those in fact that contain the personality of the cosmic life—contain also its value, and the happiness to which it gives rise. To us the divine life is revealed in beauty, in our own seasons of happiness, and in our faith in the deep roots that good has in nature. Our consciousness, however, constitutes but an echo of that consciousness in which the purpose of the world is realized; the goal of things is the happiness of God, although our happiness may to a certain extent be generously involved in it. It is an error to imagine that unless Providence works for our own highest good, and gives us all that we can well desire, then there is no God, no divine benevolence, no possible worship. This is an exaggeration of pious egoism. The divine life as Lotze conceives it and as paganism represented it, may be its own purpose, it may feel no obligation to bestow on men the greatest possible blessings, and yet it may be benevolent within limits, and regally kind:

> Denn die Unsterblichen lieben der Menschen
> Weit verbreitete gute Geschlechter,
> Und sie fristen das flüchtige Leben
> Gerne dem Sterblichen, wollen ihm gerne

Ihres eigenen, ewigen Himmels
Mitgeniessendes fröhliches Anschaun
Eine Weile gönnen und lassen.*

(Goethe, *Iphigenie auf Tauris*,
1. Aufzug, 4. Auftritt)

It is not for a realist, for one who takes this world of stars and of history for an adequate symbol of the deepest reality, to speak of the aims of the universe as identical with human aims. They must be something quite beyond our imagination; as the heavens are higher than the earth, so must nature's life be higher than our life. Only a philosophy that regards the phenomenal world as merely subjective, and allows the needs and moral impulses of man to supply the clue to the nature of the unknown and unpresentable reality, only such a phenomenalistic philosophy can expect to put God and man into close moral relations. But a naturalism like Lotze's allows only a divinity that grants to men what their life actually supplies; although it does not wholly exclude the hope of immortality. As Hercules for his virtue or Ganymede for his beauty were admitted to the company of the gods, so may any man live again in another sphere if the sense of the world, if the happiness of God, require and allow it. Anything so valuable in the eyes of the universal purpose as to deserve more than an ephemeral existence will be maintained in being. In this problematic immortality, as in much else, a striking analogy appears between Lotze's world and that of the ancients. Its religious value is not on that account small; for the religion of the pagans was a real religion, and the only sort that is possible if we admit the reality of nature such as she appears to us. All other religions have seen in nature an illusion, a temporary setting for lives that in truth belonged to a different

---

* For Immortals love the wide-spread
Worthy race of men
And long delay the flying life
For mortals and gladly wish
To grant and give a while
Of their own eternal Heaven's
Vision of gay society.

world. But if we abandon supernaturalistic conceptions we cannot establish other relations between God and man than those that experience suggests; we may trace to God the strength of the strong and the defeat of the defeated; we cannot see in him the refuge of those to whom this life is empty of great good. The spirit of this system is the ancient spirit of contentment, restraint, and silence. Religion is the sanction, not the reversal, of the judgments of the world.

No theology could more fitly crown the edifice of Lotze's thought. Throughout we see the same moderation, balance, and measured distribution of functions among various principles and instincts. Throughout is the same subtlety, fineness of perception, and modesty of judgment. If any great inherent defect can be found in this philosophy it may lie in its complexity; the equilibrium it establishes is after all not stable. Most minds need to follow more unreservedly some current of opinion; they require the support of some universal principle, of some simple and vivid conception, to give them the assurance that they possess the truth. Lotze's system of checks, of concessions, and limitations, is more fitted to serve as a check to other systems, and to obtain concessions from them, than to become itself the chief stone of the corner. Yet where men's minds are unsettled, and new principles assert themselves together with old, and no one clearly sees how far the two are compatible,—at such a time a system like Lotze's is most useful as a resting place, as a neutral spot where rival pretenders may parley, compare their claims, and attempt a reconciliation. In this way a mechanical view of nature and a moral and aesthetic conception of life meet in Lotze's philosophy; if he does not conclude a peace at least he furnishes a basis for negotiation. We need to have the various interests involved in this conflict present to our minds. The leaders of opinion in our time are too apt to simplify their problems; they propose solutions that might be accepted by beings with half our passions, half our interests, and half our ideas. Philosophy should be a social product; it should coordinate and interpret all those impressions that life makes upon mortals, and be as it were the soliloquy of man. And in such a soliloquy his instincts, his primitive convictions, his aspirations, must find expression no less than his passing thoughts and recent experience. It is Lotze's merit to have given a more human significance to philosophy, to have talked about the world we live in, rather than about some other more intelligible indeed, but not so real. Lotze takes all things into consideration, and by this single quality, quite apart from his solutions, he deserves our gratitude. Those who wish to be entertained by a new theory of the universe, or who insist on the discovery of new truths, may be disappointed in Lotze; he makes too many distinctions and too many reservations. But those who look to philosophy for the gradual clarification of our inevitable thoughts, for the cultivation and organization of perennial ideas, will find in him a stout champion, of whom they may say: Unus homo nobis cunctando restituit rem. [By delaying, one man restored our state to us.]

I. Note

Rudolf Hermann Lotze was born at Bautzen on the 21st of May, 1817. Soon after, his father, who was a doctor in the army, was removed to Zittau, and there Lotze attended the Gymnasium. He entered the University of Leipzig in 1834, where in 1838 he took the degrees of doctor of philosophy and doctor of medicine. The next year he was admitted to teach in both these faculties; in 1842 he was appointed professor of philosophy at Göttingen; there he remained until the spring of 1881, when he accepted the chair of philosophy at Berlin. He died, however, in the summer of the same year, on July 1st.

II. Titles and Dates of Lotze's Works.

1. *De futurae biologiae principiis philosophicis.* Dissertation for the medical degree, 1838.
2. *De summis continuorum.* Thesis, 1840.
3. *Gedichte.* 1840.
4. *Bemerkungen über den Begriff des Raumes.* 1841.
5. *Metaphysik.* 1841.
6. *Allgemeine Pathologie und Therapie als mechanische Naturwissenschaft.* 1842.
7. *Logik.* 1843.

8. "Herbart's Ontologie." *Zeitschrift für Philosophie und speculative Theologie.* 1843.
9. "Leben, Lebenskraft." *Wagner's Handwörterbuch der Physiologie.* 1843.
10. "Instinct." Ibidem. 1844.
11. "Seele und Seelenleben." Ibid. 1846.
12. *Ueber den Begriff der Schönheit.* 1845.
13. *Ueber Bedingungen der Kunstschönheit.* 1847.
14. *Allgemeine Physiologie des körperlichen Lebens.* 1851.
15. *Medicinische Psychologie, oder Physiologie der Seele.* 1852.
16. *Quaestiones Lucretianae.* "Philologus." 1852.
17. "Psychologische Untersuchungen." *Zeitschrift fur Phil. u. phil. Kritik.* 1853.
18. *Microcosmus.* 1856–64.
19. *Streitschriften.* 1857.
20. *Antigona Sophoclis fabula.* Latinis numeris reddidit Hermannus Lotze. 1857.
21. *Geschichte der Aesthetik in Deutschland.* 1868.
22. *System der Philosophie. Logik* 1874. *Metaphysik* 1879.
23. "De la formation de la notion de l'espace." *Revue philosophique.* Oct. 1877.
24. "Alter und neuer Glaube." *Deutsche Revue.* Mai, 1879.
25. "Anfänge spiritistischer Conjectural-Kritik." Ibid. Dec. 1879.
26. "Philosophy in the last forty years." *Contemporary Review.* Jan. 1880.
27. "L'Infini actuel est-il contradictoire?" *Revue philosophique.* Mai. 1880.
28. "Die Principien der Ethik." *Nord und Süd.* Juni. 1882.
29. *Dictate aus den Vorlesungen Lotze's* 1881–4.
[For minor articles by Lotze, see the appendix to the *Grundzüge der Aesthetik,* Leipzig, S. Hirzel, 1884.]

ERRATA ET CORRIGENDA

*The following alterations were made by the editor
in the Santayana text.*

PAGE:	LINE	COMMENT:
111	12–13	full title has been provided
112	28	insert comma (,) after "is" and after "hand"
120	25	read "were" for "we"
122	27	read "ll. (lines) 1128–1132, 1148–1149" for "v. 1127"
123	8	insert "of" after "principle"
124	15	read "superseded" for "superceded"
125	6	read "indispensable" for "indispensible"
125	25	read "determined" for "determine"
128	23	read "*Logik,* "Vorwort" " for "Logik, Voorede"
130	10	read "self-evidence" for "self evidence"
131	11	read "conclusions" for "conclusion"
131	36	read "Hierarchy" for "heirarchy"
133	19	read "postulate furnishes" for "postulates furnish"
133	31	insert "we" after "when"
133	36	read "authoritative" for "authorative"
134	2–3	read *Natural History of the Heavens* for "Natural History of the Heavens"
135	23–24	full title has been provided
137	30	delete period (.) after 43
137	32	delete "of" after "purposes"
138	12	insert comma (,) after "uniformity"
138	17	delete "in" after "consider"
138	18	delete "in" after "formalism;"
139	5	read "instruments" for "intruments"
141	7	read "is" for "are"
142	32	read "flatly" for "fatly"
146	25	insert comma (,) after "monads"
147	29	read "make" for "makes"

PAGE:	LINE	COMMENT:
148	4	read "changed" for "change"
149	18	read "receive" for "recieve"
150	17	insert "to join" after "seem"
151	33	read "but" for "by"
152	34	read "processes" for "processed"
154	5	read "self-existent" for "self existent"
155	2	delete "the" before "reality"
157	29	read "absolute" for "abs-"
158	23	insert comma (,) after "which"
159	7	read "self-existent" for "self existent"
159	25	delete "a" after "of"
160	17	read "self-sufficing" for "self sufficing"
163	7	delete comma (,) after "indeed"
165	7	insert comma (,) after "ask" and after "then"
165	8	insert comma (,) after "of"
165	11	insert "know" after "we"
165	24	delete "the" after "of"
166	25	read "indefinable" for "undefinable"
167–68	36, 1	read "regretted" for "regreted"
168	12	read "lend" for "lends"
168	16	read "treibende" for Treibende"
169	10	insert "then" after "not"
170	7	read "inadmissible" for "inadmissable"
170	11	insert "of" after "think"
171	9–10	read "pertain to" for "regard"
171	23	read "leave" for "leaves"
172	12	insert "a" after "is"
172	25	insert "a" before "molecule"
175	25	read "Lotze's for "Lotze"
175	32	read "pull" for "draw"
177	6	read "inadmissible" for "inadmissable"
177	23	after "finite space" read "possible" for "impossible"
177	33	read "shorthand" for "short hand"
177	35	read "exist" for "exists"
178	2	read "criticise" for "criticize", to be consistent with his usual spelling
183	8	delete comma (,) after "actualized"
183	13	read "is" for "in"
183	19	read "well-nigh" for "well nigh"
185	6	read "make-up" for "make up"
186	35	read "being, but not" for "being not"
186	36	read "suggests" for "suggest"
187	6–7	read "indispensable" for "indispensible"
187	13	read "One" for "one"

Errata et Corrigenda

PAGE:	LINE	COMMENT:
187	34	*ibid.*
187	34	read "places" for "place"
187	36	read "One" for "one"
188	5	read "Microcosmus" for "microcosmos"
188	23	*ibid.*
189	3	read "inadmissible" for "inadmissable"
191	22	delete repeated "not" after "does"
192	2	insert "that" after "fact"
192	3	insert comma (,) after "events"
193	2	delete repeated "and" after "description"
194	7	delete comma (,) after "account"
194	21	read "who" for "that"
195	16	read "antecedent" for "antecendent"
195	33	read "instrument" for "intrument"
196	26	read "ever-reestablished" for "ever reestablished"
197	17	read "Leibnitz'" for "Leibnitz"
197	24	*ibid.*
199	9	read "have" for "has"
199	10	read "who" for "that"
200	8	read "wherever" for "where ever"
200	11	read "instrument" for "intrument"
200	27	insert comma (,) after "world"
201	8	read "synonymous" for "synonymus"
202	29–30	read "survey" for "overlook"
203	15	read "indeterminism" for "indetermism"
203	16	read "indeterminism" for "inderterminism"
203	29	insert comma (,) after "appear"
204	14	read "once and" for "one"
206	15	read "self-determined" for "self determined"
206	19	read "affect" for "effect"
206	26	read "exist" for "exists"
207	5	insert comma (,) after "soul"
207	11	read "is" for "are"
208	27	insert "do so" after "may"
209	19	read "exaltation" for "exhaltation"
211	10–11	read "self-existent" for "self existent"
212	7	read "funds" for "finds"
212	8	read "except" for "excepts"
213	12	delete "in noting" after "than"
214	32	delete repeated "our" after "for"
215	14	read "many-sided" for "many sided"
215	36	read "seem" for "seems"
216	7	read "give" for "gives"
216	25	read "they do" for "it does"

PAGE:	LINE	COMMENT:
216	30	read "absorption" for "absorbtion"
217	22	read "or" for "of" after "greater"
218	35	insert "it is also with" after "So"
219	7	read "reverence" for "recurrence"
219	24	read "recognise" for "recognize" to be consistent with his spelling elsewhere
219	35	add "in" after "succeeded"
222	18	read "are" for "is"
222	33	insert comma (,) after "the parts"
222	34	delete "they" after "there"
224	16	read "Lotze's" for "Lotzes"
225	30	read "negotiation" for "negociation"
226	12	read "reservations" for "reserves"
227	1	read "Rudolf Hermann" for Hermann Rudolph"

Santayana is inconsistent about italicizing Latin phrases (e.g. *a priori*) but the editor has let this stand.

The quotation on pp. 223–224 is taken from Goethe's *Iphigenie auf Tauris,* Erster Aufzug, Vierter Auftritt, conclusion. Punctuation and spelling of the original varies from the text of *Goethes Werke,* Band V, Christian Wegner Verlag, Hamburg, Zweite Auflage, 1955, p. 22. The editor has altered the original quotation so as to follow the text of this edition.

The editor has italicized titles of books and journals, spelled out abbreviated German words, and placed titles of articles in quotation marks.

Lotze Bibliography

The coauthor, Mr. Charles Greaves, added many items at a time when the author had exhausted his energy and ingenuity in searching out sources of Lotze literature. The authors cannot guarantee completeness, even though many European libraries have been used, in addition to the Library of Congress and the Library of Congress Union Catalogue of American University Catalogues. The libraries of Harvard, Yale, and Princeton were especially useful. Scholars who work at Emory University are particularly grateful to Miss Ruth Walling, whose excellent Reference Department always has some way of helping even experienced scholars. The authors are grateful for the aid and example of Gregor Sebba.

Works by Rudolf Hermann Lotze

1. *Allgemeine Pathologie und Therapie als mechanische Naturwissenschaften,* 1842; Weidmann, Leipzig, 2nd ed. rev., 1848.
2. *Allgemeine Physiologie des koerperlichen Lebens,* Weidmann, Leipzig, 1851.
3. Richard Falckenberg, "Zwei Briefe von Lotze an R. Seydel und E. Arnoldt," *Philosophische Abhandlungen Christolph Sigwart zu seinem siebzigsten Geburtstag gewidmet.,* J. C. E. Mohr, Tübingen, 1900, pp. 127–132.

4. ———, "Hermann Lotze's Briefe an H. Strumpell," *Beilage zur Allgemeinen Zeitung*, 1896, No. 95.

5. ———, ed., "Lotze's Briefe an Ed. Zeller," *Zeitschrift für Philosophie und philosophische Kritik*, Vol. 113, 1899, pp. 180–190.

6. *Die Gedichte*, August Ewald, Augartenverlag, Wien, Leipzig, 1934.

7. W. Gresky, ed. with introduction, "21 Briefe von Hermann Lotze an Ernst Friedrich Apelt (1835–1841)," *Blätter für deutsche Philosophie* (Berlin), Vol. 10, 1936, pp. 319–331; Vol. 11, 1937, pp. 184–203.

8. *Geschichte der Aesthetik in Deutschland*, Cotta, München, 1868. (Reprinted by F. Meiner, Leipzig, 1913, in Hauptwerke der Philosophie in originalgetreuen Neudrucken.)

9. *Geschichte der deutschen Philosophie seit Kant*, Dictate aus den Vorlesungen von H. Lotze, S. Hirzel, Leipzig, 1882, 111 pp.; 2nd ed., Leipzig, 1894, 104 pp.

10. *Grundzüge der Aesthetik*, Dictate aus den Vorlesungen von H. Lotze, S. Hirzel, Leipzig, 1884, 113 pp.; 2nd ed., 1884, 128 pp. (Later editions after the orthographic reform spell "Diktate.")

11. Outlines of Aesthetics, dictated portions of the lectures of H. Lotze, trans. and ed. by G. T. Ladd, Ginn & Co., Boston, 1885. (No. 5 of Lotze's "Outlines of Philosophy.")

12. *Grundzüge der Logik und Encyclopädie der Philosophie*, Dictate aus den Vorlesungen von H. Lotze, Leipzig, 1883, 120 pp.; 2nd ed., S. Hirzel, Leipzig, 1885; 3rd ed., Leipzig, 1891, 123 pp.

13. Outlines of Logic and of [sic] Encyclopaedia of Philosophy, dictated portions of the lectures of H. Lotze, trans. and ed. by G. T. Ladd, Ginn & Co., Boston, 1887. (No. 6 of Lotze's "Outlines of Philosophy.")

14. *Grundzüge der Metaphysik*, Dictate aus den Vorlesungen von H. Lotze, Leipzig, 1883, 94 pp.; 2nd ed., Leipzig, 1887, 100 pp.

15. Outlines of Metaphysic, dictated portions of the lectures of H. Lotze, trans. and ed. by G. T. Ladd, Ginn, Heath & Co., Boston, 1884. (No. 1 of Lotze's "Outlines of Philosophy.")

16. *Zarys metafizyki, Dyktaty podług wykładow Hermana Lotzego. Upowąziony przykład wedtug 3-go wydania—oryginału sporządil, oraz przedmową zaopatrzyl D-r,* Adam Stögbauer, Pod redakcją Henryka Goldberga, E-Wende i sp., Warszawa, 1910.

17. *Grundzüge der Naturphilosophie*, Dictate aus den Vorlesungen von H. Lotze, H. Hirzel, Leipzig, 1882, 112 pp.; 2nd ed., 1889.

18. *Grundzüge der praktischen Philosophie*, Dictate aus den Vorlesungen von H. Lotze, Leipzig, 1882, 84 pp.; 2nd ed., Leipzig, 1884, 95 pp.; 3rd ed., Leipzig, 1899, 97 pp.

19. *Outlines of Practical Philosophy,* dictated portions of the lectures of H. Lotze, trans. and ed. by G. T. Ladd, Ginn & Co., Boston, 1885. (No. 3 of Lotze's "Outlines of Philosophy.")

20. *Grundzüge der Psychologie,* Dictate aus den Vorlesungen von H. Lotze, Leipzig, 1881, vii, 100 pp.; 3rd ed., Leipzig, 1884, 95 pp.; 5th ed., Leipzig, 1894.

21. *Outlines of Psychology,* Dictations from Lectures by Hermann Lotze, trans., with a chapter on the anatomy of the brain, by C. L. Herrick, S. M. Williams, Minneapolis, 1885.

22. *Outlines of Psychology,* dictated portions of the lectures of H. Lotze, trans. and ed. by G. T. Ladd, Ginn & Co., Boston, 1886. (No. 4 of Lotze's "Outlines of Philosophy.")

23. *Grundzüge der Religionsphilosophie,* Dictate aus den Vorlesungen von H. Lotze, Leipzig, 1882, 102 pp.; 2nd ed., Leipzig, 1884, 95 pp.; 3rd ed., Leipzig, 1894.

24. *Outlines of the Philosophy of Religion,* dictated portions of the lectures of H. Lotze, trans. and ed. by G. T. Ladd, Ginn, Heath & Co., Boston, 1885, vii, 162 pp. (No. 2 of Lotze's "Outlines of Philosophy.") Also, R. D. Dickinson, London, 1887. (Apparently London edition of G. T. Ladd's translation.)

25. *Outlines of a Philosophy of Religion,* dictated portions of the lectures of H. Lotze, trans. by F. C. and M. E. Conybeare, ed. by F. C. Conybeare, Swan Sonnenschein & Co., London, 1892; 3rd ed. 1903.

26. *Grundtræk af religionsfilosofien* (Danish), trans. and ed. by Lehmann, preface by K. Kroman, København, 1886.

27. *Kleine Schriften,* 4 vols., ed. with a preface by David Peipers, S. Hirzel, Leipzig, 1885–91.
   Contents: Vol. 1: I. De futurae biologiae principiis philosophicis dissertatio inauguralis medica, 1838; II. Recension von Carl Wilhelm Stark's allgemeiner Pathologie oder allgemeiner Naturlehre der Krankheit, 1839; III. De summis continuorum (nebst vier Thesen), 1840; IV. Bemerkungen über den Begriff des Raumes, Sendschreiben an D. Ch. H. Weisse, 1841; V. Herbart's Ontologie, 1843; VI. Leben. Lebenskraft, 1843; VII. Instinct, 1844; VIII. Recension von Amand Saintes, histoire de la vie et de la philosophie de Kant, 1844; IX. Recension von Francisque Bouillier, histoire et critique de la révolution cartésienne, 1844; X. Recension von Gustav Hartenstein, die Grundbegriffe der ethischen Wissenschaften, 1845; XI. Ueber den Begriff der Schönheit, 1845; XII. Recension von H. Krause, über die Wahrhaftigkeit, ein Beitrag zur Sittenlehre, 1846; XIII. Anzeige der zweiten Auflage von C. W.

Stark's allgemeiner Pathologie oder allgemeiner Naturlehre der Krankheit, 1846; XIV. Selbstanzeige der Abhandlung Ueber den Begriff der Schönheit, 1846; XV. Recension von Joh. Heinr. Koosen, der Streit des Naturgesetzes mit dem Zweckbegriffe in den physischen und historischen Wissenschaften, eine Einleitung in das Studium der Philosophie, 1846; XVI. Recension von Franz Biese, philosophische Propädeutik für Gymnasien und höhere Bildungsanstalten, 1846; XVII. Recension von Bordas-Demoulin, le cartésianisme ou la véritable rénovation des sciences, précédé d'un discours sur la réformation de la philosophie au dix-neuvième siècle par F. Huet, 1846.

Vol. 2: XVIII. Seele und Seelenleben, 1846; XIX. Über Bedingungen der Kunstschönheit, 1847; XX. Recension von Gustav Theodor Fechner, über das höchste Gut, 1847; XXI. Recension von Theodor Waitz, Grundlegung der Psychologie nebst einer Anwendung auf das Seelenleben der Thiere, besonders die Instincterscheinungen, 1847; XXII. Recension von H. M. Chalybäus, Entwurf eines Systems der Wissenschaftslehre, 1847; XXIII. Recension von Joseph Freiherr v. Eichendorff, über die ethische und religiöse Bedeutung der neuern romantischen Poesie in Deutschland, 1848; XXIV. Recension von F. W. Hagen, psychologische Untersuchungen, Studien im Gebiete der physiologischen Psychologie, 1848; XXV. Recension von Johann Heinr. Loosen, Propädeutik der Kunst, 1848; XXVI. Recension von Hermann Ulrici, das Grundprincip der Philosophie, kritisch und speculativ entwickelt, 1848; XXVII. Recension von Franz Vorländer, Wissenschaft der Erkenntniss, im Abriss systematisch entworfen, 1848; XXVIII. Selbstanzeige der Abhandlung über Bedingungen der Kunstschönheit, 1848; XXIX. Anzeige von Saverio Cavallari, zur historischen Entwicklung der Kunste nach der Theilung des römischen Reichs, 1848; XXX. Selbstanzeige der zweiten Auflage der allgemeinen Pathologie und Therapie als mechanische Naturwissenschaften, 1849; XXXI. Recension von Johann Heinrich Löwe, über den Begriff der Logik und ihre Stellung zu den andern philosophischen Disciplinen, 1849; XXXII. Recension von Ernst Guhl, die neuere geschichtliche Malerei und die Akademien, mit einer Einleitung von Prof. Dr. F. Kugler, 1849; XXXIII. Anzeige von Bonaventura Genelli, das Leben einer Hexe in Zeichnungen, gestochen von H. Merz und Gonzenbach, 1850; XXXIV. Recension von Ottomar Domrich, die psychischen Zustände, ihre organische Vermittelung und ihre Wirkung in Erzeugung körperlicher Krankheiten, 1850; XXXV. Recension von Theodor Waitz, Lehrbuch der Psychologie als Naturwissenschaft, 1850; XXXVI. Recension von Gustav Theodor Fechner, Nanna, oder über das Seelenleben der Pflanzen, 1850; XXXVII. Selbstanzeige der allgemeinen Physiologie des körperlichen Lebens, 1851. *Vol. 3:* XXXVIII. Selbstanzeige der medicinischen Psychologie oder Physiologie der Seele, 1852; XXXIX. Recension von Moritz Wilhelm Drobisch, erste Grundlehren der mathematischen Psychologie, 1852; XL. Recension von Hermann Ulrici, System der Logik, 1853; XLI. Psychologische Untersuchungen I. Ueber die Stärke der Vorstellungen, 1853; XLII. Quaestiones Lucretianae, 1853; XLIII. Recension von Eduard Pflüger, die sensorischen Functionen des Rückenmarks der Wirbelthiere nebst einer neuen Lehre über die Leitungsgesetze der Reflexionen, 1853; XLIV. Anzeige von Georg Meissner, Beiträge zur Physiologie des Sehorgans, 1854; XLV. Recension von W. Schlötel, die Logik neu bearbeitet, 1854; XLVI. Recension von Eduard Hanslick, vom Musikalisch-Schönen, ein Beitrag zur Revision der Aesthetik der Tonkunst, 1855; XLVII. Recension von Gustav Theodor Fechner, über die physikalische und philosophische Atomenlehre, 1855; XLVIII. Recension von Heinrich Czolbe, neue Darstellung des Sensualismus, ein Entwurf, 1855; XLIX. Recension von Albert Lemoine, du sommeil au point de vue physiologique et psychologique, 1856; L. Recension von Wilhelm Fridolin Volkmann, Grundriss der Psychologie vom Standpunkte des philosophischen Realismus, 1856; LI. Recension von Jürgen Bona Meyer, Aristoteles Thierkunde, ein Beitrag zur Geschichte der Zoologie, Physiologie und der alten Philosophie, 1856; LII. Recension von August Weber, die neueste Vergötterung des Stoffs. Ein Blick in das Leben der Natur und des Geistes, Für denkende Leser, 1856; LIII. Selbstanzeige des ersten Bandes des Mikrokosmus, 1856; LIV. Recension von Heinrich Czolbe, Entstehung des Selbstbewusstseins, Eine Antwort an Herrn Professor Lotze, 1857; LV. Selbstanzeige der lateinischen Uebersetzung der Antigone des Sophokles, 1857; LVI. Anzige von Im. Hermann Fichte, Anthropologie, Die Lehre von der menschlichen Seele, Neu begründet auf naturwissenschaftlichem Wege,—Selbstanzeige von Streitschriften, Erstes Heft, In Bezug auf Professor Fichte's Anthropologie, 1857; LVII. Selbstanzeige des zweiten Bandes des Mikrokosmus, 1859; LVIII. Recension von Immanuel Hermann Fichte, zur Seelenfrage, eine philosophische Confession, 1859; LIX. Recension von Karl Snell, die Streitfrage des Materialismus, Ein vermittelndes Wort, 1859; LX. Recension von Ch. H. Weisse's

System der Aesthetik, nach dem Collegienhefte letzter Hand herausgegeben von Rudolph Seydel, 1872; LXI. Recension von Gustav Teichmüller, neue Studien zur Geschichte der Begriffe, Erste Lieferung, Herakleitos, 1876; LXII. De la formation de la notion d'espace. La théorie des signes locaux, 1877; LXIII. Alter und neuer Glaube, Tagesansicht und Nachtansicht, Mit Beziehung auf: Die Tagesansicht gegnüber der Nachtansicht, Von G. Theodor Fechner, 1879; LXIV. Anfange spiritistischer Conjecturalkritik, Eine Geistergeschichte, 1879; LXV. Philosophy in the last forty years, First article, 1880; LXVI. Recension von Hoppe, die Scheinbewegungen, 1880; LXVII. L'infini actuel est-il contradictoire? Réponse à M. Renouvier, 1880.

Vol. 4 (Anhang) : A. Beiträge zu Werken befreundeter Verfasser: I. Vorwort zu dem anonym erschienenen Buch: Das Evangelium der armen Seele; II. Mittheilung an C. Stumpf in Betreff der Lehre von den Localzeichen; B. Nachgelassener Aufsatz zur Veröffentlichung bestimmte Arbeiten: I. Nachgelassener Aufsatz über die Principien der Ethik; II. Nachgelassener Aufsatz über Goethe (Fragment) ; C. Jugendarbeiten: I. Pensées d'un Idiote sur Descartes, Spinoza et Leibnitz; II. Geographische Phantasien (Fragment) .

28. *Logik,* Weidmann, Leipzig, 1843.
29. *Logik, Drei Bücher vom Denken, vom Untersuchen und vom Erkennen,* 1874; 2nd ed., S. Hirzel, Leipzig, 1880. ("Neuausgabe der Philosophischen Bibliothek," 1912, ed. with an introduction by Georg Misch, describing Lotze's spiritual development, as well as a German translation of Lotze's article, "Philosophy in the last forty years," Felix Meiner, Leipzig, 1928.)
30. *Logic, in three books, of Thought, of Investigation, and of Knowledge,* ed. by Bernard Bosanquet, Clarendon Press, Oxford, 1884; 2nd ed., 1887 (8) .
31. *Medicinische Psychologie, oder Physiologie der Seele,* Weidmann, Leipzig, 1852.
32. *Principes généraux de psychologie physiologique,* trans. by A. Penjon, Germer Baillière, Paris, 1876.
33. *Metaphysik,* Weidmann, Leipzig, 1841.
34. *Métaphysique,* authorized trans. by A. Duval, Firmin-Didot, Paris, 1883.
35. *Metaphysik, Drei Bücher der Ontologie, Kosmologie und Psychologie,* S. Hirzel, Leipzig, 1879; ed. by Georg Misch, with an appendix "Die Prinzipien der Ethik," Felix Meiner, Leipzig, 1912.
36. *Metaphysic in three books: Ontology, Cosmology, and Psychology,*

ed. by Bernard Bosanquet, Clarendon Press, Oxford, 1884; 2nd ed., 1887.

37. *Mikrokosmus, Ideen zur Naturgeschichte und Geschichte der Menschheit, Versuch einer Anthropologie,* S. Hirzel, Leipzig, 1856–1858, 1858–1864; 3rd ed., 3 vols., Leipzig, 1876–1880.

38. *Microcosmus: An Essay Concerning Man and His Relation to the World,* trans. by Elizabeth Hamilton and E. E. Constance Jones, Scribner and Welford, New York, 1885, 1886, 1887; 3rd ed., 1888; 4th ed., 1890; also T. & T. Clark, Edinburgh, 1885; 4th ed., 1899.

39. *Microcosmo: Idee sulla storia naturale e sulla storia dell'umanità, saggio d'antropolgia,* Mattei, Speroni, et al, Pavia, 1911–1916.

40. Russian translation of *Microcosmus,* 1866–1867.

41. *Das Dasein der Seele,* F. Meiner, Leipzig, 1923.

42. *Natur und Vermögen der Seele,* F. Meiner, Leipzig, 1930.

43. *Der Streit der Naturansichten,* F. Meiner, Leipzig, no date.

44. *Der Zusammenhang der Dinge,* Deutsche Bibliothek, Berlin, no date. (Part 9 of *Mikrokosmus.*)

45. "Microcosmus Selections," B. Rand, ed., *Modern Classical Philosophers,* 2nd ed., 1936, pp. 733–754.

46. "The Connection between Body and Soul," D. S. Robinson, ed., *An Anthology of Modern Philosophy,* 1931, pp. 764–777; 2nd ed., 1938.

47. "Idealism and Realism in Their Relation to the Theory of Knowledge," trans. from *Mikrokosmus* by Max Eberhardt, *The Journal of Speculative Philosophy,* Vol. 6, 1872, pp. 4–18. (This is the first translation into English that we have discovered.)

48. Henry Churchill King, *An Outline of the Microcosmus of Hermann Lotze,* based upon the English translation, Pearce & Randolph, Oberlin, Ohio, 1895; 2nd ed., L. D. Harkness, Oberlin, Ohio, 1900.

49. *Sophocles' Antigona,* Latinis numeris reddidit H. Lotze, H. Wigand, Göttingen, 1857.

50. *Streitschriften,* Part 1 of Prof. J. H. Fichte's *Anthropologie,* S. Hirzel, Leipzig, 1857. (No more was published.)

51. *System der Philosophie,* 2 vols., Drei Bücher der Logik, Drei Bücher der Metaphysik, S. Hirzel, Leipzig, 1874–1879; 2nd ed., 1880.

52. *System of Philosophy,* ed. by Bernard Bosanquet, Clarendon Press, Oxford, Part 1 (Logic), 1884; Part 2 (Metaphysic), 1884. Parts listed separately above; 2nd ed., 1887.

53. *Ueber Bedingungen der Kunstschönheit,* Vanderhoeck und Ruprecht, Göttinger Studien, 1847.

54. *Ueber den Begriff der Schönheit,* Vanderhoeck und Ruprecht, Göttinger Studien, 1845.

Secondary Literature

55. Theodor Achelis, "Hartmann wider Lotze," *Preussische Jahrbücher,* Vol. 63, 1889.
56. ———, "Hermann Lotze," *Westermann's illustrierte deutsche Monatshefte für die gesamte geistige Leben der Gegenwart,* Vol. 66, 1889, pp. 744–753.
57. ———, "Lotzes Philosophie," *Vierteljahrsschrift für wissenschaftliche Philosophie,* Vol. 6, 1882, pp. 1–27.
58. ———, "Lotze's praktische Philosophie in ihren Grundzügen," *Philosophische Monatshefte,* Vol. 22, 1886, pp. 577–609.
59. ———, review, "*Hermann Lotze* by R. Falckenberg," *Beilage zur Allgemeinen Zeitung,* No. 211, 1901, pp. 2–3.
60. Erwin Ackerknecht, *Die Theorie der Lokalzeichen,* J. C. B. Mohr, Tübingen, 1904, p. 88.
61. G. P. Adams and W. P. Montague, eds., *Contemporary American Philosophy,* Macmillan, New York, 1930, Vol. 1, pp. 119, 122, 124.
62. Robert Adamson, *The Development of Modern Philosophy,* Vol. 1, William Blackwood, Edinburgh, 1903.
63. ———, review, "Hermann Lotze's *Logic* trans. by B. Bosanquet," *Mind,* o.s.Vol. 10, 1885, pp. 100–115. (Reprinted in his *A Short History of Logic,* 1911.)
64. ———, review, "Hermann Lotze's *Metaphysic* trans. by B. Bosanquet," *Mind,* o.s.Vol. 10, 1885, pp. 573–588.
65. S. Alexander, *Space, Time and Deity,* Macmillan, London, 1920; The Humanities Press, New York, 1950, passim.
66. M. Allihn, "Die Theorien der Künste nach Lotze," *Zeitschrift für exakte Philosophie,* Vol. 8, 1868, pp. 281–299.
67. L. Ambrosi, *Ermanno Lotze e la sua filosofia,* Società editrice Dante Alighieri, Albrighi, Segati e C, Milano, 1912.
68. ———, "Metafisica dello spazio e del tempo secondo Ermanno Lotze," *Annali dell, Università Toscana,* Vol. 7, 1922, pp. 1–61.
69. ———, "Il mondo della realtà secondo il Lotze," *Cultura filosofica,* Vol. 10, 1916, pp. 32–49.
70. L. Ambrosi, "Per una monographi ital. s. H. Lotze," *Cultura filosofica,* Vol. 3, 1909.

71. Henri Frederic Amiel, *The Private Journal*, trans. by Van Wyck Brooks, Macmillan, New York, 1935, pp. 244–245.

72. Hosang An, *Hermann Lotzes Bedeutung für das Problem der Beziehung* (Diss. Jena), Thüringer Verlagsanstalt, Jena, 1929. (Reprinted in *Abhandlungen zur Philosophie, Psychologie und Pädagogik*, Vol. 36, Bouvier, Bonn, 1967.)

73. Anonymous, "Goethe, Kant, Lotze," *Lehre und Wehre*, Vol. 65, 1922, p. 127.

74. Anonymous, "Lotze," *Chambers's Encyclopaedia*, G. Newnes, London, new ed., 1955, Vol. 8, p. 695.

75. Anonymous, "Lotze," *Appleton's New Practical Cyclopedia*, Appleton, New York, 1910, Vol. 4, p. 111.

76. Anonymous, "Von und über H. Lotze," *Neue evangelische Kirchenzeitung*, 1882, column 737.

77. Anonymous, review, "*Geschichte der Aesthetik in Deutschland* (1913) by Hermann Lotze," *Philosophie der Gegenwart*, Vol. 5, 1916, p. 233.

78. Anonymous, review, "*Grundzüge der Metaphysik* (1910) by H. Lotze," *Philosophie der Gegenwart*, Vol. 4, 1914, p. 41.

79. Anonymous, review, "*Kant, Lotze und Ritschl* by L. Stählin," *Evangelische Kirchenzeitung*, Vol. 122, 1888, p. 488.

80. Anonymous, review, "*Hermann Lotze* by R. Falckenberg," *Die Grenzboten, Zeitschrift für Politik, Litteratur und Kunst*, No. 8, 1901, pp. 368–371.

81. Anonymous, review, "*Hermann Lotze* by R. Falckenberg," *Litterarisches Centralblatt für Deutschland*, 1901, p. 1494.

82. Anonymous, review, "*Lotze's Religionsphilosophie* by P. Gese," *Theologie Studien*, Vol. 34, 1918, p. 249.

83. Leo Baerwald, *Die Entwicklung der Lotzeschen Psychologie* (Diss. Erlangen), Koebner'sche Buchhandlung, Breslau; H. Fleischmann, Breslau, 1905.

84. John Bailiee, *The Interpretation of Religion*, Scribner's, New York, 1936, pp. 278–287.

85. James Mark Baldwin, ed., *Dictionary of Philosophy and Psychology*, Macmillan, New York, 1901–1902; reprinted by Peter Smith, New York, 1940, "Lotze," Vol. 2, p. 31.

86. ———, *History of Psychology, a Sketch and an Interpretation*, Vol. 2, *From John Locke to the Present Time*, G. P. Putnam's Sons, New York, 1913, pp. 82–86.

87. Fritz Bamberger, *Untersuchungen zur Entstehung des Wertproblems in der Philosophie des 19. Jahrhunderts: Lotze* (Diss. Berlin,

1923), M. Niemeyer, Halle a.S., 1924. (Only Vol. 1 was published.)

88. F. Bantalli, *Introduzione alla tradizione italiano del Microcosmo*, Pavia, 1911.

89. F. Barone, "Lotze," *Enciclopedia Filosofica*, Istituto per la Collaborazione Culturale, Venezia-Roma, 1957, Vol. 3, pp. 168–170.

90. Fr. Bartels (Pastor), *Lotze's religionsphilosophische Gedanken im Lichte der göttlichen Offenbarung betrachtet*, H. Feesche, Hannover, 1884.

91. ———, "Dr. R. Hermann Lotze," *Rheinische Blätter für Erziehung und Unterricht*, Vol. 62, 1888, pp. 66–73, 141–157.

92. ———, review, *"Das Gefühl in seiner Eigenart und Selbständigkeit mit besonderer Beziehung auf Herbart und Lotze* by J. Hübener," *Rheinische Blätter für Erziehung und Unterricht*, Vol. 70, 1900, pp. 40–43.

93. Friedrich Bartels (of Gera), *Pädagogische Psychologie nach Hermann Lotze in ihrer Anwendung auf die Schulpraxis und auf die Erziehung*, F. Mauke (A. Schenk), Jena, 1891, 1892.

94. B. Bauch, "Lotze's Logik und ihre Bedeutung in deutschem Idealismus," *Beiträge zu Philosophie des deutschen Idealismus*, Vol. 1, 1919, pp. 45–58.

95. Julius Baumann, "Persönliche Erinnerungen an Hermann Lotze," *Annalen der Naturphilosophie, Leipzig*, Vol. 8, 1909, pp. 175–182.

96. ———, "Zum Gedächtnis Lotze's," *Philosophische Monatshefte*, Vol. 17, 1881, pp. 613–623.

97. E. Becher, "Hermann Lotze," *Erich Becher: Deutsche Philosophen*, 1929, pp. 47–72.

98. ———, "Lotze und seine Psychologie," *Die Naturwissenschaften*, Vol. 5, 1917, pp. 325–334.

99. Beermann, "Lotze und das Judentum," *Israelitische Wochenschrift*, Vol. 13, 1904, p. 401.

100. A. F. O. Belau, *Ueber die Grenzen der mechanischen Geschehens im Seelenleben der Menschen nach Lotze* (Diss. Erlangen), R. G. Brandt, Flatow, 1901.

101. I. Benrubi, *Philosophische Strömungen der Gegenwart in Frankreich*, Felix Meiner, Leipzig, 1928, p. 403.

102. Joseph L. Blau, *Men and Movements in American Philosophy*, Prentice-Hall, New York, 1952, pp. 199–201. (Re Bowne and Lotze, see #110.)

103. Friedrich G. R. Bocksch, *Zur Raumtheorie Hermann Lotzes* (Diss. Greifswald), Julius Abel, Greifswald, 1889.

104. Walter Boerl, *Das Problem der Willensfreiheit in der Philosophie Lotzes* (Diss. Halle), Heinrich John, Halle a.S., 1910.
105. Böhmer, review, *"Hermann Lotze* by R. Falckenberg," *Hamburger Correspondent,* No. 26, 1901.
106. Hermann Bohner, *Die Grundlage der Lotzeschen Religionsphilosophie* (Diss. Erlangen), Borna-Leipzig, 1914.
107. John Elof Boodin, *A Realistic Universe: An Introduction to Metaphysics,* Macmillan, New York, 1916, p. 63.
108. L. Bornemann, "Lotze's 100. Geburtstag," *Christliche Welt,* Vol. 31, 1917, p. 418.
109. Bernard Bosanquet, "The History of Philosophy," C. H. Herford, ed., *Germany in the Nineteenth Century,* Manchester University Press, Manchester, 1915.
110. Borden Parker Bowne, *Metaphysics: A Study in First Principles,* Harper, New York, 1882. "Dedicated in grateful recollection to the memory of my friend and former teacher, Hermann Lotze." (Re Bowne and Lotze, see # 102, 148, 230, 247, 318, 533.)
111. Ernest G. Braham, *Personality and Immortality in Post-Kantian Thought,* George Allen and Unwin, London, 1926, Ch. 3, "Personality in Hermann Lotze's Idealistic Monism. Link with Hegel"; Ch. 4, "The Reaction Against Monistic Idealism."
112. O. Braun, review, *"Geschichte der Aesthetik in Deutschland* (1913) by H. Lotze," *Monatsschrift für höhe Schulen,* 1915, p. 122.
113. Emile Bréhier, *Histoire de la Philosophie,* II, Presses Universitaires de France, Paris, 1948, pp. 993–996.
114. Hedwig Breilmann, *Lotzes Stellung zum Materialismus, unter besonderer Berücksichtigung seiner Controverse mit Czolbe* (Diss. Münster), Joseph Jansen, Telgte in W., 1925. (Re Czolbe and Lotze, see #27-Vol. 3 XLVIII, LIV, #134.)
115. Franz Brentano, *Die Lehre vom richtigen Urteil,* ed. by Franziska Mayer-Hillebrand (pseud.), Franke Verlag, Bern, 1956, pp. 134, 157.
116. George S. Brett, *History of Psychology,* 3 vols., 1912–1921; abridged in one volume, ed. by R. S. Peters, George Allen and Unwin, London; Macmillan, New York, 1953; rev. ed., 1962, pp. 591–600.
117. Werner Brock, *An Introduction to Contemporary German Philosophy,* Cambridge University Press, Cambridge, 1935.
118. Brügel, review, *"Mikrokosmus* (5th ed.) by H. Lotze," *Neue Blätter aus Sud-Deutschland für Erziehung und Unterricht,* 1912, p. 40.
119. Budde, "Charakter der Lotze'sche Philosophie speziell die Psy-

chologie," *Rheinische Blätter für Erziehung und Unterricht,* Vol.
69, 1895, pp. 394–411.

120. Vincent Buranelli, *Josiah Royce,* Twayne Publishers, New York,
1964. (Re Royce, see #397.)

121. B. C. Burt, *A History of Modern Philosophy,* A. C. McClung,
Chicago, 1892, Vol. 2, pp. 173–199.

122. Busse, review, *"Hermann Lotze* by R. Falckenberg," *Deutsche
Literatur-Zeitung,* No. 16, 1901.

123. Mary Whiton Calkins, *A First Book in Psychology,* Macmillan,
New York, 4th ed., 1919.

124. C. Cantoni, "Terenzio Mamiani e Ermanno Lotze, o il mondo
secondo la scienza e secondo il sentimento," *Nuova Antologia,*
Vol. 11, June and July, 1869, pp. 237–281, 563–587.

125. Myrick H. Carré, *Phases of Thought in England,* Clarendon Press,
Oxford, 1949, p. 363.

126. M. Carriere, "Lotze's Metaphysik," *Deutsche Revue,* Vol. 4, 1880,
pp. 131–138.

127. O. Caspari, *Hermann Lotze in seiner Stellung zu der durch Kant
begründeten neuesten Geschichte der Philosophie und die philosophische Aufgabe der Gegenwart,* 1883; 2nd ed., Eduard Tre-
wendt, Breslau, 1894.

128. Franz Chelius, *Lotzes Wertlehre* (Diss. Erlangen), Junge und
Sohn, Erlangen, 1904.

129. E. Chiocchetti, "Recenti contributi allo studio della filosofia di
H. Lotze," *Rivista di filosofia neo-scolastica,* Vol. 4, 1912, pp. 240–
251.

130. Frederick Copleston, *A History of Philosophy,* Vol. 8, *Bentham to
Russell,* Burnes and Oates, London, 1966, pp. 247, 268, 291, 381.

131. H. T. Costello, *Josiah Royce's Seminar,* 1913–1914, ed. by Grover
Smith, Rutgers University Press, New Brunswick, N.J., 1963, p.
183. (Re Royce and Lotze, see #397.)

132. J. H. Cotton, *Royce on the Human Self,* Harvard University Press,
Cambridge, Mass., 1954, p. 4. (Re Royce and Lotze, see #397.)

133. Agnes Cuming, "Lotze, Bradley and Bosanquet," *Mind,* Vol. 26,
1917, pp. 162–170.

134. Heinrich Czolbe, M.D., *Entstehung des Selbstbewusstseins. Eine
Antwort an Herrn Professor Lotze,* H. Costenoble; Otto Purfürst,
Leipzig, 1856. (Re Czolbe and Lotze, see #27-Vol. 3 XLVIII, LIV,
#114.)

135. P. Devaux, *Lotze et son influence sur la philosophie anglo-saxonne,
contribution a l'étude historique et critique de la notion de va-
leur,* Maurice Lamartin, Bruxelles, 1932.

136. John Dewey, *Essays in Experimental Logic,* University of Chicago Press, Chicago, 1916; Dover Publications, New York, 1953.

137. ———, *Leibniz's New Essays Concerning the Human Understanding, A Critical Exposition,* S. C. Griggs and Co., Chicago, 1888, pp. 260–338.

138. ———, *Studies in Logical Theory,* University of Chicago Press, Chicago, 1903, Chap. 1–4. (Re Dewey and Lotze, see #360, 417.)

139. Gudrun Diem, "Hermann Lotze," *De Homine, Der Mensch im Spiegel seines Gedankens,* Michael Landmann et al., Freiburg, 1962, pp. 446–461.

140. Th. W. Drobisch, "Über Lotze's psychologischen Standpunkt," *Zeitschrift für Philosophie und philosophische Kritik,* Vol. 34, 1859, pp. 1–40.

141. Johanna Droop, *Die Erkenntnisstheorie, insbesondere das Realisierungsproblem bei Lotze* (Diss. Bonn), A. & W. Opitz, Bielefeld, 1920.

142. James Drummond, *The Life and Letters of James Martineau,* and a survey of his philosophical work by C. B. Upton, 2 vols., Dodd, Mead and Co., New York, 1902.

143. A. Eastwood, "Lotze's Antithesis between Thought and Things," *Mind,* Vol. 1, 1892, pp. 305–324, 470–488.

144. Albin Elgström, *Hermann Lotzes uppfattning af människans valfrihet,* Gleerupska Universitets-bokhandeln, Lund, 1892.

145. Johann Eduard Erdmann, *Grundriss der Geschichte der Philosophie,* Hertz, Berlin, rev. 3rd ed., 1878.

146. ———, *A History of Philosophy,* trans. by W. S. Hough, Swan Sonnenschein, London, 1890; 2nd ed., 1890, pp. 298–327.

147. M. Ettlinger, "Lotze's Lehre vom Zusammenhang der Dinge," *Hochland,* Oct. 1913, pp. 118.

148. Rudolf Eucken, "The Work of Borden Parker Bowne," R. T. Flewelling, ed., *Personalism and the Problems of Philosophy,* Methodist Book Concern, New York, 1915. (Re Bowne and Lotze, see #110.)

149. A. Ewald, "Hermann Lotze," *Das deutsche Wort (Die literarische Welt),* Vol. 10, 1934, No. 20, p. 4.

150. Richard Falckenberg, *Geschichte der neueren Philosophie von Nikolaus von Kues bis zur Gegenwart,* Veit and Co., Leipzig, 1908, pp. 567–572; 1927 ed., pp. 616–622.

151. ———, *Hermann Lotze, Das Leben und die Entstehung der Schriften, nach den Briefen,* Frommanns Klassiker der Philosophie, Stuttgart, 1901. (For reviews see #59, 80, 81, 105, 122, 192, 317, 370, 433, 442, 527.)

152. ———, "Die Entwicklung der Lotze'schen Zeitlehre," *Zeitschrift für Philosophie und philosophische Kritik*, Vol. 105, 1895, pp. 178–221.

153. ———, "Hermann Lotze," *Illustrierte Zeitung*, 1917, No. 3855.

154. ———, "Lotze's Philosophie," *Zeitschrift für Philosophie und philosophische Kritik*, Vol. 98, 1890, pp. 221–225.

155. ———, "Hermann Lotze, sein Verhältnis zu Kant und Hegel und zu den Problemen der Gegenwart," Vortrag gehalten auf der Generalversammlung der Kant-Gesellschaft am 19. April 1913 in Halle, *Zeitschrift für Philosophie und philosophische Kritik*, Vol. 150, 1913, pp. 37–56.

156. ———, review, *"Kausalproblem in Lotze's Philosophie* by E. Wentscher," *Zeitschrift für Philosophie und philosophische Kritik*, Vol. 125, 1905, pp. 79–80.

157. Fr. Fauth, "Verwendbarkeit der Lotze'sche Philosophie für die Theologie," *Theologische Studien und Kritiken*, Vol. 45, 1872, pp. 520–534.

158. Joseph Feiten, *Die aesthetische Gerechtigkeit bei Hermann Lotze* (Diss. Bonn), Junfermannsche Buchdruckerei, Paderborn, 1926.

159. S. Ferenczi, "Aus der Psychologie von Lotze," *Imago, Zeitschrift für Anwendungen der Psychoanalyse*, Vol. 2, 1913, p. 238.

160. J. Ferreol, review, *Lotze's Metaphysik* by H. Schön, *Pädagogisches Archiv und Centralorgan für das Interessen des Realschulwesens*, 1902, pp. 467–468.

161. Max Harold Fisch, ed., *Classic American Philosophers: Peirce, James, Royce, Santayana, Dewey, Whitehead*, selections from their writings with introductory essays, Appleton-Century-Crofts, New York, 1951, pp. 3, 17, 18, 182.

162. Hubert Fischer, "Die Pathologie als mechanische Naturwissenschaft bei Rudolf Hermann Lotze," typescript München 1952. (Medical faculty dissertation, not for exchange.)

163. ———, "Die psychophysischen Korrelationen bei R. H. Lotze," *Philosophia Naturalis* (Meisenheim/Glan), Vol. 4, 1957, pp. 151–157.

164. Florence Mary Fitch, *Der Hedonismus bei Lotze und Fechner* (Diss. Berlin), E. Ebering, Berlin, 1903.

165. John Carl Flügel, *A Hundred Years of Psychology, 1833–1933*, Macmillan, New York; Gerald Duckworth, London, 1933; 2nd ed., 1951, 1953.

166. O Flügel, "Einige Bemerkungen über Lotze's Ansicht vom Zu-

sammenhange der Dinge," *Zeitschrift für exakte Philosophie,* Vol. 8, 1868, pp. 36–59.

167. G. Fonsegrive, "La logique de Lotze," *Revue philosophique,* Vol. 21, 1886, pp. 618–634.

168. Frank Hugh Foster, *The Doctrine of the Transcendent Use of the Principle of Causality in Kant, Herbart and Lotze* (Diss. Leipzig), Ackermann and Glaser, Leipzig, 1882.

169. Johannes Franke, *Über Lotze's Lehre von der Phänomenalität des Raumes* (Diss. Erfurt), J. G. Cramer, Erfurt, 1884.

170. O. Freund, "Herbart und Lotze," *Pädagogische Reform,* Vol. 15, 1891, No. 49, Vol. 16, 1892, No. 18.

171. Otto Heinrich Frommel, *Das Verhältnis von mechanischer und teleologischer Naturerklärung bei Kant und Lotze* (Diss. Erlangen), E. T. Jacob, Erlangen, 1898.

172. ———, review, "*Problem des Wirkens und die monistischen Weltanschauung mit Beziehung an Lotze* by M. Wartenberg," *Kantstudien,* Vol. 6, 1901, pp. 305–313.

173. Elizabeth Smith Gates, *The Life of George Augustus Gates,* The Pilgrim Press, New York, 1915, pp. 5–6.

174. Felix M. Gatz, *Die Begriffe der Geltung bei Lotze* (Diss. Erlangen, originally R. Noske, Borna-Leipzig, 1918), F. Enke, Stuttgart, 1929.

175. Reinhold Geiger (K. R. Geijer), *Hermann Lotzes tankar om tid och timlighet i kritisk belysning,* 1885–1886, in Lund-Karolinska Universitet Årsskrift (*Acta Universitatis Lundensis*), Vol. 22, Part 1, No. 1, Lund, 1886.

176. ———, "Darstellung und Kritik der Lotze'schen Lehre von den Localzeichen," *Philosophische Monatshefte,* Vol. 20, 1885, pp. 513–560.

177. ———, "Einige Bemerkungen zu Falckenberg's Abhandlung über die Entwicklung der Lotze'schen Zeitlehre," *Zeitschrift für Philosophie und philosophische Kritik,* Vol. 106, 1895, pp. 90–92.

178. ———, "Hermann Lotze's lara om rummet," *Nytt Svensk Tidskrift,* Uppsala, Vol. 5, Vol. 7, 1880.

179. Ferdinand Geisler, "Der Gottesbegriff A. Ritschl's und seine Abhängigkeit von der Philosophie H. Lotze's" (Diss. Halle), typescript, 1925.

180. G. Gentile, "Francesco Bonatelli e l'influsso di Lotze in Italia," *La Critica,* Jan. 20 and March 20, 1907.

181. ———, "Carlo Cantoni e l'influsso di Lotze in Italia," *La Critica,* May 20 and July 20, 1907.

182. H. Gercken, *Beitrag zur Würdigung der Erkenntnisstheorie Lotzes,* Perleberg, 1885.

183. Paul Gese, *Lotzes Religionsphilosophie* (Diss. Halle), Lucka S.-A.; R. Berger, Leipzig, 1916.

184. Katherine Everett Gilbert and Helmut Kuhn, *A History of Esthetics,* Macmillan, New York, 1939, pp. 508–512; revised and enlarged, Indiana University Press, Bloomington, Indiana, 1954.

185. Hermann Glockner, *Die europäische Philosophie von den Anfängen bis zur Gegenwart,* Reclam-Verlag, Stuttgart, 1958, Chap. 48, "Fechner, Lotze und Planck," pp. 965–980.

186. ———, "Lotze's Deutung der Platon Ideen," *Die Pädagogische Hochschule,* Vol. 2, 1930, pp. 7–16.

187. M. Glossner, review, *"Lotze und Wundt* by A. Lichtenstein," *Jahrbuch für Philosophie und spekulative Theologie,* Vol. 16, 1901, pp. 201–205.

188. Rolf W. Göldel, *Die Lehre von der Identität in der deutschen Logik-Wissenschaft seit Lotze. Beitrag zur Geschichte der modernen Logik und philosophische Systematik* (Diss. Leipzig), Leipzig, 1935.

189. Felix M. Goldner, *Die Begriffe der Geltung bei Lotze* (Diss. Erlangen), Noske, Borna-Leipzig, 1918.

190. Rubin Gotesky, "Lotze, Rudolf Hermann," *The Encyclopedia of Philosophy,* Paul Edwards, ed., Macmillan, New York, 1967, Vol. 5, pp. 87–89.

191. Ernst Gundelach, *Die Verfassung der Göttinger Universität,* Otto Schwarz, Göttingen, 1955, Vol. 16, Göttinger Rechtwissenschaftliche Studien, "Wiedererstarken des akademischen Regiments nach der Revolution von 1848," pp. 103 ff.

192. C. Gutberlet, review, *"Hermann Lotze* by R. Falckenberg," *Philosophisches Jahrbuch der Görres-Gesellschaft,* Vol. 14, 1901, p. 336.

193. August F. C. Haeger, *Lotzes Kritik der Herbartischen Metaphysik und Psychologie* (Diss. Greifswald), F. W. Kunike, Greifswald, 1891.

194. Gustav Hahn, *Der Allbeseelungsgedanke bei Lotze* (Diss. Tübingen), W. Kohlhammer, Stuttgart, 1925.

195. Viscount Richard Burdon Haldane, *An Autobiography,* Doubleday, Garden City, N.Y., 1929, pp. 12–25, 33.

196. ———, *The Pathway to Reality,* John Murray, London, 1905, Vol. 1, pp. 141–143.

197. ———, *Universities and National Life,* John Murray, London, 1912. (Re Haldane and Lotze, see #314.)

Lotze bibliography

198. Granville Stanley Hall, *Founders of Modern Psychology*, Appleton, New York and London, 1912, pp. 65–121.

199. ———, *Die Begründer der modernen Psychologie, Lotze, Fechner, Helmholtz, Wundt*, trans. by R. Schmidt, 1914. (German translation of #198.)

200. J. Halpern, review, "*Logik* (1912) by H. Lotze," *Archiv für Geschichte der Philosophie*, Vol. 26, 1913, pp. 385–387.

201. Karl Hanser, *Das Wahrheitsproblem bei Lotze im problemgeschichtlichen Zusammenhang* (Diss. Freiburg/Br., 1929), Wernigerode, 1928.

202. Samuel Harris, *The Philosophical Basis of Theism*, Scribner's, New York, rev. ed., 1886 (c 1883).

203. (Karl Robert) Eduard von Hartmann, *Lotze's Philosophie*, W. Friedrich, Leipzig, 1888.

204. G. Hartung, "E. von Hartmann und Lotze, Metaphysische Studie," *Philosophische Monatshefte*, Vol. 21, 1885, pp. 1–20.

205. Edna Heidbreder, *Seven Psychologies*, Appleton-Century, New York, 1933, pp. 97–98.

206. Walther Herbertz, *Der Zweckbegriff bei Lotze* (Diss. Breslau), Adolf Stenzel, Breslau, 1901. (For review see #233.)

207. Gustav Julius Moritz Hermann, *Das Verhältnis des Ewigen und des Historischen in der Religionsphilosophie Kants und Lotzes* (Diss. Erlangen), Junge und Sohn, Erlangen, 1898.

208. P. Hermant and A. Van de Waele, *Les principales théories de la logique contemporaine*, Paris, 1909, pp. 81–126.

209. G. Dawes Hicks, *Critical Realism: Studies in the Philosophy of Mind and Nature*, Macmillan, London, 1938.

210. G. Hinsche, review, "*Geschichte der Aesthetik in Deutschland* (Vol. 1, 1913) by H. Lotze," *Archiv für die gesamte Psychologie*, Vol. 32, 1914, pp. 73–76.

211. Harald Høffding, *Den nyere Filosofis Historie, etc.*, 2 vols., København, 1894–1895; 3rd ed., 1921.

212. ———, *A History of Modern Philosophy. A sketch of the history of philosophy from the close of the Renaissance to our own day*, 2 vols. trans. from German ed. by B. E. Meyer, Macmillan, London, 1900; reissue 1908; 1924, Vol. 2, pp. 508–524.

213. ———, *A Brief History of Modern Philosophy*, authorized trans. by Charles Finley Sanders, Macmillan, New York, 1912, pp. 272–275.

214. ———, *Histoire de la philosophie moderne . . .* , trans. by P. Bordier, with preface by V. Delbos, 2 vols., Alcan, Paris, 1906.

215. ———, *Geschichte der neueren Philosophie, eine Darstellung der*

Geschichte der Philosophie von dem Ende der Renaissance bis zu unseren Tagen, trans. from Danish ed. by F. Bendixen, O. R. Reisland, Leipzig, 1895–1896.

216. ———, *Storia della filosofia moderna, esposizione della storia della filosofia dalla fine del Rinascimento fino ai giorni nostri,* 2 vols., trans. by P. Martinetti, fratelli Bocca, Torino, 1906, Vol. 2, pp. 490–502.

217. ———, *Psykologi i Omrids paa Grundlag af Erfaring,* København og Kristiania, rev. 5th ed., 1898; rev. 6th ed., 1911.

218. ———, *Outlines of Psychology,* trans. by Mary E. Lowndes, Macmillan, London, 1891.

219. ———, *Esquisse d'une psychologie fondée sur l'expérience,* trans. from 4th Danish ed. by Léon Poitevin, with a preface by Pierre Janet, Alcan, Paris, 1900; 2nd ed., 1903; 3rd ed., 1906.

220. ———, *Psychologie in Umrissen auf Grundlage der Erfahrung,* trans. from 2nd Danish ed. by F. Bendixen, Altenburg (printed), Leipzig, 1887; rev. 2nd ed. from rev. 3rd Danish ed., O. R. Reisland, Leipzig, 1893, pp. 274–276.

221. ———, "Lotze og den Svenske Filosofi," *Nordisk Tidskrift,* 1888, pp. 148–162.

222. ———, "Lotze und die schwedische Philosophie," *Philosophische Monatshefte,* Vol. 26, 1890.

223. P. Th. Hoffmann, "Lotze, Zu 100. Geburtstag," *Deutscher Wille,* Vol. 30, May, 1917, pp. 158–161.

224. George W. Howgate, *George Santayana,* University of Pennsylvania, 1938, on the Lotze book, pp. 34–37. (Re Santayana and Lotze, see #406–408.)

225. J. Hübener, *Das Gefühl in seiner Eigenart und Selbständigkeit mit besonderer Beziehung auf Herbart und Lotze,* Bleyl und Kaimmerer, Dresden, 1898. (For reviews see #92, 365.)

226. Reinhard Hülse, "Lebenskraft, Sensibilität," typescript, Saarbrücken 1964 (Universitet des Saarlandes, medical faculty dissertation, not for exchange.)

227. Edmund Husserl, *Logische Untersuchungen,* 2 vols., M. Niemeyer, Halle, Germany, 1900–1901.

228. Ernst Jaeger, *Kritische Studien zu Lotzes Weltbegriff* (Diss. Leipzig), Triltsch, Würzburg, 1937.

229. William James, *A Pluralistic Universe,* Longmans Green, New York, 1920, pp. 54–55. (Re James and Lotze, see #362, 257–260.)

230. Gilbert Haven Jones, *Lotze und Bowne, eine Vergleichung ihrer philosophischen Arbeit* (Diss. Jena), Thomas, Weida i.Th., 1909. (Re Bowne and Lotze, see #110).

231. Sir Henry Jones, *A Critical Account of the Philosophy of Lotze,* J. Maclehose & Sons, Glasgow; Macmillan, New York, 1895. (For review see #379.)

232. H. W. B. Joseph, *An Introduction to Logic,* Oxford University Press, Oxford, 2nd ed., 1916.

233. R.K., review, *"Der Zweckbegriff bei Lotze* by W. Herbetz," *Revue internationale de théologie,* 1901, pp. 811–814.

234. Paul Kalweit, *Die praktische Begründung des Gottesbegriffs bei Lotze* (Diss. Jena), A. Kampfe, Jena, 1900.

235. Joseph Keller, *Raum und Zeit bei Lotze* (Diss. Bonn), Bonn, 1926.

236. Thomas R. Kelly, "The Place of Value Judgments in Lotze's Philosophy," typescript (Diss. Hartford Theological Seminary, 1924).

237. ———, "Lotze and the One and the Many," *Philosophical Review,* Vol. 40, 1931, pp. 430–443.

238. R. Keussen, "Lotze's Religionsphilosophie," *Deutscher Merkur,* 1917, p. 81.

239. F. Kirchner, "H. Lotze," *Illustrierte Zeitung,* Vol. 77, 1881, p. 74.

240. A. Kirstein, "Lotze, ein Repräsentant der modernen deutschen Philosophie," *Der Katholik,* Vol. 16, 1897, pp. 289–308.

241. R. Kita, "Geltungsbegriff bei Lotze und der Badischen Schule," *Ex-Oriente,* Vol. 1, 1925, pp. 65–80.

242. Maximilian Klein, *Lotzes Logik vom Sein und Geschehen in ihrem Verhältnis zur Logik Herbarts,* M. Breitkreuz, Berlin, 1890.

243. ———, *Lotze's ontologische Ansichten in ihrem Verhältnis zur Lehre Herbarts* (Diss. Berlin), M. Breitkreuz, Berlin, 1890.

244. Otto Klemm, *Geschichte der psychologie,* B. G. Teubner, Leipzig and Berlin, 1911.

245. ———, *A History of Psychology,* trans. by Emil Carl Wilm and Rudolf Pintner, Scribner's, New York, 1914.

246. E. T. Knower, "Lotze's Logic," *Philosophical Review,* Vol. 42, 1933, pp. 381–398.

247. Albert C. Knudson, *The Philosophy of Personalism,* Abingdon Press, New York, 1927. (Re Bowne and Lotze, see #110.)

248. Otto Koeper, *Lotzes geschichtsphilosophische Auseinandersetzung mit Hegel* (Diss. Münster).

249. Fritz Kögel, *Lotzes Aesthetik,* Vanderhoeck und Ruprecht, Göttingen, 1886.

250. ———, "Ueber Lotze's kleine Schriften," *Grenzboten, die Zeitschrift für Politik, Literatur und Kunst,* Vol. 45, 1886, pp. 204–213.

251. F. Köhler, "Rudolf Hermann Lotze," *Deutsche Blätter für erziehenden Unterricht,* 1917, p. 337.

252. W. Koppelmann, "Lotze's Stellung zu Kant's Kriticismus," *Zeitsch-*

rift für Philosophie und philosophische Kritik, Vol. 88, 1886, pp. 1–46.

253. A. Korman, review, "Logik (1912) by H. Lotze," Preussische Jahrbücher, May 1913, p. 291.

254. Kowalewski, review, "Logik (1912) by H. Lotze," Theologische Literaturzeitung, 1916, p. 141.

255. ———, review, "System der Philosophie (Vol. 2, 1912) by H. Lotze," Theologische Literaturzeitung, 1916, p. 141.

256. Emil Kramm, De ideis Platonis a Lotzei judicio defensis (Diss. Halle), Holae, 1879.

257. Otto F. Kraushaar, "Lotze as a Factor in the Development of James's Radical Empiricism and Pluralism," Philosophical Review, Vol. 47, 1938, pp. 517–526; Vol. 48, 1939, pp. 455–471.

258. ———, "Lotze's Influence on the Pragmatism and Practical Philosophy of William James," Journal of the History of Ideas, Vol. 1, 1940, pp. 439–458.

259. ———, "Lotze's Influence on the Psychology of William James," Psychological Review, Vol. 43, 1936, pp. 235–257.

260. ———, "What James's Philosophical Orientation Owed to Lotze," Philosophical Review, Vol. 47, 1938, pp. 517–525. (Re James and Lotze, see #230.)

261. Otto Krebs, Der Wissenschaftsbegriff bei Hermann Lotze (Diss. Zürich), S. Geibel, Altenburg, 1897.

262. ———, "Der Wissenschaftsbegriff bei Lotze," Vierteljahrsschrift für wissenschaftliche Philosophie, 1897, pp. 26–78, 191–226.

263. Kresto K. Krestoff, Lotze's metaphysicher Seelenbergriff (Diss. Leipzig), Karras, Halle a.S., 1890.

264. A. Krohn, "Zur Erinnerung an H. Lotze," Zeitschrift für Philosophie und philosophische Kritik, Vol. 81, 1882, pp. 56–94.

265. Moritz Kronenberg, Moderne Philosophen: Porträts und Characteristiken, Beck, München, 1898, pp. 1–75.

266. ———, "Fechner und Lotze," Die Naturwissenschaften, Vol. 13, 1925, pp. 957–964.

267. ———, "Lotze als Dichter," Beilage zur Allgemeinen Zeitung, 1891, No. 224, 225.

268. ———, "Philosophie innerhalb der modernen Weltanschauung," Christlicher Welt, Vol. 1, 1887, pp. 199, 206 ff.

269. ———, "Weltanschauung und Geistesart," Beilage zur Allgemeinen Zeitung, 1892, Part 2, No. 93, 95 ff.

270. ———, "Zu Gedächtnis Lotze's," Vossische Zeitung, Sonntagsbeilage, 1897, No. 21.

271. Hans Kronheim, Lotzes Kausaltheorie und Monismus, Abhandlun-

gen zur Philosophie und ihrer Geschichte, Part 15, 7, Quelle und Meyer, Leipzig, 1910.

272. ———, *Lotzes Lehre von der Einheit der Dingen* (Diss. Erlangen), Quelle und Meyer, Lipzig, 1910.

273. B. Krstitsch, *Der Seelenbegriff bei Hermann Lotze: Eine kritische Darstellung* (Diss. Bern), Bern, 1914.

274. Hans Josef Krupp, "Die Gestalt des Menschen, ihr immanenter Wert und ihre Symbolik bei R. H. Lotze," typescript, not for exchange (Diss. Bonn, 1941).

275. Oswald Külpe, *Die Philosophie der Gegenwart in Deutschland,* B. G. Teubner, Leipzig, 1902; 5th ed., 1911, pp. 87–94. (*Aus Natur und Geisteswelt,* Vol. 41.)

276. ———, *The Philosophy of the Present in Germany,* trans. from 5th German ed. by Maud Lyall Patrick and G. T. W. Patrick, George Allen and Unwin, London; Macmillan, New York, 1913, pp. 160–174.

277. Paul G. Kuntz, ed., "G. Santayana: Unity and Beauty of the World," *Review of Metaphysics,* Vol. 19, 1966, pp. 425–440. (This is Chap. 5, "Lotze's System of Philosophy," from the present work by Santayana, with a new title and a preface.) (Re Santayana and Lotze, see #406–408.)

278. George Trumbull Ladd, *A Theory of Reality,* Scribner's, New York, 1899.

279. ———, "Lotze's Microcosmus," *New Englander,* Vol. 45, 1886, pp. 318–336.

280. John Laird, *Problems of the Self,* Macmillan, London, 1917.

281. ———, *Theism and Cosmology,* George Allen and Unwin, London, 1950, pp. 180–181.

282. E. Paolo Lamaura, *Storia della Filosofia, La Filosofia del Novecento,* Felici le Monnier, Firenze, 1963, p. 605.

283. Paul Lang, *Lotze und der Vitalismus* (Diss. Bonn), Ludwig, Bonn, 1913.

284. Fr. A. Lange, *Geschichte des Materialismus,* J. Baedecker, Iserlohn and Leipzig, 1866; 2nd ed., 1873–1875.

285. ———, *Histoire du matérialisme,* trans. by B. Pommerol, C. Reinwald, Paris, 1879, Vol. 2, pp. 127–128.

286. Paul Lange, *Die Lehre vom Instincte bei Lotze und Darwin,* R. Gaertner, Berlin, 1896.

287. Gerhard Lehmann, *Die Deutsche Philosophie der Gegenwart,* Alfred Kroner Verlag, Stuttgart, 1943.

288. Johannes W. Lemcke, *Die skeptischen Momente bei H. Lotze* (Diss. Erlangen), H. Laupp, Tubingen, 1914.

289. Sali Levi, *Lotze's Substanzbegriff* (Diss. Erlangen), D. Straus, Heidelberg, 1906.

290. Abraham Lichtenstein (Lichtstein), *Lotze und Wundt; eine vergleichende philosophische Studie* (Diss. Bern), Berner Studien zur Philosophie und ihrer Geschichte, Vol. 24, C. Sturzenegger, Bern, 1900.

291. Helmut Liedtke, "Die Exposition ontologischer Probleme bei Hermann Lotze und ihre Bedeutung für die gegenwärtige philosophische Systematik," typescript (Diss. Köln, 1949).

292. Bruno Lind, *Vagabond Scholar*, Seven Sirens Press, New York, 1962, pp. 49–50. (Re Santayana and Lotze, see #406–408.)

293. James Lindsay, *A Philosophical System of Theistic Idealism*, William Blackwood and Sons, Edinburgh and London, 1917, passim.

294. T. M. Lindsay, "Hermann Lotze," *Mind*, o.s. Vol. 1, 1876, pp. 363–382.

295. Th. Litt, "Lotze," *Handbuch der Philosophie*, Part 3, Dec. 1930, p. 157.

296. Heinrich Max Lohan, *Die Gottesidee Lotzes* (Diss. Marburg, Universität Dissertationen, Vol. 13, No. 7), Hoffman & Reiber, Marburg, 1888.

297. Donald M. Love, *Henry Churchill King of Oberlin*, Yale University Press, New Haven, 1956.

298. Arthur Löwenstamm, *Lotzes Lehre vom Ding an sich und Ich an sich* (Diss. Erlangen), H. Fleischmann, Breslau, 1906.

299. Walter Löwig, *Ueber Teleologie und Mechanismus in der Philosophie Lotzes* (Diss. Breslau), H. Fleischmann, Breslau, 1901.

300. W. Lutoslawski, "Über Lotze's Begriff der metaphysischen Einheit aller Dinge," *Zeitschrift für Philosophie und philosophische Kritik*, Vol. 114, 1899, pp. 64–77.

301. Cecil Alec Mace, "Lotze," *Encyclopedia Britannica*, Encyclopedia Britannica Corp., Chicago, 1960, Vol. 14, pp. 406–407.

302. Henry M. MacCracken, "Kant and Lotze," *Christian Thought*, November–December, 1885, pp. 161–180.

303. J. S. MacKenzie, *Elements of Constructive Philosophy*, George Allen and Unwin, London, 1917.

304. H. R. Mackintosh, *Types of Modern Theology*, Nisbet and Co., London, 1937.

305. Robert Mackintosh, *Albrecht Ritschl and His School*, Chapman and Hall, London, 1915, pp. 40 ff.

306. J. K. Majumdar, "Idealism of Leibniz and Lotze," *Philosophical Review*, Vol. 38, 1929, pp. 456–468.

307. Gregor Malantschuk, *Die Kategorienfrage bei Lotze* (Diss. Berlin), Graphisches Institut Paul Funk, Berlin, 1934.

308. Terenzio Mamiani della Rovere, *Ermanno Lotze,* Notizie biografische del socio Terenzio Mamiani lette nella seduta del 18 guigno 1882, in *Atti della R. Accademia dei Lincei,* Memorie della Classe di scienze morali, storiche e filologiche, Roma, 1882, Ser. 3, Vol. 10, pp. 237–240.

309. S. Mandl, *Kritische Beiträge zur Metaphysik Lotzes* (Diss. Bern), K. J. Wyss, Bern, 1888.

310. S. Marck, review, *"Logik* (1912) by H. Lotze," *Deutsche Literatur-Zeitung,* 1913, p. 916.

311. Jacques Maritain, *La philosophie morale: Examen historique et critique des grandes systèmes,* Librairie Gallimard, Paris, 1960, p. 327.

312. ———, *Moral Philosophy: An Historical and Critical Survey of the Great Systems,* Geoffrey Bless, London, 1964, p. 261.

313. Amédée Matagrin, *Essai sur l'esthétique de Lotze,* G. Baillière et cie., Alcan, Paris, 1901.

314. Sir Frederick Maurice, *The Life of Viscount Haldane of Cloan,* K.T., O.M., Faber and Faber, London, 1937. (Re Haldane and Lotze, see #195–197.)

315. Agnes Maxsein, *Die Entwicklung des Begriffs "A priori" von Bolzano über Lotze zu Husserl und den von ihm beeinflussten Phänomenologen* (Diss. Giessen), Giessen, 1933.

316. ———, "Der Begriff der "Geltung" bei Lotze," *Der Görres-Gesellschaft philosophisches Jahrbuch* (Fulda), Vol. 51, 1938, pp. 457–470.

317. Mayer, review, *"Hermann Lotze* by R. Falckenberg," *Theologische Zeitung,* No. 6, 1901.

318. Francis John McConnell, *Borden Parker Bowne, His Life and Philosophy,* Abingdon Press, New York, 1929. (Re Bowne and Lotze, see #110.)

319. P. Mehlhorn, "Ein deutscher Idealist," *Universum,* Vol. 33, 1917, No. 19.

320. P. Mentz, review, *"Problem des Wirkens und die monistischen Weltanschauung mit Beziehung an Lotze* by M. Wartenberg," *Vierteljahrsschrift für wissenschaftliche Philosophie,* 1901, p. 109.

321. John Theodore Merz, *A Fragment on the Human Mind,* Scribner's, New York, 1920, "Preface" on Lotze, passim.

322. ———, *History of European Thought in the Nineteenth Century,* William Blackwood, London, 3rd ed., 1907–1914.

323. ——— and Henry Sturt, "Lotze, Rudolf Hermann," *Encyclopaedia Britannica*, 11th ed., 1910–1911, Vol. 17, pp. 23–26.

324. Rudolf Metz, *Die Philosophischen Strömungen der Gegenwart in Grossbritannien*, 2 vols., Meiner, Leipzig, 1935.

325. ———, *A Hundred Years of British Philosophy*, trans. by J. W. Harvey, T. E. Jessop, ed. by J. H. Muirhead, George Allen and Unwin, London; Macmillan, New York, 1938.

326. Taylor E. Miller, "An Evaluation of Lotze's Theism," *Anglican Theological Review*, Vol. 36, 1954, pp. 292–298.

327. D. P. Mirtov, *Lotze's Lehre vom menschlichen und absolutlichen Geist* (Russian), St. Petersburg, 1914.

328. G. Misch, *Einleitung zu seiner Ausgabe von Lotze's Logik*, Leipzig, 1912. (see #29.)

329. St. George Mivaet, "Hermann Lotze and the Mechanical Philosophy," *Fortnightly Review*, Vol. 42, 1887, pp. 696–702.

330. Vida Frank Moore, *The Ethical Aspect of Lotze's Metaphysics*, Cornell Studies in Philosophy, No. 4, Macmillan, New York, 1901.

331. José Ferrater Mora, *Diccionario de Filosofia*, Editorial Sudamericana, Buenos Aires, 4th ed., 1958, pp. 831–832.

332. J. H. Muirhead, *Contemporary British Philosophy*, George Allen and Unwin, London, 1925.

333. ———, *German Philosophy in Relation to the War*, John Murray, London, 1915, pp. 6–7.

334. ———, *The Platonic Tradition in Anglo-Saxon Philosophy: Studies in the History of Idealism in England and America*, George Allen and Unwin, London, 1931.

335. Ad. Müller, "Die Behandlung der Hauptprobleme der Metaphysik bei Lotze," *Archiv für systematische Philosophie*, Vol. 7, 1901, pp. 88–113.

336. Gustav E. Müller, *Amerikanische Philosophie*, Fr. Frommanns Verlag, Stuttgart, 1936, 2nd ed., 1950, p. 172.

337. Richard Müller-Freienfels, *Die Hauptrichtungen der gegenwärtigen Psychologie*, Quelle and Meyer, Leipzig, 1929.

338. ———, *The Evolution of Modern Psychology*, trans. by W. Béran Wolfe, M.D., Yale University Press, New Haven, 1935.

339. Gardner Murphy, *Historical Introduction to Modern Psychology*, Harcourt Brace and Co., New York, 1949.

340. Andrew H. Murray, *The Philosophy of James Ward*, Cambridge University Press, Cambridge, 1937, passim. (Re Ward and Lotze, see #501–506.)

341. Max Nath, *Die Psychologie Hermann Lotzes in ihrem Verhältnis zu Herbart* (Diss. Halle-Wittenberg), Beilage zum Jahresbericht

der Ritter-Akademie zu Brandenburg a.H., Brandenburg a.d. Havel, 1887; also Berlin, 1887; Halle a.S., 1892.

342. Edmund Neuendorff, "Anmerkungen zu Lotze's Weltanschauung mit besonderer Berücksichtigung des Wartenbergschen Buches: *Das Problem des Wirkens usw.*," *Zeitschrift für Philosophie und philosophische Kritik*, Vol. 121, 1902, pp. 36–70.

343. ———, "Lotze's Kausalitätslehre," *Zeitschrift für Philosophie und philosophische Kritik*, Vol. 115, 1899, pp. 41–144.

344. ———, review, "*Darstellung der Seinslehre Lotzes in ihrem Verhältnis zu der Herbart* by Th. Simon," *Zeitschrift für Philosophie und philosophische Kritik*, Vol. 116, 1900, pp. 134–136.

345. ———, review, "*Lotze's Gottesbegriff* by M. Wentscher," *Zeitschrift für Philosophie und philosophische Kritik*, Vol. 116, 1900, pp. 140–142.

346. ———, review, "*Lotzes Stellung zum Occasionalismus* by E. Tuch," *Zeitschrift für Philosophie und philosophische Kritik*, Vol. 116, 1900, pp. 137–139.

347. Jens Nörregård, *Studier over Spencer, Lotze og Grundtvig*, K. Schønberg, København, 1890.

348. Taugott Konstantin Oesterreich, ed., *Friedrich Ueberwegs Grundriss der Geschichte der Philosophie*, Vol. 4, *Die Deutsche Philosophie des 19. Jahrhunderts und der Gegenwart*, E. S. Mittler & Sohn, Berlin (12th ed.), 1923, pp. 299–309, 703–705, passim. (Benno Schwabe & Co., Basel/Stuttgart, 1951).

349. Jacob Ohse (J. Ozé), *Proektivizm i personalizm v metafizike Lotse*, 4 vols., K. Mattiesen, Jurjew (= Tartu, Estonia), 1893–1896.

350. ———, *Personalisme i proektivisme v metafisické Lotze*, 1 vol., Derpt, 1896. (For review see #353.)

351. O. Opable, "Die Idee der Ganzheit bei den Philosophen Trendelenburg und Lotze," *Die Ganzheitsschule*, Vol. 8, 1950–1960, pp. 97–102.

352. Ossip-Lourié, review, "La métaphysique de Lotze" (*Personalisme i proektivisme v metafisiké Lotze* by J. Ozé [J. Ohse]), *Revue philosophique de la France et de l'étranger*, Vol. 49, 1897, pp. 327–329.

353. Ostermann, "Lotze's Weltanschauung," *Die Deutsche Schule*, 1902, pp. 7–22, 65–81, 129–152.

354. Clemens H. A. M. Otto, *Hermann Lotze über das Unbewusste* (Diss. Erlangen), A. Straube, Labes, 1900.

355. Heinrich Pannier, *Lotzes Gottesbegriff: genetisch dargestellt unter besonderer Berücksichtigung von Chr. Hermann Weisse* (Diss. Erlangen), E. R. Herzog, Meerane Sa., 1921.

356. Georg J. K. W. Pape, *Lotzes religiöse Weltanschauung,* Thormann & Goetsch, Berlin, 1899.

357. John Passmore, *A Hundred Years of Philosophy,* Gerald Duckworth, London, 1957.

358. Heinrich Pattgen, *Gesamtdarstellung und Würdigung der Ethik Lotzes* (Diss. Bonn, 1929), L. Neuendorff, Bonn, 1928.

359. Friedrich Paulsen, *An Autobiography,* trans. by Theodor Lorenz, Columbia University Press, New York, 1938.

360. C. S. Peirce, *Collected Papers,* ed. by Arthur W. Burks, Harvard University Press, Cambridge, Mass., 1958, Vol. 8, p. 184. (Re Dewey and Lotze, see #136.)

361. A. Penjon, "La metaphysique de Lotze," *Revue philosophique,* Vol. 21, 1886, pp. 348–366.

362. Ralph Barton Perry, *The Thought and Character of William James,* Little, Brown, Boston, 1935. (Re James and Lotze, see #229.)

363. Christian F. Pfeil, *Der Einfluss Lotzes auf die logische Bewegung der Gegenwart, dargestellt am Begriff der "Geltung" und am Begriff der Wahrheit und der Apriori* (Diss. Erlangen), Laupp, Tübingen, 1914.

364. O. Pfister, "Wechselwirkung und Gottesbegriff" (especially about Lotze and Bolliger), *Schweizerische theologische Zeitschrift,* 1901, pp. 168–185.

365. Chr. D. Pflaum, review, *"Das Gefühl in seiner Eigenart und Selbständigkeit mit besonderer Beziehung an Herbart und Lotze* by J. Hübener," *Vierteljahrsschrift für wissenschaftliche Philosophie,* 1900, p. 356.

366. E. Pfleiderer, *Lotze's philosophische Weltanschauung nach ihren Grundzügen,* G. Reimer, Berlin, 1882; 2nd ed., 1884.

367. W. Pieth, "Kritik der Lotzeschen Psychologie in der Analyse ihrer Grundlagen," *Archiv für systematische Philosophie,* Vol. 17, 1911, pp. 461–472.

368. W. B. Pillsbury, *The History of Psychology,* W. W. Norton, New York, 1929, pp. 149–152.

369. Karl Pira, *Framställning och Kritik af J. St. Mills, Lotzes och Sigwarts Läror om begreppsbildningen i Logiken, etc.* (Diss. Uppsala), P. Palmquists Aktienbolag, Stockholm, 1897.

370. Ed. Platzhoff, review, *"Hermann Lotze* by R. Falckenberg," *Christliche Welt,* 1901, p. 671.

371. G. A. Pochmann, *German Culture in America,* University of Wisconsin Press, Madison, 1957.

Lotze bibliography

372. Hans Adam Pöhlmann, *Die Erkenntnistheorie Rudolf Hermann Lotzes* (Diss. Erlangen), August Vollrath, Erlangen, 1897.

373. Friedrich Pol, *Lotzes Ansicht über die Reproduction der Vorstellungen und Vergleich derselber mit den gegenwärtigen Lehren der Psychologie* (Diss. Erlangen), Soltau, Norden, 1903, Psychological tracts, Vol. 3.

374. E. Pololsky, "Rudolph Hermann Lotze," *Medical Record*, Vol. 152, 1940, p. 379.

375. Joseph Horace Powers, *Kritische Bemerkungen zu Lotzes Seelenbegriff* (Diss. Göttingen), Dietrich'sche Univ.-Buchdruckerei, Göttingen, 1892.

376. von Prantl, "R. Hermann Lotze," *Sitzungsberichte der philosophische-philologische und historische Classe d.k.b. Akademie der Wissenschaft zu München*, Vol. 12, 1882, pp. 400–403.

377. A. Seth Pringle-Pattison, *The Balfour Lectures on Realism*, ed. with a "Memoir of the Author" by G. F. Barbour, William Blackwood and Sons, Edinburgh and London, 1933, pp. 29–30.

378. ———, review, "*A Critical Account of the Philosophy of Lotze* by H. Jones," *Mind*, Vol. 4, 1895, pp. 515–533. (Reprinted in *The Philosophical Radicals and Other Essays*, William Blackwood and Sons, Edinburgh, 1907, pp. 147–177.)

379. Franz Prosenc, *Eine vergleichende Darstellung der Psychologischen Hauptlehren bei Herbart und Lotze*, K. K. Staats-gymnasium, Mähr.-Weisskirchen, 1907.

380. Benjamin Rand, *The Classical Psychologists: Selections Illustrating Psychology from Anaxagoras to Wundt*, Houghton Mifflin, Boston, 1912.

381. William L. Raub, *Die Seelenlehre bei Lotze und Wundt* (Diss. Strassburg), C. & J. Goeller, Strassburg, 1901.

382. E. Rehnisch, *Bilder von Hermann Lotze*, A. T. Engelhardt, Leipzig, 1896 (*Göttinger Anzeigen*, No. 4202, June 26, 1896).

383. E. Rehnisch, "Hermann Lotze," *Neues Lausitzisches Magazin*, Vol. 77, 1901, pp. 203–215.

384. Ernst Reinhardt, *Lotzes Stellung zur Offenbarung* (Diss. Erlangen), H. Kraatz, Berlin, 1897.

385. Charles Renouvier, "L'infini actuel est-il contradictoire?—Réplique à M. Lotze," *Revue Philosophique*, 1880.

386. ———, "L'infinité de l'espace et du temps dans la métaphysique de M. H. Lotze," *Critique Philosophique*, Vol. 17, 1880. No. 3–5, pp. 33–40, 49–55, 65–72.

387. Theodule Ribot, *La psychologie allemande contemporaine*, G. Ballière, Paris, 1879, pp. 67–102.

388. ———, *German Psychology of To-Day: The Empirical School,* trans. by J. M. Baldwin, Preface by James McCosh, Scribner's, New York, 1886, "Lotze: Theory of Local Signs," pp. 68–95.

389. Fritz-Joachim von Rintelen, "Wertphilosophie," in *Die Philosophie im 20. Jahrhundert,* Ernst Klett Verlag, Stuttgart, 1959, p. 443.

390. A. A. Roback, *History of American Psychology,* Library Publishers, New York, 1952, pp. 93–94.

391. Edwin P. Robins, *Some Problems of Lotze's Theory of Knowledge,* ed. with a biographical introduction by J. E. Creighton, Cornell Studies in Philosophy, No. 1, Macmillan, New York, 1900.

392. Daniel S. Robinson, *Crucial Issues in Philosophy,* Christopher Publishing House, Boston, 1955, Chap. 28, "Hermann Lotze and Albert Lange as Interpreters of the Crisis in Western Civilization," pp. 222–233.

393. Hilario Rodriguez Sanz, "El concepto de valor en la filosofia de Lotze," *Philosophia* (Mendoza, Argentine Republic, Universidad Nacional de Cuyo, Facultad de filosofía y letras, Vol. 5, 1948, pp. 88–103.

394. (Oscar Heinrich) Julius Röhr, *Kritische Untersuchungen über Lotze's Ästhetik* (Diss. Halle a.S., 1890).

395. Georg Gustav Alexander Rosenqvist, *Den Filosofiska Grundvalen för Albrecht Ritschl och Lotze,* Osakeyhtiö Weilen & Göös Aktiebolag, 1902.

396. ———, *Lotzes Religionsfilosofi framstäld och bedömd,* J. C. Frenckell & Son, Helsingfors (Akademisk afhandling Helsingfors), 1889.

397. Josiah Royce, "Present Ideals of American University Life," *Scribner's Magazine,* X (1891), p. 383. (Re Royce and Lotze, see #120, 131, 132.)

398. Alois Ruescher, *Die Teleologie in ihrem Verhältnis zur Gottesidee, mechanischen Naturansicht und göttlichen Notwendigkeitsweltanschauung. Eine principielle Untersuchung mit besonderer Berücksichtigung von Haeckel, Wundt, Lotze und Fechner,* Mueller, Zürich, 1902.

399. Guido de Ruggiero, *La Filosofia contemporanea,* 2 vols., G. Laterza & figli, Bari, rev. 3rd ed., 1929; 5th ed., 1947.

400. ———, *Modern Philosophy,* trans. by A. Howard Hannay and R. G. Collingwood, George Allen and Unwin, London, 1921.

401. Bertrand Russell, *An Essay on the Foundations of Geometry,* Cambridge University Press, Cambridge, 1897; Dover Publications, New York, 1956.

402. ———, *The Principles of Mathematics,* Cambridge University Press, Cambridge, 1903; 2nd ed., George Allen & Unwin, London, 1937, Chap. 51, "Logical Arguments against Points," pp. 445–455.

403. ———, *A Critical Exposition of the Philosophy of Leibniz,* Cambridge University Press, Cambridge, 1900; new ed., George Allen & Unwin, London, 1937.

404. ———, *History of Western Philosophy,* George Allen & Unwin; Simon and Schuster, New York, 1945, pp. 585, 721. (Russell writes, on p. 811: "Santayana, whose doctor's thesis William James had described as 'the perfection of rottenness.'" This has become a widespread confusion. The remark is quite contrary to James's high opinion of Santayana on Lotze.) (Re Russell and Lotze, see #420.)

405. R. Salinger, "Lotze als Berliner Universitätslehrer," (*Alt-Berlin*) *Mitteilungen des Vereins für Geschichte Berlins,* Vol. 34, 1917, p. 34.

406. George Santayana, *The Last Puritan: A Memoir in the Form of a Novel,* Scribner's, New York, 1936, pp. 83–87.

407. ———, *Persons and Places,* Vol. 2, *The Middle Span,* Scribner's, New York, 1945, pp. 152–153.

408. ———, "Lotze's Moral Idealism," *Mind,* o.s.Vol. 15, 1890, pp. 191–212. (Re Santayana and Lotze, see #225, 278, 293.)

409. Paul Schaaf, *Herder und Lotze, Wegweiser in die Ästhetik der Gegenwart,* typescript, 1924 (Diss. Bonn).

410. Fritz Schäfer, *Lotze's Lehre vom Absoluten* (Diss. Erlangen), Junge, Erlangen, 1895.

411. Walter Scheller (O.F.W.W.), *Die kleine und die grosse Metaphysik Hermann Lotzes: eine vergleichende Darstellung* (Diss. Erlangen), Buchdruckerei Heinrich Ludwig, Bonn, 1912.

412. F. C. S. Schiller, *Studies in Humanism,* Macmillan, London, 2nd ed., 1912, pp. 434–435. (Chap. 4, "Lotze's Monism," is a reprint of "Lotze's Monism," *The Philosophical Review,* May, 1896.)

413. ———, "Reply to W. J. Wright: Lotze's Monism," *Philosophical Review,* Vol. 6, 1897, pp. 62–64. (See Wright #537.)

414. Roland W. Schilling, *Die realistischen Elemente der Lotzeschen Ontologie* (Diss. Leipzig), Jachner und Fischer, Leipzig, 1909.

415. Paul Arthur Schilpp, *The Philosophy of C. D. Broad,* Tudor, New York, 1959, p. 50.

416. ———, *The Philosophy of Ernst Cassirer,* Library of Living Philosophers, Evanston, Ill., 1949.

417. ———, *The Philosophy of John Dewey,* Library of Living Phi-

losophers, Evanston, Ill., 1939, pp. 32 f, 80. (Re Dewey and Lotze, see #136.)

418. ———, *The Philosophy of Karl Jaspers*, Tudor, New York, 1957, p. 120.

419. ———, *The Philosophy of G. E. Moore*, Tudor, New York, 1952, p. 17.

420. ———, *The Philosophy of Bertrand Russell*, Tudor, New York, 1951, pp. 10, 171–173, 263. (Re Russell and Lotze, see #401–404.)

421. Johannes Schmidt, *Leibniz und Baumgarten, ein Beitrag zur Geschichte der deutschen Aesthetik, Hierin eine ausführliche Kritik ästhetischer Grundanschauung Lotze's und Zimmermann's*, Lippert, Halle a.S., 1875.

422. John. Wilh. Schmidt-Japing, *Lotzes Religionsphilosophie in ihrer Entwicklung*, Vanderhoeck und Ruprecht, Göttingen, 1925.

423. T. Schmitz, "Lotze, sprachphilosophische Untersuchungen," *Germanromanische Monatsschrift*, Vol. 3, 1911, pp. 129–137, 193–207.

424. C. M. Schneider, review, "*Problem des Wirkens und die monistischen Weltanschauung mit Beziehung an Lotze* by M. Wartenberg," *Jahrbuch für Philosophie und spekulative Theologie*, Vol. 15, 1900, p. 473.

425. Herbert W. Schneider, *A History of American Philosophy*, Columbia University Press, New York, 1946; 2nd ed., 1963, passim.

426. Henri Schön, *La métaphysique de Hermann Lotze: ou, La philosophie des actions et des réactions réciproques*, Thèse de la Faculté des Lettres de Paris, Fischbacher, Paris, 1902.

427. ———, *Lotze's Metaphysik oder Philosophie der Wechselwirkung*, Edinburgh, 1902. (For reviews see #160, 439.)

428. ———, *Les origines historique de la théologie de Ritschl*, Fischbacher, Paris, 1893.

429. Gustav Schöneberg, *Vergleichung der ersten drei Auflagen von Lotzes Mikrokosmus* (Diss. Erlangen), George Chasté, Berlin, 1903.

430. Arthur E. G. Schröder, *Geschichtsphilosophie bei Lotze* (Diss. Leipzig), F. A. Wilhelm, Leipzig, 1896.

431. ———, review, "*Mikrokosmus* by H. Lotze," *Leipzig. Neuest. Nachr.*, 1924, Vol. 13, No. 3.

432. G. von Schulteis, "Religionsphilosophische Grundgedanken H. Lotze's," *Theologische Zeitschrift aus der Schweiz*, Vol. 2, 1885, pp. 274–302.

433. W. P. Schumann, review, "*Hermann Lotze* by R. Falckenberg," *Vierteljahrsschrift für wissenschaftliche Philosophie und Soziologie*, 1902, p. 468.

434. Schummert, "Beurteilung des Wertes der Lotzesche Lokalzeichen-theorie vom Standpunkt der experimentischen Psychologie," *Pädagogische Werke* 1903, pp. 505–515.

435. Johann Friedrich Schwarz, *Lotzes Geschichtsphilosophie in ihrem Verhältnis zu seiner Religionsphilosophie und Metaphysik* (Diss. Giessen), Joh. Wirth'sche Hofbuchdruckerei, Mainz, 1901.

436. Else Schwedler, "Die Lehre von der Beseeltheit des Atome bei Lotze," *Zeitschrift für Philosophie und philosophische Kritik,* Vol. 121, 1902, pp. 66–92, 156–160. (see also Else [Schwedler] Wentscher, #515.)

437. Max Schweinitz, *Die Bedeutung von Lotzes Philosophie für eine Theorie der Bildung* (Diss. Leipzig, 1931), Emil Hampel, Weiss-wasser O.-L., 1930.

438. E. Schwertfeger, review, *"Lotze's Metaphysik oder Philosophie der Wechselwirkung* by H. Schön," *Zeitschrift für Philosophie und Pädagogik,* Vol. 10, 1903, pp. 161–166.

439. Karl F. L. Seibert, *Lotze als Anthropologe* (Diss. Erlangen), H. Ferger, Wiesbaden, 1900. (For review see #528.)

440. R. Seydel, "R. Hermann Lotze," *Nord und Süd,* Vol. 20, 1882, No. 63.

441. ———, "Hermann Lotze's System der Philosophie," *Die Grenzbo-ten, Zeitschrift für Politik, Literatur und Kunst,* Vol. 40, 3rd quarter, 1881, pp. 283–297.

442. Seydl, review, *"Hermann Lotze* by R. Falckenberg," *Der Katho-lik,* 3rd series, Vol. 24, 1902, pp. 164–167.

443. Paul Sickel, "Das Verhältnis des Pantheismus zum Theismus in Lotzes Lehre vom Absoluten," *Zeitschrift für Philosophie und philosophische Kritik,* Vol. 130, 1906, pp. 113–141.

444. O. Siebert, "Lotze's Lehre von der Existenz der Seele," *Kirchliche Wochenschrift für evangelische Christen,* 1901, No. 19, 20.

445. Eduard Hermann Simon (i.e. C.E.H.), *Lotzes Verhältnis zu Leibniz* (Diss. Erlangen), August Hoffmann, Leipzig-Reudnitz, 1904.

446. Theodor Simon, *Darstellung der Seinslehre Lotzes in ihrem Verhältnis zu der Herbarts* (Diss. Erlangen), August Hoffmann, Leipzig-Reudnitz, 1892. (For review see #344.)

447. ———, *Leib und Seele bei Fechner und Lotze als Vertreteren zweier massgebenden Weltanschauungen,* Vanderhoeck und Ru-precht, Göttingen, 1894.

448. ———, *Der Monismus* (Gegenwartsfragen Part 7), Greiner und Pfeiffer, 1904.

449. ———, "Widerspruche und Schwankungen in Lotzes Lehre von

den Dingen," *Zeitschrift für exakte Philosophie*, Vol. 20, 1893, pp. 300–317.

450. May Sinclair, *The New Idealism*, Macmillan, New York, 1922, p. 235.

451. James H. Snowden, *The World A Spiritual System: an Outline of Metaphysics*, Macmillan, New York, 1910.

452. Hugo Sommer, *Die Neugestaltung unserer Weltansicht durch die Erkenntniss der Idealität des Raumes und der Zeit . . .* , G. Reimer, Berlin, 1882.

453. ———, *Der Pessimismus und die Sittenlehre*, Theological Society of Haarlem, Haarlem: Harrassowitz, Leipzig, Berlin, 1882; 2nd ed., 1883.

454. ———, *Ueber das Wesen und die Bedeutung der menschlichen Freiheit und deren moderne Widersacher*, G. Reimer, Berlin, 1882; 2nd ed., 1885.

455. Hugo Sommer, "Dem Andenken Lotze's," *Im neuen Reich*, Vol. 11, No. 36, 1881, pp. 345–360.

456. ———, "Hermann Lotze," *Preussische Jahrbücher*, Vol. 47, 1881, pp. 177–195.

457. ———, "Die Lotze'schen Philosophie und ihre Bedeutung für das geistliche Leben der Gegenwart," *Preussische Jahrbücher*, Vol. 36, 1875.

458. ———, "Zum Andenken Lotze's," *Preussische Jahrbücher*, Vol. 49, 1882, pp. 655–662.

459. William R. Sorley, "James Ward, 1843–1925," *Proceedings of the British Academy*, 1925, Humphrey Milford, London, 1927. (Re Ward and Lotze, see #502–506.)

460. Staffel, "Rudolf Hermann Lotze," *Preussische Jahrbücher*, Dec. 1918, pp. 328–336.

461. Leonhard Stählin, *Kant, Lotze, Albrecht Ritschl—Eine kritische Studie*, Dörffling und Franke, Leipzig, 1888.

462. ———, *Kant, Lotze and Ritschl*, trans. by D. W. Simon, T. and T. Clark, Edinburgh, 1889.

463. Steichen, review, "*Grundzüge der Naturphilosophie* (2nd ed., 1889) by H. Lotze," *Scholastik*, 1931, p. 466.

464. Johannes A. Steinbach, *Apologetische Tendenzen in Lotzes Philosophieren* (Diss. Göttingen), E. A. Huth, Göttingen, 1919.

465. Kurt Fritz Theodor Steinbrück, *Grundzüge der Musikästhetik Hermann Lotzes* (Diss. Erlangen, 1917), Herrmann, Berlin-Lichterfelde, 1918.

466. Johannes August Stier, *Das Unbewusste bei Lotze* (Diss. Erlangen), Grunert, Berlin, 1897.

Lotze bibliography

467. G. F. Stout, *Analytic Psychology*, 2 vols., Swan Sonnenschein, London, 1896.

468. ———, *God and Nature*, ed. by A. K. Stout, Cambridge University Press, Cambridge, 1952, "The Monadism of Leibniz and Lotze," pp. 215–218.

469. ———, *A Manual of Psychology*, revised in collaboration with C. A. Mace, University Tutorial Press, London, 5th ed., 1938.

470. Eleonora Stratilescu, *Die physiologische Grundlage des Seelenlebens bei Fechner und Lotze* (Diss. Berlin), Schade, Berlin, 1903.

471. Carl Stumpf, "Zum Gedächtnis Lotzes," *Kantstudien*, Vol. 22, 1917, pp. 1–26.

472. Franz Stumpf, *Die Gotteslehre von Hermann Lotze und Gustav Theodor Fechner, eine vergleichende religionsphilosophische Untersuchung* (Diss. Giessen), F. Ussner, Schotten, 1925.

473. H. Sturt, *Personal Idealism*, Macmillan, London, New York, 1902.

474. ———, *The Principles of Understanding*, Cambridge University Press, Cambridge, 1915, p. 27.

475. Albert Temple Swing, *The Theology of Albrecht Ritschl*, Longmans Green, New York, 1901, pp. 67–76.

476. Einar Tegen, *Moderne Willenstheorien*, Uppsala Universitēts Arsskrift, Part 1, 1934.

477. Gustav Teichmueller, *Logik und Kategorienlehre*, Kaunas, Amsterdam, Leipzig, 1939. (*Archiv für spiritualistische Philosophie und ihre Geschichte*, Vol. 1.)

478. Karl P. A. F. Thieme, *Glaube und Wissen bei Lotze*, Dörffling & Franke, Leipzig, 1888.

479. ———, *Der Primat der praktischen Vernuft bei Lotze* (Diss. Leipzig), Ackermann & Glaser, Leipzig, 1887.

480. Evan E. Thomas, *Lotze's Theory of Reality*, Longmans Green, London, 1921.

481. ———, "Lotze's Relation to Idealism," *Mind*, Vol. 24, 1915, pp. 186–206, 367–385, 481–497.

482. Tyler Thompson, *Lotze's Conception of the Self* (Diss. Boston University, 1950).

483. Alfred Tienes, *Lotze's Gedanken zu den Principienfragen der Ethik*, J. Hörning, Heidelberg, 1896.

484. Felice Tocco, *Lo spiritualismo del Lotze*, Napoli, 1887.

485. Alexander C. F. Trommsdorff, *Lotzes Bedeutung für die Pädagogik* (Diss. Jena), B. Vopelius, Jena, 1902.

486. Erika Tubbesing "Hermann Lotze, Wurzeln, Werk und Wirkungen seiner mechanistischen Naturauffassung," typescript, not for exchange (Medical faculty Diss. Münster, 1964).

487. Ernst Tuch, *Lotzes Stellung zum Occasionalismus. Die Bedeutung der occasionalistischen Theorie in Lotzes System* (Diss. Erlangen), Mayer und Müller, Berlin; Deutschländer und Kompanie, Nachfl., Hamburg, 1897. (For review see #346.)

488. J. E. Turner, "Lotze's Theory of the Subjectivity of Time and Space," *Monist*, Vol. 29, 1919, pp. 579–600.

489. Friedrich Ueberweg, *Grundriss der Geschichte der Philosophie*, E. S. Mittler, Berlin, 1st ed., 1862–1866; 4th ed., 1871. (See also Oesterreich's editions, #348.)

490. ———, *A History of Philosophy from Thales to the Present Time*, 2 vols., authorized translation from 4th German edition by George S. Morris, Scribner's, New York, 1871–1873, Vol. 2, pp. 312–321.

491. W. M. Urban, *The Intelligible World: Metaphysics and Value*, George Allen and Unwin, London, 1929, pp. 162–163.

492. C. W. Valentine, *The Philosophy of Lotze in its Theological Aspects*, R. Maclehose & Co., Glasgow, 1911.

493. Otto Veeck, "Zu Lotze's Religionsphilosophie," *Protestantische Kirchen-Zeitung*, 1892, No. 24–27.

494. G. Mourly Vold, "R. H. Lotze's Ontologie," *Norske Universitets-og Skole Annaler*, 1879.

495. Gustav Vorbrodt, *Principien der Ethik und Religionsphilosophie Lotzes*, Rich. Kahle's Verlag, Dessau-Leipzig, 1891.

496. Jean Wahl, *Les Philosophies Pluralistes d'Angleterre et d'Amérique*, Alcan, Paris, 1920.

497. ———, *The Pluralist Philosophers of England and America*, trans. by Fred Rothwell, Open Court, London, 1925, pp. 50–55.

498. F.J.K.G. Wahn, *Kritik der Lehre Lotzes von der menschlichen Wahlfreiheit*, Heynemann, Halle a.S., 1888.

499. ———, "Kritik der Lehre Lotze's von der menschlichen Wahlfreiheit," *Zeitschrift für Philosophie und philosophische Kritik*, Vol. 94, 1888, pp. 88–141.

500. William Wallace, *Lectures and Essays on Natural Theology*, Oxford University Press, Oxford, 1898.

501. Thomas Friedrich Walter, *Die religionsphilosophischen Grundgedanken Hermann Lotze's* (Diss. Erlangen), K. Henn, Freiburg i. Br., 1901.

502. James Ward, *Naturalism and Agnosticism*, 2 vols., Macmillan, New York, 1899.

503. ———, *Psychological Principles*, Cambridge University Press, Cambridge, 1919.

504. James Ward, *The Realm of Ends—or Pluralism and Theism*, Cambridge University Press, Cambridge, 1911.

505. ———, *Essays in Philosophy*, ed. by W. R. Sorley and G. F. Stout, with a "Memoir" by Olwen Ward Campbell, Cambridge University Press, Cambridge, 1927.

506. ———, "A Theistic Monadism," *Contemporary British Philosophy*, Vol. 2, ed. by J. H. Muirhead, George Allen and Unwin, London, 1925, 1953. (Re Ward and Lotze, see #340, 459.)

507. Mscislaw Wartenberg, *Das Problem des Wirkens und die monistischen Weltanschauung mit besonderer Beziehung an Lotze. Eine historischkritische Untersuchung zur Metaphysik*, H. Haacke, Leipzig, 1900. (For reviews see #172, 320, 342, 424.)

508. John Watson, *An Outline of Philosophy*, James Maclehose, Glasgow, 3rd ed., 1901, Chap. 10, "Lotze's Theory of Knowledge," pp. 431–449.

509. Robert I. Watson, *The Great Psychologists: From Aristotle to Freud*, J. B. Lippincott, Philadelphia, 1963, p. 269.

510. O. Weder, "Hermann Lotze und die höhe Schule," *Neue Jahrbücher für das klassische Altertum, Geschichte und deutsche Literatur und für Pädagogik*, Vol. 40, 1917, pp. 153–162.

511. Karl Weidel, *Mechanismus und Teleologie in der Philosophie Lotzes* (Diss. Breslau, 1903), O. Gutsmann, Breslau, 1904.

512. ———, "Mechanismus und Teleologie in der Philosophie Lotzes," *Archiv für Geschichte der Philosophie*, Vol. 19, 1906, pp. 1–98.

513. Ch. H. Weisse, review, "*Mikrokosmus* by H. Lotze," *Zeitschrift für Philosophie und philosophische Kritik*, Vol. 47, 1865, pp. 272–315.

514. R. M. Wenley, *The Life and Work of George Sylvester Morris: A Chapter in the History of American Thought in the Nineteenth Century*, Macmillan, New York, 1917.

515. Else (Schwedler) Wentscher, *Geschichte des Kausalproblems in der neueren Philosophie*, F. Meiner, Leipzig, 1921. (For review see #156.)

516. ———, *Das Kausalproblem in Lotzes Philosophie*, Max Niemeyer, Halle a.S., 1903.

517. ———, review, "*Mikrokosmus* by H. Lotze," *Frauenbildung*, 1910, p. 395. (See also Else Schwedler #436.)

518. Max Wentscher, *Fechner und Lotze*, (*Geschichte der Philosophie in Einzeldarstellung*), E. Reinhardt, München, 1925.

519. ———, *Hermann Lotze*, Vol. 1, *Lotze's Leben und Werke*, Carl Winter Universitätsbuchhandlung, Heidelberg, 1913. (Only Vol. 1 was published.)

520. ———, *Lotze's Gottesbegriff und dessen metaphysische Begrün-*

dung (Diss. Halle-Wittenberg), C. A. Kaemmerer, Halle a.S., 1893. (For review see #345.)

521. ———, "Lotze," James Hastings, ed., *Encyclopedia of Religion and Ethics*, T. and T. Clark, Edinburgh, 1916, Vol. 8, pp. 146–148.

522. ———, "Lotze's Optimismus im Zusammenhang mit seiner Ethik," *Synthesen in der Philosophie des Gegenwart*, 1926, pp. 145–163.

523. ———, "Lotze's Theismus," *Archiv für die gesamte Psychologie*, Vol. 77, 1930, pp. 273–290.

524. ———, "Das Problem der Willensfreiheit bei Lotze," Sonderabzug aus *Philosophische Abhandlungen dem Andenken Rudolf Hayms gewidmet*, M. Niemeyer, Halle a.S., pp. 155–202.

525. ———, "Zur Weltanschauung Lotze's," *Zeitschrift für Philosophie und philosophische Kritik*, Vol. 117, 1901, pp. 224–231. (Answer to E. Neuendorff's review of *Lotze's Gottesbegriff*, see #345.)

526. ———, review, *"Geschichte der Aesthetik in Deutschland (1913)* by H. Lotze," *Deutsche Literatur-Zeitung*, 1913, pp. 2842–2844.

527. ———, review, *"Hermann Lotze* by R. Falckenberg," *Zeitschrift für Philosophie und philosophische Kritik*, Vol. 125, 1904, pp. 203–204.

528. ———, review, *"Lotze als Anthropologe* by F. Seibert," *Zeitschrift für Philosophie und philosophische Kritik*, Vol. 118, 1901, pp. 126–128.

529. Alban G. Widgery, *A Philosopher's Pilgrimage*, Thomas Y. Crowell Co., New York, 1961.

530. ———, "Lotze," *The Encyclopedia Americana*, Americana Corp., New York, 1967, Vol. 17, p. 774.

531. H. Wiedenmann, *Grundzüge der Lotze'schen Psychologie und ihre Bewertung*, Bielefeld, 1911.

532. Wilke, review, *"Mikrokosmus* (3 vols., 6th ed., 1923) by H. Lotze," *Hefte für Büchereiwesen* Österreich Schulbücher, 1925, pp. 52–54.

533. Emil Carl Wilm, *Studies in Philosophy and Theology by Former Students of Borden Parker Bowne*, Abingdon Press, New York, 1922. (Re Bowne and Lotze, see #110.)

534. John Cook Wilson, *Statement and Inference*, ed. by A. S. L. Farquharson, Clarendon Press, Oxford, 1926.

535. Selmar Witkowski, *Ueber den Zusammenhang von Lotzes medizinisch-physiologischer Anschauung mit seiner Auffassung vom Entstehen und Fortleben der Seele* (Diss. Giessen), E. Ebering, Berlin, 1924.

536. J. Wolff, "Lotze's Metaphysik," *Der Görres-Gesellschaft philosophische Jahrbuch* (Fulda), Vol. 4, 1891, pp. 138–160, Vol. 5, 1892, pp. 26–41, 133–151, 285–315.

537. W. J. Wright, "Lotze's Monism," *Philosophical Review,* Vol. 6, 1897, pp. 57–61. (For a reply by F. C. S. Schiller, see #412.)

538. Albert Eduard Wruck, *Die Ethik Rudolf Hermann Lotzes in ihren pädagogischen Konsequenzen* (Diss. Bonn), Wendt Groll, Marienwerder, 1928.

539. Paul Wrzecianko, *Die philosophischen Wurzeln der Theologie Albrecht Ritschls: ein Beitrag zum Problem des Verhältnisses von Theologie und Philosophie im 19. Jahrhundert,* Theologische Bibliothek Töpelmann, Berlin, 1964, "Die Philosophie Hermann Lotzes," pp. 52–120.

540. Hugo Zellner, "Lotze's Stellung zum Unsterblichkeitsgedanke," typescript (Diss. Erlangen, 1922).

541. V. V. Zenkovsky, *A History of Russian Philosophy,* trans. by George L. Kline, Columbia University Press, New York, 1953, pp. 200, 548, 646–647.

542. Werner Ziegenfuss und Gertrud Jung, *Philosophen-Lexikon: Handwörterbuch der Philosophie nach Personen,* Walter de Gruyter, Berlin, 1950, Vol. 2, pp. 80–87.

543. Th. Ziegler, "Zu Lotze's Gedächtnis," *Protestantische Monatshefte,* 1917, pp. 161–169.

544. E. Zoeller, "Der Gottesbegriff in der neueren schwedischen Philosophie, mit besonderer Berücksichtigung der Weltanschauungen Boströms und Lotzes," *Philosophische Gesellschaft zu Berlin,* C. E. M. Pfeffer (R. Stricker), Halle a.S., 1888.

545. Egon Zoeller, "Schwedische Schriften über Lotze," *Zeitschrift für Philosophie und philosophische Kritik,* Vol. 95, 1889, p. 106.

546. Zschau, *Lotze's Ethik,* Meerane i.S., 1885.

INDEX

References pp. 3–105 are to Kuntz' Introduction, references pp. 109–226 are to Santayana's text.

Absolute, 42–45, 157
Adamson, Robert, 54, 59
Aesthetics, 15–16, 123–124, 128, 143, 218–220, 222
Anglo-American philosophy, 48–67
Aristotle, 23, 87, 100
Atomism, 147–150, 155–181

Bacon, Francis, 121
Bergson, Henri, 56, 72
Berkeley, George, 38, 177
Bosanquet, Bernard, 48
Bowne, Borden Parker, 52
Broad, C. D., 56–57
Browning, Robert, 52

Caspari, O., 109
Causality, 45–46, 80–81, 103, 123, 187–195, 201–202
Chaos, 29
Classical realism, 100–101
Comte, Auguste, 32
Consciousness, 71, 150–151, 154, 218, 223
Conservation of energy, 126
Contiguity, 146
Conybeare, F. C. and E. M. M., 58
Cook Wilson, John, 54, 57–58
Cosmos, 33, 211, 222

Darwin, Charles, 32, 121
Descartes, René, 160
Design, 30 ff
Devaux, Philippe, 68
Dialectic, 19–20

Eliot, T. S., 3
Empiricism, 112
Evolutionary hypothesis, 119–122
Extension, 160–176

Falkenberg, Richard, 69
Fallacies, 16–19, 45–47, 78, 83
Fechner, Gustav Theodor, 13, 163
Fichte, J. G., 13, 17, 135, 137, 142
Fisch, Max H., 86
Formalism, 134–139
Freedom, 132

Gates, George A., 53
German philosophy, 4, 17, 48, 51, 140–142
God, 83, 111, 112, 153, 199, 215–217, 220–221, 223–225
Goethe, J. W. von, 9, 42, 223–224
Green, T. H., 6, 57–58

Haldane, R. B. (Lord H. of Cloan), 7–8, 49
Hamilton, Elizabeth, 58

Harmony, 195–198, 203
Hegel, G. W. F., 3, 15, 28, 31, 39–
40, 62, 96, 126, 131, 137, 142,
213, 219
Herbart, Johann Friedrich, 10–11,
12, 131, 134, 142–152, 154, 157–
159, 181
Howison, George H., 54
Hume, David, 96, 191–192, 212

Ideal, 101, 200–201, 202, 204, 207–
208, 213, 219, 222
Idealism, 38–47, 60–62, 156
Idealism/Realism, 26–29, 33, 45,
59–60, 126, 152–153, 157, 159–
160, 163, 164, 165, 168, 177–180,
198
Indeterminism, 198–199, 203, 206–
209

James, William, 3, 5, 8, 12, 16, 45,
48, 65, 105
Jaspers, Karl, 5
Jones, E. E. Constance, 58

Kant, Immanuel, 12, 40–41, 96,
126–127, 142, 130–154, 163, 177
King, Henry Churchill, 7
Kraushaar, Otto, 49

Ladd, George T., 6–7, 52
Lange, F. A., 19
Law, 183, 189, 204, 216, 218–219
Leibniz, Gottfried Wilhelm, 13,
41–42, 131, 134, 146, 196–198,
203
Linguistic philosophy, 11 f, 100,
102, 104
Locke, John, 179
Logic, 61, 95
Lotze, Rudolf Hermann: simi-
larity to James, 4–5; motivation
in philosophy, 5; reputation, 6;
theism explains popularity in
American colleges, 6–7; empiri-

cist and anti-rationalist, 12, 16,
136; humanist, 12; Leibnizian,
13; anti-Hegelian, 15, 28, 31;
aesthetician, 15; pluralist, 16;
systematic?, 17; not anti-
mechanist, 19; logician, not
dialectician, 19 ff; eclectic?, 22;
Aristotelian, 23; Whiteheadian
(before Whitehead), 26; idealist and realist, 28, 38 ff, 127,
129; no Darwinian, 32; self-
contradictory, 33–34, 45–46; in
Lovejoy's terms, 45; personal influence, 48–49, 54–57; students,
49–53; books translated, 57–58;
critical studies of, 59–61; relation to Royce and James, 62–
67; influence underestimated,
68; contemporary relevance, 68–
70; process philosopher, 70–75;
influence on Ward, 76–77; and
Whitehead, 77–83; idealistic
realist, 77; monistic monadist,
80 f
Lovejoy, Arthur O., 45
Lucretius, 9, 13, 122

Malebranche, Nicholas, 194–195
Materialism, 148, 158, 159, 163,
167, 213, 215
Mechanism, 31, 43, 115, 123, 199–
201, 205
Merz, John Theodore, 32, 54
Metaphysical foundation of logic
and knowledge, 116
Metaphysics, 9–10, 22, 35, 69 ff,
113, 143–144, 155–160, 167, 168
Methods in Philosophy, 16–21,
113, 131 ff, 156
Monism, 42, 46–47, 80, 182–187,
190, 195, 197–198, 203, 205–207,
211–215, 217
Moore, G. E., 56–57
Moral idealism, 129
Moralism, 144

Moral postulates, 133–135, 137, 143
Muirhead, John, 53
Mysticism, 214

Nature (laws, uniformity), 32–33, 117–119, 138, 224

Objective world, 130
Order (concept defined), 21 ff, 29, 30–31, 138

Pantheism, 138
Passmore, John, 49
Peirce, Charles Sanders, 14
Pepper, Stephen C., 22
Perry, Ralph Barton, 65
Pfleiderer, E., 109
Phelps, William Lyon, 7
Phenomenalism, 96–97, 141, 157, 191, 193, 224
Plato, 23, 44, 70, 87, 100
Pluralism (metaphysical), 21–22, 42, 46–47, 80, 82, 104
Positivism, 141
Practical reason, 132
Pragmatism, 45–46, 62, 67, 99
Principles of explanation, 115–120
Pringle-Pattison, Andrew Seth, 49, 53
Process philosophy, 11–13, 22–24, 70–83, 103, 150–153

Rationalism, 13, 15, 16, 136
Realism, 126–127, 155, 158, 159, 160, 162, 163, 167, 176, 224. *See* Idealism/Realism
Relations, 22, 35–36, 38, 69, 138, 152, 157–161, 174, 176, 182, 206
Religion, 6–8, 49–50, 51, 55, 58, 63
Renouvier, Charles, 14
Ritschl, Albrecht, 6, 58
Robertson, George Croom, 54, 55
Root metaphor, 22–23

Royce, Josiah, 3, 12, 29, 48, 63
Russell, Bertrand, 29, 56–57, 78

Santayana, George: subject of doctoral dissertation, 3–5, 8–9; estimate of Lotze an exception to *Egotism in German Philosophy*, 4; discusses Lotze in *The Last Puritan*, 7–8; *Lotze's System of Philosophy* and later works, 4, 9; style of writing, 10–11; student in Germany, 48; hostile to process philosophy, particularly Bergson, 72, 86, 101; hostile to Lotze's moralism, 84; weaknesses as critic, 85–86; marginalia reveal how he read Lotze's texts, 98–105; phenomenalism influenced by Hume and Kant, 96–97; scepticism, 97–98; voluntarism influenced by James, 98–99; reduction of logical to psychological, 99; defender of Plato and Aristotle, 100–101; criteria of the real, 101–102; linguistic turn, 102; sympathy with all perspectives, 103–105
Scepticism, 97–98
Schiller, F. S. C., 45, 55
Schopenhauer, Arthur, 3, 8, 10, 13, 142
Schurman, Jacob Gould, 53
Science, 112
Sidgwick, Henry, 55
Sorley, W. R., 55
Soul, 19, 34, 37, 146–150, 207
Space, 147
Spinoza, Baruch, 42
Substance, 39, 145–147, 150–153, 160
Sufficient reason, 125

Teleology (purpose), 118–120, 128–129, 200, 205
Theism, 56

Truth: correspondence *vs.* coherence theory, 59–61

Unity, 150

Value-theory, 50, 200–201, 202–
204, 208–209
Voluntarism, 98–99

Ward, James, 55–56, 76
Weisse, Hermann, 13, 15
Wenley, Robert M., 54
Whitehead, Alfred North, 25–26,
68, 69–83
Winckelmann, Johann Joachim,
16
Wundt, Wilhelm, 5